THE GUARDIAN YEAR 2005

THE GUARDIAN YEAR 2005

EDITED BY GILES FODEN

theguardian

Atlantic Books
London

First published in hardback in Great Britain in 2005 by Atlantic Books on behalf of Guardian Newspapers Ltd. Atlantic Books is an imprint of Grove Atlantic Ltd.

The moral right of Giles Foden to be identified as the editor of this work has been asserted in accordance with the Copyright, Designs and Patents Act of 1988.

The Guardian is a registered trademark of the Guardian Media Group Plc. Guardian Books is an imprint of Guardian Newspapers Ltd.

9 8 7 6 5 4 3 2 1

A CIP record for this book is available from the British Library.

ISBN 1 84354 061 4

Printed and bound in Great Britain by William Clowes Ltd, Beccles, Suffolk
Text design: www.carrstudio.co.uk

Atlantic Books
Grove Atlantic Ltd
Ormond House
26–27 Boswell Street
London WC1N 3JZ

CONTENTS

A NEW BEGINNING

IN TENEBRIS

Having once, for other sins, edited *The Guardian Century*, I thought a *Guardian Year* would be a piece of cake. Not a crumb of it. Deciding on the most important events of the last twelve months has been much more difficult. Hindsight is a wonderful thing, and I wish I had more of it. But one must deal with what is in front of one, making one's cuts and selections, as one is disposed, in the time available.

This particular year begins in October 2004, just after the execution of Kenneth Bigley. His death set the tone for much of what was to come. For this was a year in which, as Katharine Viner puts it in a different context in these pages, 'Disaster followed disaster'. Viner was reviewing her teenage diary of 1988 ('Piper Alpha, Lockerbie, Armenia, Clapham, Jamaica, Bangladesh, Sudan, Northern Ireland still'), the year the *Guardian's Weekend* magazine was launched, which she currently edits.

Our present list of doom would run: Iraq (still), the execution of Margaret Hassan, the tsunami, the Zimbabwean clearances, two London bombings, the shooting of Jean-Charles de Menezes, a dramatic increase in the rate of global warming and, perhaps confirming this, a devastating hurricane on America's Gulf coast – followed by an inadequate rescue response that made a public disgrace of the world's moral policeman, George W. Bush. Sometimes, it seemed that we only had a 'choice of catastrophes', to borrow the title of a book by Isaac Asimov about the disasters that threaten our world.

Is the failure of the European Union constitution a disaster? To answer that question would require the prescience of an Asimov. We can be more positive about the end of armed struggle in Northern Ireland, but seeing as we have been here before, phlegmatism is probably the right attitude. Even the unexpected triumph of London's Olympic bid was immediately marred by the bombings that followed.

How to leaven all this misery? Or at least find those stories which point us to a better place, allowing us to feel, if only for a while, that we live in blessed times. I'm reminded of a line from Thomas Hardy's poem sequence 'In Tenebris': 'If way to the better there be, it exacts a full look at the worst.'

Although previous editors of the *Guardian Year* have often, and quite legitimately, chosen to arrange their items by theme rather than chronologically, I have taken the latter route. I wanted this book to be a reading experience *in toto*. I wanted it to be a narrative that, in its own terms, evokes and recaptures the rhythm and mood of the year as it happened. It has many of the highlights, then, but it is not a 'highlights DVD' of the kind John Lanchester refers to in the book's last sentence.

So this time we run from autumn to autumn. In part this is because of the peculiar timing of two events: the Boxing Day tsunami and the London bombings in July. Both tragedies occurred in holiday periods usually thought of as news-shy. They stood out as narratives in their own right, and they were as newsworthy as Zeus' thunderbolts. And both sets of events set off echoes, lines of thought, patterns of connection.

'If a bomb goes off, the fear I have is that everyone will say, "You're completely wrong,"' Adam Curtis, writer of *The Power of Nightmares* documentary, tells Andy Beckett in this collection. 'We have all become trapped . . . by a fear that is completely irrational.' Well, have we? wonders Mark Lawson, reviewing a contradictory documentary (*The New Al-Qaeda*) in the wake of the London attacks. Meanwhile, as if to prove that the greatest terror is not human in origin, we were swept from the ravages of the tsunami at the end of 2004 to Hurricane Katrina at the close of this book.

The points of connection bifurcate: climate change, terrorism and Iraq all came up at the G8 summit, which was, of course, interrupted by the London bombings. Some argued the attacks were a direct response to Iraq (a view strenuously denied by Tony Blair). Later in the year, the accusation was levelled at the US administration that it could not respond to Hurricane Katrina because it had overextended itself in Iraq.

Oil was another filament linking one story to another. Hurricane Katrina severely damaged America's refinery capacity, at a time of rising oil prices (see Nils Pratley on White Nile fever), themselves a function of decreased Iraqi production. Another reason oil prices shot up was because of rapid industrial growth in China, a picture of which was given in a special supplement of *G2* published from Shanghai this year (from which Esther Addley's piece is taken). In pictures, too, the links are there – from the bus exploded in the London bombing to that which carried victorious Flintoff and friends through Trafalgar Square.

That there should be such links is no surprise. But some of the connections which the year threw up were very unexpected. Who would have thought that the same John McCririck, the Channel 4 racing commentator, would both be needling Germaine Greer out of *Big Brother* and giving an oration at the funeral of Robin Cook?

For Libby Brooks, seeing her feminist icon on *Celebrity Big Brother* left her feeling that 'Nothing is allowed to mean anything any more.' This having been another year in which what she calls 'our ghastly witness culture' has held sway, I recommend her recipe for staving off the postmodern blues: 'When I'm feeling especially dismal I imagine what it must have been like to have been born before the days of triangulation, irony, multiple referencing and every other post-post-blah that empties out the truth and replaces it with a terribly handsome void.'

The true ghastliness of this witness culture was evident in the filmed executions released on the Internet, often preceded by the victims pleading for their lives (as in the case of Margaret Hassan). Since newspapers, as much as broadcasters, are in the business of representation, they must handle such images and their context with care. It is a proviso of which the *Guardian* is acutely aware. A similar one must be attached to reporting the private lives of individuals (even if they are celebrities), lest this too becomes a function of what one might term 'the amoral gaze': that sense one gets, while watching *Big Brother* or reading *Heat*, that one is consuming a type of pornography.

The growth in reality-TV formats would appear to suggest that the witness culture is here to stay, but there is no obligation for an editor to follow the herd. If it is important to report a pattern, it is equally important to not become enslaved by it. That is probably the hardest job for editors these days: to maintain detachment, refusing to be absorbed by the hypnotic lure of a mass media culture, but knowing when to recognise important developments in it.

As a reader one occasionally finds oneself in need of a pit stop (see Michael Hann on Little Chefs) or a pause for a quizzical smile (see Amelia Gentleman on the *Mona Lisa*). One might be tempted by a daydream: what if the US election had turned out differently (read Suzanne Goldenberg on the lost hope of John Kerry)? Or to look back with flinty fondness at the lost world of Mitchell and Kenyon, in the distinguished company of Ian Jack.

One thing that didn't get lost was the Ashes series, coming along at last to lift our spirits. It is something about which one can feel a degree of modest pride. England's glorious victory brought the trophy back to these shores for the first time since 1987. These are indeed blessed times – or at least it seemed a good place to end this book.

In the history of the *Guardian* itself, 2005 was not a year to be modest. It proved a historic moment for us and for the newspaper industry generally. On 12 September we switched to a new format, midway between tabloid and broadsheet, which required the construction of a new press centre. This enabled the *Guardian* to become the only full-colour national newspaper in the UK. Together, these moves can only strengthen its reputation for serious journalism, independent of proprietors and other *partis pris*. Obviously, as a member of staff, I am *parti pris* and they have paid me to write this. At 50 pence a word I could have produced yards of it, but unfortunately that rate is only available to those freelance writers who will walk naked through battlefields or work for six months as Bruce Springstein's valet.

Joking apart, this new format represents another significant milestone for the *Guardian*, perhaps even more important than the launch of the *Weekend* magazine (1988), the *G2* supplement (1991) and the *Guardian Unlimited* network of websites (1999). All of which were implemented or overseen by Alan Rusbridger, either as editor of the individual section or as editor of the newspaper as a whole, a position he has held since 1995.

That was the year I myself joined the *Guardian* and a decade has gone by in a flash. There have been many changes, and as we turn another page in the *Guardian*'s history (the paper was founded in 1821), it is worth reflecting once again on its guiding principles. Always, our job has been the conveyance of the truth. In C. P. Scott's famous phrase, 'Comment is free, but facts are sacred.' He made this observation in 'A Hundred Years' (1921), an essay to celebrate the centenary of the *Guardian* and his fiftieth anniversary as its editor.

Scott's dictum still applies, even at a time when what constitutes a fact is under increasing pressure from postmodernists, the owners of media conglomerates and politicians adept at spin. Another threat to the fact may be that very human desire – more prevelant still today, in an interdependent network society – to make patterns of fact: to grab information from here and there without regard for where it came from, or who provided it and why. These patterns suggest – even create – a world-view, which is a heavy responsibility: one I have felt in selecting the items for this anthology. For the plain truth is, facts cannot walk alone in the world. More than ever before, faithful context is everything. It surrounds a fact like an aura; take the proper context away, and the fact is no longer sacred.

Readers are part of the context. They find expression in another profound change the *Guardian* has undergone this year: it is listening more than ever to its readers, interacting with them in chatrooms and by e-mail, adding a new dimension to the already revolutionary presence of a readers' editor. In addition to this, efforts are being made to harness the energy of blogs, as what the *Guardian* says is cited and recited on the worldwide web, with approval or disapproval, as the case may be.

I hope, in this instance at least, you approve. If not, I refer you to Blake Morrison's piece on editing, which is nothing if not a hostage to fortune. No, not nothing; a beam of light, in fact, like all the best pieces of journalism. Here, in a year we wanted torches to guide us, is a fair gathering of some of them.

giles.foden@guardian.co.uk

AUTUMN

BEGINNING WITH A SIGH

Simon Hoggart

Lord Whitty, who proposed the second reading of the hunting bill in the Lords, began with a long, loud sigh, rather like Mr Bennet hearing another of his daughters knock on his study door in search of cash for a new dress. Everyone was familiar with the bill, he said – why, it was exactly the same as the one they had pondered last year. Was there any real need to consider it all again? The Commons had voted seven times, by huge majorities, for a ban on hunting. Can't we all, his body language, indeed his actual vocabulary, seemed to say, pack it in and go home?

Fat chance. The Lords regard this bill as slightly less important than, say, female emancipation, but rather more important than the abolition of the slave trade. They believe they are not talking about a few dozen furry animals, but the eternal flame of human liberty. As Baroness Mallalieu, a Labour peer and herself a huntsperson, put it: 'The stench of this bill, if it ever becomes law, will pollute the record of this government.'

What? More than the 45-minute claim, which only a few hours before Jack Straw had been obliged to disown in the Commons, laying it fastidiously to one side, as one might dispose of a smelly old fox fur discovered in the attic of a recently deceased aunt? More than that?

Baroness Byford, who kicked off for the Tories, warmed up on the pitch with a few observations about 'this ancient parliament', always a sign that we're going to get some gorgeous, hand-stitched march-of-time-type tapestry. 'They have abandoned the principle of concern for minorities, they are crushing civil liberties.' She asked who could doubt that horse racing would be banned next. Up to a point, I thought. Horse racing doesn't yet end up with the horse being torn to shreds by dogs. On the other hand, horses don't overturn your dustbins. The

Bishop of Chelmsford, if I understood him correctly, thought you couldn't go round banning things just because you didn't like them. You might as well ban adultery, gambling and tobacco. Each to his own. But it sounds as if a weekend in the bishop's palace at Chelmsford might be fun.

Lord Mancroft was very cross indeed. He denounced Sir Gerald Kaufman for calling the hunt protesters 'racist, larcenous scum', adding, 'if that sort of language were used about any other minority – gay people, black people or, God forbid, Jewish people . . .' He somehow forgot to mention that Sir Gerald was describing an event when hunt protesters had thrown anti-Semitic abuse at him, while one of them tried to steal his wallet. Lord Mancroft accused the Government of 'behaving like a fascist dictatorship'. The hyperbole in that line seems to me to imply a certain anti-Semitism, but no doubt unconscious.

David Steel made one of the more reasonable pro-hunting speeches, arguing that John Prescott had demonstrated that the bill wasn't really meant to abolish hunting, but to abolish toffs. 'A bill to abolish toffs might seem to have a rationale, unlike this bill,' he said. Of course. Ministers have been trying and failing to abolish toffs for years.

One of the most thoughtful contributions came from Lord Burns, whose report on hunting declared that it 'seriously compromised the welfare of the fox'. As any fox will tell you. Basically, he told the peers that they had made a huge tactical error by not accepting a compromise earlier, and now they were going to pay with a complete ban on hunting. You could almost hear the chill run round the chamber.

15 October 2004

THE POWER OF NIGHTMARES

Andy Beckett

Since the attacks on the United States in September 2001, there have been more than a thousand references in British national newspapers, working out at almost one every single day, to the phrase 'dirty bomb'. There have been articles about how such a device can use ordinary explosives to spread lethal radiation, about how London would be evacuated in the event of such a detonation, about the Home Secretary David Blunkett's statement on terrorism in November 2002 that specifically raised the possibility of a dirty bomb being planted in Britain, and about the arrests of several groups of people, the latest only last month, for allegedly plotting exactly that.

Starting next Wednesday, BBC2 is to broadcast a three-part documentary series that will add further to what could be called the dirty bomb genre. But, as its title suggests, *The Power of Nightmares: The Rise of the Politics of Fear* takes a different view of the weapon's potential.

'I don't think it would kill anybody,' says Dr Theodore Rockwell, an authority on radiation, in an interview for the series. 'You'll have trouble finding a serious report that would claim otherwise.' The American department of energy, Rockwell continues, has simulated a dirty bomb explosion, 'and they calculated that the most exposed individual would get a fairly high dose [of radiation], not life-threatening.' And even this minor threat is open to question. The test assumed that no one fled the explosion for one year.

During the three years in which the 'war on terror' has been waged, high-profile challenges to its assumptions have been rare. The sheer number of incidents and warnings connected or attributed to the war has left little room, it seems, for heretical thoughts. In this context, the central theme of *The Power of Nightmares* is riskily counterintuitive and provocative. Much of the currently perceived threat from international terrorism, the series argues, 'is a fantasy that has been exaggerated and distorted by politicians. It is a dark illusion that has spread unquestioned through governments around the world, the security services, and the international media.' The series' explanation for this is even bolder: 'In an age when all the grand ideas have lost credibility, fear of a phantom enemy is all the politicians have left to maintain their power.'

Adam Curtis, who wrote and produced the series, acknowledges the difficulty of saying such things now. 'If a bomb goes off, the fear I have is that everyone will say, "You're completely wrong," even if the incident doesn't touch my argument. This shows the way we have all become trapped, the way even I have become trapped by a fear that is completely irrational.'

So controversial is the tone of his series, that trailers for it were not broadcast last weekend because of the killing of Kenneth Bigley. At the BBC, Curtis freely admits, there are 'anxieties'. But there is also enthusiasm for the programmes, in part thanks to his reputation. Over the past dozen years, via similarly ambitious documentary series such as *Pandora's Box*, *The Mayfair Set* and *The Century of the Self*, Curtis has established himself as perhaps the most acclaimed maker of serious television programmes in Britain. His trademarks are long research, the revelatory use of archive footage, telling interviews, and smooth, insistent voiceovers concerned with the unnoticed deeper currents of recent history, narrated by Curtis himself in tones that combine traditional BBC authority with something more modern and sceptical: 'I want to try to make people look at things they think they know about in a new way.'

The Power of Nightmares seeks to overturn much of what is widely believed about Osama Bin Laden and al-Qaeda. The latter, it argues, is not an organised international network. It does not have members or a leader. It does not have 'sleeper cells'. It does not have an overall strategy. In fact, it barely exists at all, except as an idea about cleansing a corrupt world through religious violence.

Curtis's evidence for these assertions is not easily dismissed. He tells the story of Islamism, or the desire to establish Islam as an unbreakable political framework, as half a century of mostly failed, short-lived revolutions and spectacular but politically ineffective terrorism. Curtis points out that al-Qaeda did not even have a name until early 2001, when the American government decided to prosecute Bin Laden in his absence and had to use anti-Mafia laws that required the existence of a named criminal organisation.

Curtis also cites the Home Office's own statistics for arrests and convictions of suspected terrorists since 11 September 2001. Of the 664 people detained up to the end of last month, only 17 have been found guilty. Of these, the majority were Irish Republicans, Sikh militants or members of other groups with no connection to Islamist terrorism. Nobody has been convicted who is a proven member of al-Qaeda.

In fact, Curtis is not alone in wondering about all this. Quietly but increasingly, other observers of the war on terror have been having similar doubts. 'The grand concept of the war has not succeeded,' says Jonathan Eyal, director of the British military think-tank, the Royal United Services Institute. 'In purely military terms, it has been an inconclusive war . . . a rather haphazard operation. Al-Qaeda managed the most spectacular attack, but clearly it is also being sustained by the way that we rather cavalierly stick the name al-Qaeda on Iraq, Indonesia, the Philippines. There is a long tradition that if you divert all your resources to a threat, then you exaggerate it.'

Bill Durodie, director of the international centre for security analysis at King's College London, says: 'The reality [of the al-Qaeda threat to the West] has been essentially a one-off. There has been one incident in the developed world since 9/11 [the Madrid bombings]. There's no real evidence that all these groups are connected.' Crispin Black, a senior government intelligence analyst until 2002, is more cautious but admits the terrorist threat presented by politicians and the media is 'out of date and too one-dimensional. We think there is a bit of a gulf between the terrorists' ambition and their ability to pull it off.'

Terrorism, by definition, depends on an element of bluff. Yet ever since terrorists in the modern sense of the term (the word 'terrorism' was actually coined to describe the strategy of a government, the authoritarian French revolutionary regime of the 1790s) began to assassinate politicians and then members of the public during the nineteenth century, states have habitually overreacted. Adam Roberts, professor of international relations at Oxford, says that governments often believe struggles with terrorists 'to be of absolute cosmic significance', and that therefore 'anything goes' when it comes to winning. The historian Linda Colley adds: 'States and their rulers expect to monopolise violence, and that is why they react so virulently to terrorism.'

Britain may also be particularly sensitive to foreign infiltrators, fifth columnists and related menaces. In spite, or perhaps because of, the absence of an actual invasion for many centuries, British history is marked by frequent panics about the arrival of Spanish raiding parties, French revolutionary agitators, anarchists, Bolsheviks and Irish terrorists. 'These kinds of panics rarely happen without some sort of cause,' says Colley. 'But politicians make the most of them.'

They are not the only ones who find opportunities. 'Almost no one questions this myth about al-Qaeda because so many people have got an interest in keeping it alive,' says Curtis. He cites the suspiciously circular relationship between the security services and much of the media since September 2001: the way in which official briefings about terrorism, often unverified or unverifiable by journalists, have become dramatic press stories which – in a jittery media-driven democracy – have prompted further briefings and further stories. Few of these ominous announcements are retracted if they turn out to be baseless: 'There is no fact-checking about al-Qaeda.'

In one sense, of course, Curtis himself is part of the al-Qaeda industry. *The Power of Nightmares* began as an investigation of something else, the rise of modern American conservatism. Curtis was interested in Leo Strauss, a political philosopher at the university of Chicago in the 1950s who rejected the liberalism of post-war America as amoral and who thought that the country could be rescued by a revived belief in America's unique role to battle evil in the world. Strauss's certainty and his emphasis on the use of grand myths as a higher form of political propaganda created a group of influential disciples such as Paul Wolfowitz, now the US deputy defense secretary. They came to prominence by talking up the Russian threat during the Cold War and have applied a similar strategy in the war on terror.

As Curtis traced the rise of the 'Straussians', he came to a conclusion that would form the basis for *The Power of Nightmares*. Straussian conservatism had a previously unsuspected amount in common with Islamism: from origins in the 1950s, to a formative belief that liberalism was the enemy, to an actual period of Islamist-Straussian collaboration against the Soviet Union during the war in Afghanistan in the 1980s (both movements have proved adept at finding new foes to keep them going). Although the Islamists and the Straussians have fallen out since then, as the attacks on America in 2001 graphically demonstrated, they are in another way, Curtis concludes, collaborating still: in sustaining the 'fantasy' of the war on terror.

Some may find all this difficult to swallow. But Curtis insists, 'There is no way that I'm trying to be controversial just for the sake of it.' Neither is he trying to be an anti-conservative polemicist like Michael Moore: '[Moore's] purpose is avowedly political. My hope is that you won't be able to tell what my politics are.' For all the dizzying ideas and visual jolts and black jokes in his programmes, Curtis describes his intentions in sober, civic-minded terms. 'If you go back into history and plod through it, the myth falls away. You see that these aren't terrifying new monsters. It's drawing the poison of the fear.'

But whatever the reception of the series, this fear could be around for a while. It took the British government decades to dismantle the draconian laws it passed against French revolutionary infiltrators; the Cold War was sustained for almost half a century without Russia invading the West, or even conclusive evidence that it ever intended to. 'The archives have been opened,' says the Cold War historian David Caute, 'but they don't bring evidence to bear on this.' And the danger from Islamist terrorists, whatever its scale, is concrete. A sceptical observer of the war on terror in the British security services says: 'All they need is a big bomb every 18 months to keep this going.'

The war on terror already has a hold on western political culture. 'After a 300-year debate between freedom of the individual and protection of society, the protection of society seems to be the only priority,' says Eyal. Black agrees: 'We are probably moving to a point in the UK where national security becomes the electoral question.' Some critics of this situation see our striking susceptibility during the 1990s to other anxieties – the millennium bug, MMR, genetically modified food – as a sort of dress rehearsal for the war on terror. The press became accustomed to publishing scare stories and not retracting them; politicians became accustomed to responding to supposed threats rather than questioning them; the public became accustomed to the idea that some sort of apocalypse might be just around the corner. 'Insecurity is the key driving concept of our times,' says Durodie. 'Politicians have packaged themselves as risk managers. There is also a demand from below for protection.' The real reason for this insecurity, he argues, is the decay of the twentieth century's political belief systems and social structures: people have been left 'disconnected' and 'fearful'.

Yet the notion that 'security politics' is the perfect instrument for every ambitious politician from Blunkett to Wolfowitz also has its weaknesses. The fears of the public, in Britain at least, are actually quite erratic: when the opinion pollsters Mori asked people what they felt was the most important political issue, the figure for 'defence and foreign affairs' leapt from 2 per cent to 60 per cent after the attacks of September 2001, yet by January 2002 had fallen back almost to its earlier level. And then there are the twin risks that the terrors politicians warn of will either not materialise or will materialise all too brutally, and in both cases the politicians will be blamed. 'This is a very rickety platform from which to build up a political career,' says Eyal. He sees the war on terror as a hurried improvisation rather than some grand Straussian strategy: 'In democracies, in order to galvanize the public for war, you have to make the enemy bigger, uglier and more menacing.'

Afterwards, I look at a website for a well-connected American foreign policy lobbying group called the Committee on the Present Danger. The committee features in *The Power of Nightmares* as a vehicle for alarmist Straussian propaganda during the Cold War. After the Soviet collapse, as the website puts it, 'The mission of the committee was considered complete.' But then the website goes on: 'Today radical Islamists threaten the safety of the American people. Like the Cold War, securing our freedom is a long-term struggle. The road to victory begins . . .'

SMILE, PLEASE

Amelia Gentleman

Objectively, this is a very bad tourist experience. At least at the Eiffel Tower, the other highlight of travel-brochure Paris, you get the excitement of the lift and an incredible view. Here you get one small, dark picture surrounded by a jostling crowd of hundreds. It is hard to see how anyone can genuinely enjoy looking at the painting in these circumstances, which probably explains why most people don't. A few seconds, a few photographs and the line moves on. The speed with which the majority of visitors deal with this tourist obligation is astonishing. And yet, unless they have anarchist tendencies, no first-time visitor to Paris would consider skipping it.

The *Mona Lisa* remains the most famous painting in the world. This year the crowds lining up to see it have grown thicker than ever, with the influx of millions of new Chinese tourists into Europe. A day spent in the room where the picture hangs reveals much about the global tourist industry – illustrating which countries are doing well enough economically to allow their middle classes the chance to visit France. It casts only scant light on why people still bother to come in their thousands to pay homage to the painting. If you start queuing well before the Louvre's doors open at 9 a.m., and walk briskly through a network of long galleries that stand between the entrance hall and the first-floor room where the painting hangs, you can reach the *Mona Lisa* at about 9.09, before anyone else. For a short few minutes it is cool and quiet. A guard is rearranging the crowd barriers in the centre of the room with careful precision.

Four Chinese tourists are the first visitors at 9.11. They arrive, visibly delighted, and begin to examine the picture, holding their hands up to shield their eyes against a sun which isn't there. They take a few pictures of the painting and then of each other in front of the painting.

Their delight lasts for about 50 seconds, after which they hurry off. The rumble of dozens of approaching feet is already audible by 9.14, as dozens of people make their way rapidly down the grand gallery, rushing past Caravaggios, Bellinis, Raphaels and a few other da Vincis, guided by the *Mona Lisa* signposts. By 9.20 there is a group of 28 people standing in front of the painting and fathers are already having to hold their children above the crowd so that they can see.

'People come because she is famous. Period,' says Pete Brown, a retired businessman from Iowa, with some irritation. 'But you want my opinion honestly? I'm not overly impressed.'

At 9.30 the crowd has grown to about 47. Mobile phones are used to take pictures. Children show their parents how to use the equipment. The noise of the clicking of shutters, the buzzing of zooms whirring in and out, the satisfied pips of the machinery signalling its readiness, becomes overwhelming. Some couples kiss as they walk away, happy that another part of the Paris experience has been completed. At 10.14 the mass of people is twelve rows deep; 15 minutes later there are so many people elbowing from behind that it becomes uncomfortable to stand at the curved wooden barrier by the front of the picture. 'She must be one of the ugliest women in the world,' a teenager mutters.

Waiting to see the *Mona Lisa* has all the thrill of standing in an airport check-in queue. The crowd pushes forward, cattle-like and unquestioning, performing a ritual they know they have to go through with in order to complete a preordained tourist experience. By midday the room is seething with visitors, the line heaves towards the front, a slow, weary museum trudge, and around 70 more people file in every minute. Caged in a box of bullet-proof glass, the picture looks unimpressive under the harsh institutional lighting. Winking dots of red and orange reflected camera eyes dance across the canvas and every few seconds the *Mona Lisa*'s face is obscured by another flash.

'I don't know why they keep coming,' says Stephane, a security guard who has worked for the Louvre for the past two years. 'It's a nice painting, but there are many more interesting pictures elsewhere in the museum. People don't look at it anyway. They come in, take a picture and leave. It takes 15 seconds.'

'People no longer study it. It is no longer a painting, but has become a symbol of a painting,' says Darian Leader, author of *Stealing the Mona Lisa: What Art Stops Us from Seeing*. Looking at the visitors at the front of the crowd, about half have their faces pressed into a camera. Those at the back arch onto tiptoes, hold their arms far above their head and take a picture, paparazzi-style.

You have to feel sorry for Salvator Rosa, whose pictures hang to the left and the right of the *Mona Lisa*. No one spares a glance for the enormous *Heroic Battle* (1652) to the left, with its dramatic portrayal of carnage. There must have been a time when this would have been the more obvious crowd-gatherer, but a sequence of quite random events has transformed the *Mona Lisa* over the past century into a celebrity painting.

Before the 1789 revolution, scarcely anyone had access to it. Then, with the creation of the Louvre, it was for some time kept in the curator's bureau, away from the hordes, and valued much less than Leonardo's *Virgin and Child with St Anne*. But as the romantic poets of the nineteenth century began to be obsessed with the femme fatale, the *Mona Lisa* was seized on as an ideal of womanhood, her smile and the eyes venerated. The confusion over quite who she was increased her allure.

Donald Sassoon, author of *Becoming Mona Lisa: The History of the World's Most Famous Painting*, points out that such was the profusion of religious paintings of saints, famous royals, skinny Dutch women and obese Rubens females, that there weren't that many other paintings of unknown, beautiful women to choose as the object of male fantasies. Then just as the painting was gaining mass recognition, it was stolen in 1911, at a time when popular newspapers were booming. The image was reproduced globally as the search began. Such was the painting's new significance that people lined up to stare at the empty space where the picture had been hanging. The story of the theft and its rediscovery inspired dozens of books and films. Then came the lampooning of the work by Marcel Duchamp, the appropriation of the image by surrealists, pop artists and finally by the advertising industry.

Art historian E. H. Gombrich says the picture has become so worn out by all these references that it's almost impossible 'to see it with fresh eyes'. But the reality is that in the Louvre you cannot really see the painting at all for the far more practical reason that there are too many other people in front of it. Some visitors are quite open about their frustration. 'The *Mona Lisa* is probably the single most disappointing piece of work in the entire world,' says Guy Kress, an experimental psychologist from California. 'The picture everyone has in their minds is much larger and brighter.' It is true that the poster reproduction in the museum shop is a much bolder image. With this fresh in your mind, the original looks dour and gloomy.

Moonkyou Kim, a tour guide with a group of 16 tourists from Seoul, taking a 10-day whirlwind tour of Europe with 24 hours in France, says the anticlimax is palpable. 'People aren't very happy when they see it. It's too small. They don't believe it's the original.' But of the 51 people approached randomly over the day, the majority still say the picture is wonderful and they are thrilled to have seen it. Despite the crush and the inconvenience, there is for many a reluctance to question the value of the experience.

To doubt that the *Mona Lisa* is worth seeing is a bit like asking whether it's worth coming to Paris at all. The *Mona Lisa* is a key part of the Paris package and one of the reasons why you come to France, why you come to Europe. For most tourists, this moment will be a critical part of their memory of France as a whole. To come here and not be amazed or delighted is in some way to admit that the whole Paris experience is somehow not as great as it's cracked up to be. Most people know this is illogical and yet they buy into it anyway. 'When you come to Paris for the first time, you have to see the clichés. You can't be too proud,' says Oded Hauptaman, an ophthamologist from Melbourne.

Among the thousands who process past throughout the day, there are very few who pause to look hard. Takuya Sejima is an exception, stopping for over 30 minutes, holding his hand up towards his eyes at different angles, using his museum plan to help measure different sections of the painting, making notes. Next to the rushing masses, his behaviour looks eccentric, verging on the insane. An 18-year-old art student from Tokyo, he wants to assess why da Vinci made the left hand so much larger than the right hand, and so out of proportion with the face. 'It's marvellous. It's difficult to express why in words,' he says.

Later the tourists become wearier, their legs heavier, more prone to squabbling with their partners. The number of tour groups dwindles. The number of French visitors increases. Leading away his small group of French art enthusiasts, Bruno de Baecque explains: 'People invest a lot of hope into the prospect of seeing the *Mona Lisa* for the first time. It becomes a quasi-sacred experience. They're ready to suffer considerable discomfort to extract some pleasure from the experience. No one can really know if they're disappointed. I tell people to try to enjoy the thrill of seeing the painting surrounded by crowds.'

By 9.30 p.m. there are only about ten people left in the room, and for the first time all day there's time to really examine the painting. But as closing time approaches, guards shoo the remaining visitors away so that only Mohamed Elabdi, the night cleaner, remains, sweeping away the mound of rubbish discarded over the day at the foot of the painting. After 30 years in France he saw the painting for the first time three days ago when he started this new job with the Louvre. 'It's hard to understand what the fuss is about,' he says. 'But the way that the eyes follow you around the room as you work is disconcerting.'

21 October 2004

OPERATION CLARK COUNTY

Ian Katz

Blimey. I think I have an idea as to how Dr Frankenstein felt. By the beginning of this week, a quixotic idea dreamed up last month in a North London pub had morphed into a global media phenomenon complete with transatlantic outrage, harrumphing over journalistic ethics, grave political predictions – and thousands of people from every corner of the planet writing personal, passionate letters to voters in a tiny American district few outside Ohio had heard of ten days ago.

I realised just how much momentum our project to match concerned non-Americans with voters in a marginal US county had acquired when I arrived in Shanghai on Sunday to be handed a message from a local reporter. I rang back expecting a few desultory questions about why a group of *Guardian* journalists were visiting China but the reporter had a bigger story in her sights: 'Is it possible to make interview about Operation Clark County?' (There was no sign in her voice of the mild irony with which we had chosen the project's quasi-military name.) When I rang a colleague in London the next morning to tell him about the strangely surreal encounter, he reported that he had just said goodbye to a crew from Japanese TV. CNN were on their way.

It's been like that for the best part of a week: Canadian newspapers, Irish radio, US TV networks. Fox has been frothing. Rush Limbaugh has been raving. A quick Google search as I write this produces the *Washington Post* wondering, 'Can the Brits swing Ohio?', and the *New York Times* reporting, in unusually demotic voice, 'British Two Cents Draws, in Sum, a Two-Word Reply: Butt Out'. Elsewhere, detailing the robust response to our campaign, the *Arab News* in Saudi Arabia asks gravely: 'Can the "special" US-UK relationship survive?'.

Even before the *Springfield News Sun* of Clark County splashed our campaign across its front page (the paper's charming crime correspondent was assigned to the story because, 'There was no crime in the county today'), it was pretty clear that we had touched off something bigger than we had anticipated. In the first 24 hours after we published details of the campaign, more than 4,000 people visited our website to be matched with a Clark County voter. A day later the figure had reached 7,000, and by this Sunday, when the site was attacked by a (presumably politically inspired) hacker, we had sent out the names of more than 14,000 undecided voters. Not all of them will be acquiring foreign pen pals; right-wing bloggers have been urging Republicans to sign up themselves, and prevent names falling into the hands of Euroweenie leftists. But extrapolating from the hundreds of people who have gone to the trouble of copying us their letters, it's a good bet that several thousand will.

The letters have made rather stirring reading – sensitive, thoughtful and warm, if occasionally prone to propaganda, too. 'I'm a cartographer who specialises in digital mapping,' began one Welsh correspondent. 'Parts of the US are almost as familiar to me as Wales. It's a small country but it was the ancestral home of 18 out of the 56 delegates who signed your Declaration of Independence.' Another, from Leicester, wrote: 'Please forgive this intrusion. I am writing to you because I care about America a great deal. Let me tell you why. I lived and worked in the USA for 22 years. My dearest friends are American and some of my best memories are of 4 July parties, Memorial Day picnics, and the Thanksgiving feasts partaken with the welcoming families of friends. I close my eyes and I still see the woods and lakes of Connecticut.'

At first the letters came almost exclusively from Britain, but as word spread our inbox began to look more and more like a UN telephone directory. In one of those bits of casual alliteration to which journalists are prone, I had introduced the project with the suggestion that it would offer a way for 'people from Basildon to Botswana to campaign in the presidential race'. Suddenly, they were. 'My country is a new democracy,' wrote a South African. 'When we set about building our nation from the ruins of apartheid, we looked long and hard at the lessons the people of the USA have learned from more than 200 years of self-government and democracy.' From Chile came this: 'As someone who has lived in the United States and loves it dearly, events over the recent years have caused great concern to many of us in the world.' They kept coming, from Norway and Germany and Morocco and Australia and Uruguay and Sweden and Singapore and China and Brazil and Italy and, yes, France, too.

Then came the backlash. We had expected it, of course. Fox-viewing America was never going to embrace our modest sortie into US politics and we knew full well that any individual voter might take exception to the idea of a foreigner writing to offer some advice on how they should vote – our website explicitly urged participants to 'imagine how you would feel if you received a letter from an American urging you to vote for Tony Blair . . . or Michael Howard.' But you couldn't fail to be a little shocked by the volume and pitch of the invective directed our way. Most of it was coordinated by a handful of resourceful bloggers – the ringleader of whom is fittingly published on a site called 'spleenville' – and much of it was eye-wateringly unpleasant. 'I hope your earholes turn to arseholes and shit on your shoulders,' was one, more repeatable example of the scatological genre. Another memorable mail asked: 'How secure is your building that contains all you morons??? Do you have enough security?? ARE YOU SURE ??? Are you VERY sure??'

Interestingly, one of the recurrent themes running through the onslaught was an ardent admiration for Tony Blair from the kind of people who might feel slightly out of place in even the biggest of New Labour big tents. Another was a curious obsession with the state of British dentistry: 'MAY YOU HAVE TO HAVE A TOOTH CAPPED. I UNDERSTAND IT TAKES AT LEAST 18 MONTHS FOR YOUR GREAT MEDICAL SERVICES TO GET AROUND TO YOU.' At times, it felt as though whole swathes of America had suffered an epidemic of Tourette's syndrome.

So far, so bad. The e-mail onslaught was pretty unpleasant and inconvenient for the 53 *Guardian* colleagues whose addresses were targeted by the rightwing spammers – several of us received more than 700 mails – but by and large they were the sort of missives that left you feeling relieved you were not on the same side of the argument (indeed, any argument) as the sender. The same could be said of the news this week that Rush Limbaugh had devoted virtually all of one of his three-hour shows to our Clark County project. But a much smaller number of responses demanded to be taken more seriously. Some of them, a trifle portentously, questioned whether something such as the Clark County project is an appropriate thing for a newspaper to be doing at all. Others, a small but increasing number of Democrats among them, suggested that our campaign could be dangerously counterproductive. Americans don't like being told what to do, the argument went. If a load of foreigners write telling the voters of Clark County to vote Kerry, they are liable to do precisely the opposite. Or, as Sharon Manitta, spokeswoman in Britain for Democrats Abroad, put it with preternatural confidence: 'This will certainly garner more votes for George Bush.' Yikes.

It's not as if we didn't consider the possibility that our project might have precisely the opposite effect to that intended. The feature introducing the project included notes of caution from Manitta's colleague, Rachelle Valladares, and a University of Columbia professor. It's just that we didn't believe it. For one thing, it seemed unlikely that our campaign would ever reach a scale that would have any real impact on the election, one way or another. For another, it seemed spectacularly patronising to suggest that the people of Clark County would be so volatile that they would vote one way simply because an individual several thousand miles away had suggested they do the opposite.

Finally, there was the special nature of the Anglo-American relationship. I suppose it might be possible, after that nasty business in the run-up to the Gulf war, to imagine a less internationally minded American voter taking umbrage at the very idea of receiving a letter from a Frenchman, but aren't we the staunchest and most longstanding of allies? Surely a letter from a concerned Brit would be received more like a plea from an old friend. (And surely it was important that Americans, who have been reminded repeatedly during this campaign of Tony Blair's legitimising support for George Bush's Iraqi adventure, should know that a majority of the British public did not share their prime minister's analysis of world affairs.)

Well, it's true that we may have underestimated the number of people willing to put pen to paper and shell out 47p for an airmail stamp, and it's true, too, that one or two residents of Clark County may get a letter from a cheese-eating surrender monkey, but I would still bet my last € 10 that none of them will make their election decision by reversing whatever our long-distance lobbyists suggest. Consider the first reports of Clark County residents receiving *Guardian*-inspired letters. 'When Dawn Brink went to her mailbox and found a letter from Germany, she was surprised because she knows no one from there,' relates the *Springfield News Sun*. 'When she opened it, she was even more surprised to find someone asking her to vote for Kerry. "It caught me off guard," she said. "But I'm always open to listening to other points of view."' And here's James Chapman, who got a letter from a woman in Yorkshire on Saturday: 'She said it was an important election and asked me to vote for Kerry. It was very nicely written.' Chapman already planned to vote for Kerry so the letter was pushing at an open door. Two other residents were less thrilled by their missives but did not think anyone would vote differently as a result of them.

As for the question of whether any newspaper should be attempting to influence a foreign election in the first place, I'm torn between answering, 'Yes' and 'Puleeeeeese'. Yes, because I can't see any qualitative distinction between what newspapers have always done without controversy – attempt to sway the few foreign readers they have with leaders urging them to back one candidate or another – and our Clark County project. Some time in the next ten days or so, the *Guardian* will run one urging its American readers – several million of them now, thanks to the long arm of the Internet – to back John Kerry. In what way is Operation Clark County any more than an inventive way of empowering individuals to do the same?

Puleeeese, because we're in danger of taking all this too seriously. It's always tricky, and usually disingenuous, to suggest when something has been taken very seriously indeed, that actually it was all a bit of a joke. Operation Clark County was not a joke, but neither was it entirely po-faced – it was a light-hearted attempt to make some quite serious points. There were plenty of clues to its intended spirit in the feature which launched it. The cover, among other things, featured a bumper sticker, *Kentish Town for Kerry* – a gentle joke at our own expense, given the London district's reputation as the heartland of Britain's liberal chattering classes. The introduction to the project itself, meanwhile, began: 'Where others might see delusions of grandeur, we saw an opportunity for public service . . .'

Somewhere along the line, though, the good-humoured spirit of the enterprise got lost in translation. It's easier perhaps for British readers to recognise that a project launched in *G2* – the same section which sought to save Tory leader Iain Duncan Smith by persuading him to pose in front of a poster which read, *It rained less under the Conservatives* – was not to be taken in deadly earnest. Reading some American correspondence, you might believe that the editor of the *Guardian* himself was secreted in a subterranean war room plotting George Bush's demise.

Oddly, it seems that it is the folks in Clark County itself who have best recognised the spirit of the enterprise. Local media coverage has been consistently fair and good-humoured. Even the spokesman for Ohio's Bush-Cheney campaign replied to the first query about our effort with a wry reference to the events of 1776: 'The last time the Brits tried to persuade us to do something, we started a revolution.' Nevertheless it feels as if the time has come to let the good people of the county make their minds up in peace. Since sending a *Guardian* delegation to the county in the last week of the campaign would be bound to prolong the media brouhaha, with unknowable consequences, and since some of the mail we have received brings to mind the old joke about unenviable holidays (first prize one week, second prize two weeks), we have decided that our competition winners will be watching the last days of the campaign from another, more tranquil, corner of the American electoral battlefield.

We set out to get people talking and thinking about the impact of the US election on citizens of other countries, and that is what we have done. For the *Guardian* to have experienced such a backlash to an editorial project is extraordinary, but the number of complaints is thoroughly outdone by the number of people who engaged positively with the project. What other lessons can we draw from Operation Clark County? I guess we will have to wait till 3 November to find out for sure, but here's a provisional stab: there are a huge number of people around the world who are profoundly dismayed by the prospect of another four years of a Bush White House and who are desperate for a way to do something about it. *Guardian* readers are a reassuringly engaged, resourceful and largely charming bunch; parts of America have become so isolationist that even the idea of individuals receiving letters from foreigners is enough to give politicians the collywobbles and perhaps, in the digital age, little acorns can turn into big trees very, very quickly.

Got to run now – the Finnish local elections are coming up on Sunday.

THIS IS NO PASSING PHASE

Jonathan Freedland

Once it looked like an aberration. Now it is an era. George W. Bush's tenure of the White House was born in 2000 to an electoral quirk, the fruit of a Florida fiasco, the arcane algebra of the US electoral system, and a split decision of the Supreme Court. It seemed to be the accidental presidency, one that would stand out in the history books as a freak event.

Yesterday that changed, changed utterly. President Bush and his Republican army recorded a famous victory, one that may come to be seen as more than a mere election triumph – rather, a turning point in American life, a realignment. For twelve hours that fact was obscured by the fate of Ohio and the desperate Democratic desire to see if that pivotal state might be wrested from Republican hands. By late morning the challenger John Kerry realised it was a vain hope. This was no Florida 2000.

For George Bush had done more than rack up the requisite numbers in the electoral college. He had done what he signally failed to do four years ago: win the popular vote – and not by a sliver, but by a 3.5 million margin. Bush had also achieved what no one had managed since his father in 1988, winning more than 50 per cent of the vote. But, of course, he had outdone his father, becoming a member of that surprisingly small, select club of presidents who have won two full terms. That alone would ensure that this first decade of the twenty-first century would become the Bush era, just as the 1980s belonged to Ronald Reagan, and the 1990s to Bill Clinton. But there was more.

The Republicans expanded their presence in the 100-seat Senate from 51 to 55 seats, beating Democrats in almost every close contest and toppling their senate leader. They increased their majority in the House of Representatives, too. Under Bush the Republican Party has won clear control of both the legislative and executive branches of the US government – with a mandate whose legitimacy no one can doubt. But the Republican revolution will not stop there. A subplot to this week's drama has been playing out at the Supreme Court, where the 80-year-old Chief Justice, William Rehnquist, has been incapacitated by thyroid cancer. Few expect him to serve for much longer, giving President Bush the chance to appoint a successor. A social conservative, such as White House counsel, Alberto Gonzales, is a likely nominee.

Other vacancies on the bench are imminent. Once filled, Bush will have overturned the court's wafer-thin moderate majority. The court could set to work unravelling a 50-year settlement that has asserted the rights of women, black Americans and, more recently, homosexuals. Opposition to affirmative action or abortion rights has, until now, been a minority position in America's highest court. That could change. And the conservative takeover of all three branches of the American government (executive, legislative and judiciary) would be complete. So George Bush will be no footnote to history: he is instead making it.

Those outside America, in the chanceries of Europe and beyond, who hoped that this would be a passing phase, like a Florida hurricane that wreaks havoc only to blow over, will instead have to adjust to a different reality. For four years many hoped that the course charted by President Bush – a muscular go-it-alone view of a world divided between the forces of darkness and those of light – would prove to be a blip. Come 2 November 2004, they wanted to believe, normal service would be resumed. The United States would return to the old way of doing business, in concert with allies and with respect for the international system the US itself had done so much to create. The norms of foreign policy pursued by every president from Roosevelt to Clinton, including the first George Bush, would be revived. Senator Kerry promised as much.

Now that fantasy will be shelved. The White House is not about to ditch the approach of the last four years. Why would it? Despite the mayhem and murder in Iraq, despite the death of more than 1,000 US soldiers and countless (and uncounted) Iraqis, despite the absence of weapons of mass destruction, despite Abu Ghraib, the Bush administration won the approval of the American people. If Bush had lost, the neo-conservative project would have been buried for ever. But he won and the neo-cons will welcome that as sweet vindication. So it will be full steam ahead. 'There are real threats that have to be dealt with,' Danielle Pletka of the impeccably neo-con American Enterprise Institute told the *Guardian* yesterday. Iran would not go away – indeed, Ms Pletka warned, 'force might be the only option' – nor would North Korea. 'We can't all pretend that the world would be a prettier place if only George W. Bush was not the president.'

There were plenty of people around the globe who used to think precisely that way, hoping that the past four years were a bad dream which would end yesterday. Now they have to navigate around a geopolitical landscape in which President Bush is the dominant, fixed feature. But yesterday's victory also signalled a shift in America itself. It has been under way for several decades, but now it is revealed in all its clarity. The electoral map showed it in full colour: 'blue' coasts where the Democrats won; vast 'red' swathes of the Republican heartland everywhere else.

Democrats need to stare long and hard at that map and at this comprehensive defeat. Exit pollsters, who failed so dismally to predict the result, made some telling discoveries. Many Bush voters admitted their unhappiness on Iraq and confessed to great economic hardship – two issues which ordinarily would be enough to defeat an incumbent. But these voters backed Mr Bush because he reflected something they regarded as even more important: their values. Those values can be boiled down to issues – abortion, guns, gays – but they represent a larger, cultural difference. One Republican analyst asks people four questions. Do you have a friend or relative serving in the military? Do you have any personal ties to rural America? Do you attend religious services on a weekly basis? Do you own a gun? Answer yes to most or all of those and you are 'a cultural conservative' and most likely vote Republican. Answer no and the chances are you live on the east or west coast and vote Democrat. In 2000 this cultural split was dead-even: 50-50 America. This time it was 51-49 America, with the conservatives in the majority.

Put plainly, the US is moving steadily and solidly to the Right. That poses a problem for Democrats, who have to learn to speak to the people of those red states if they are ever to hold power again. But it also poses a problem for America, which has somehow to house two radically diverging cultures in one nation. And it may even pose a problem for the rest of the world's peoples as they watch the sole superpower, the indispensable nation, chart a course they fear – and barely understand.

4 November 2004

I WISH THINGS HAD TURNED OUT DIFFERENTLY

Suzanne Goldenberg

Ever the dutiful soldier, John Kerry delivered the most painful speech of his life yesterday, choking back the tears and the bitter aftertaste of defeat as he appealed to fellow Democrats – and his rival George Bush – to work to heal America's divide. Amid the raw emotions that occasionally overwhelmed him, forcing Mr Kerry to gaze up at the ceiling for composure, the senator apologised to his dejected supporters for coming up short, but said it was time to admit defeat. He had done so in a brief phone call to President Bush earlier in the morning, praising his opponent, but urging him to heal the divisions in the country. It was a theme he took up in his concession speech, saying it was imperative to banish the rancour of the past four years – especially while America remained at war.

'In the days ahead, we must find common cause,' Mr Kerry said. 'We must join in common effort, without remorse or recrimination, without anger or rancour. America is in need of unity and longing for a larger measure of compassion. I hope President Bush will advance those values in the coming years.' It was, in many ways, Mr Kerry's finest appearance – the flinty New Englander's feelings on full display for perhaps the first time in his candidacy. And it was when he spoke directly to his supporters, some tearful, some defiant, all deflated, that his voice choked. But for all the anguish and agonising, he stressed that the legal challenges that beset the 2000 election had no place here.

'In America it is vital that every vote counts and that every vote be counted, but the outcome should be decided by voters, not a protracted legal fight,' he said. 'I would not have given up this fight if there was a chance we would prevail, but it is now clear that if all the provisional ballots were counted, which they will be, there won't be enough outstanding votes for us to win Ohio, and therefore we can't win the election.' It was the end of an odyssey and the feeling of deflation was palpable. Some spoke wearily of leaving the country, others vowed to stay and maintain the fight.

It was a far cry from the euphoria of a few hours earlier, when Mr Kerry's running mate, John Edwards, had told the crowd in the dark hours of Wednesday morning that they would 'continue to fight for every vote'. For several hours it seemed that this election would be a rerun of the 2000 vote – albeit with a change in venue from Florida to Ohio – with recounts and legal challenges and no clear election victory for days to come. But in the harsh dawn of the day, it was clear that victory was beyond Mr Kerry's grasp. Even the Democrats' eleventh-hour scenario of demanding a count of the provisional ballots cast in Ohio would not bring home the votes that Mr Kerry needed.

After studying the returns and consulting with Republican as well as Democratic politicians in the state, Mr Kerry's aides advised him to surrender. The concession speech, delivered in the eighteenth-century splendour of Boston's Faneuil Hall meeting place, was a rare encounter with failure for Mr Kerry. The product of a privileged New England upbringing, a graduate of Yale, a Vietnam War hero and husband to two heiresses, Mr Kerry has lost just one election in his political career, and that was around 30 years ago. But in ending the quest that has consumed him for more than half of his lifetime, the Democratic leader found an eloquence, a connection with ordinariness that has sometimes eluded him. And while he tried to stage a graceful exit from the presidential race and was full of praise for his campaign staff and for the support of American voters, there remained an abiding sense of wistfulness. The Massachusetts senator who entered this race with a reputation for thoughtfulness and for enjoying a grasp of complex issues, somehow was never able to communicate his strengths to the ordinary American voter.

'I did my best to express my vision and my hopes for America,' he said. 'I wish things had turned out differently.'

WRITING BY NUMBERS

Richard Eyre

Popular novels have taught me a lot. I'd know nothing of Moscow police procedure without *Gorky Park*. I'd be familiar with barely three, let alone 55 words, to describe snow without *Miss Smilla's Feeling for Snow*, and without *The Da Vinci Code* I'd be ignorant of the secret of the *Mona Lisa*'s smile. These aren't insignificant additions to my knowledge of the world even if, like Donald Rumsfeld, US defense secretary, I can only remember that these are things that I know that I know but can't quite recall.

The Da Vinci Code has now reached the *ultima Thule* of popularity – read on the Tube and the beach by those who don't read books, featured in broadsheet editorials, the object of a plagiarism suit and the subject, in this newspaper, of a piece castigating those who, like me, are snooty about its popularity. There's even a spin-off publishing industry – books describing the 'facts' behind the novel, exposing its 'hoax', expounding its 'truth'. That the book is compulsively readable is indisputable, but equally so is the fact that it is, from first sentence ('Renowned curator Jacques Sauniere staggered through the vaulted archway of the Museum's Grand Gallery') to last ('For a moment, he thought he heard a woman's voice . . . the wisdom of the ages . . . whispering up from the chasms of the earth'), quite astonishingly badly written. It is, to borrow from *Blackadder*, as badly written as the most badly written bad book that you've ever thrown across a room in disgust. It's as bad as a bad novel by Jeffrey Archer. It's so bad that even Erik von Däniken would scorn its prose. It belongs, as Joe Queenan said, to 'that category of things that suck so bad even your kids know they suck'.

Given the popularity of the book, describing the plot is probably redundant. But for the disenfranchised: the body of the curator of the Louvre ('the most famous art museum in the world'), splayed out in the shape of Da Vinci's sketch of a male nude enclosed by a circle, is discovered at the foot of the 'famous' *Mona Lisa*, with further clues written in blood by the dead man on the parquet floor. Sophie Neveu, the victim's granddaughter and a ('glamorous') French police cryptographer and Robert Langdon ('Harrison Ford in Harris tweed'), a Harvard professor of religious symbology, unravel these cryptic clues and initiate an investigation that develops into a treasure hunt for the 'fabled' Holy Grail. With 'a dogged determination bordering on the obstinate', the two protagonists follow the trail from the Louvre to a Swiss bank, a chateau in Versailles, the Temple Church, Westminster Abbey and the Rosslyn chapel – all in the space of two days.

Labyrinthine conspiracies and religious relics are unearthed, truths of the ages are untangled. The 'mysterious' Catholic secret societies, Opus Dei and the Priory of Sion, provide obstacles to the truth, while spurious information about the nature of original sin, the 'obliteration of the sacred feminine', Vatican politics, Rosicrucianism, Range Rovers and Hawker 731 jets, rains down mercilessly on the reader. The novel is not so much peopled as infested by an amoebic cast of characters – stocky detective, alluring cryptologist, dashing academic, sinister bishop, albino thug, camp aristocratic historian (English naturally) – who make Tarot cards look as vivid as Tolstoy. It doesn't even put the boot into the Vatican or Opus Dei: they're fine organisations plagued by the odd bad apple.

Nevertheless, in spite of the novel's clockwork plot and *Hello!* magazine prose, I was enslaved by it. Picture Angelina Jolie as Sophie Neveu – 'her cryptological senses tingling as she studied the printout' – and you will understand that the scheme of the writing takes its model from *Tomb Raider*. It isn't a novel, it's a computer game. Each chapter is a new level of the game presenting new challenges to be overcome before the next level is achieved, and each challenge encourages in the reader the same solipsistic absorption. I'm familiar with this sensation: I once spent three days in self-enforced solitary confinement playing a computer game in which you had to found cities, irrigate grassland, send settlers to colonise your territory, diplomats to negotiate with other empires and armies to kill barbarians. With no irony but much prescience the game was called *Civilisation*.

That *The Da Vinci Code* should remind me of a computer game is not surprising. In Chapter 95 (of 107) the two protagonists enlist the Google search engine to aid their quest and it becomes apparent that the co-author of the book is Google him/her/itself. A crude scaffolding of plot has been plastered with cryptic clues and decorated with otiose knowledge, name checks and local colour – 'Langdon vaguely recalled the Chapter House as a huge octagonal hall where the original British Parliament convened in the days before the modern Parliament existed' – all plucked off Google's shelves. The age of the DIY novel has arrived.

Many people – appalled (or inspired) by the success of Jeffrey Archer novels – have thought it possible to manufacture popular fiction in this way, but they miss the one unfakeable ingredient: that it has to be done with utter sincerity – in good faith, as our prime minister might say – allied to wilful self-belief. The readership will smell out the bogus. There is no clearer indication of this than the story of Archer lunching with an eminent publisher in the days before he was a novelist or a criminal. Archer gave him lunch and after some idle political gossip, said to the publisher: 'I'm thinking of writing a novel.'

'Ah,' he flinched.

'Do you think,' said Archer, 'do you think, that after writing several novels, that I might –'

And here he paused and there was an awkward silence as the publisher waited for the inevitable request not only to read the novel but to publish it. 'Do you think,' said Archer, 'that I might ever win the Nobel Prize for Literature?'

11 November 2004

IF I LIKE A GUY ENOUGH

Esther Addley

Catherine Liu is 28 and a little nervous, she says, because two weeks ago she split up with her boyfriend and it is making her twitchy about her prospects. 'In England, it is OK until 35 not to be married?' she asks, slightly awed. 'In China, it is only until 30.' Then, a little forlornly, 'My mother is worried about me.'

Catherine is a Shanghai success story – well educated, sophisticated, with a high-profile job for a British company that has given her opportunities to travel the world. She is also unsettlingly fluent in the language that every woman of a certain age who wants to be married prefers not to utter aloud: how she is getting older every year, how she saves a sum each month towards an imagined future with an imagined husband, how she is looking for a guy who understands her, but who also has a solid career and promising earning potential.

She liked her boyfriend, she says, but he wasn't quite up to the mark. And so she is glad that during their four-year relationship, although they travelled together and frequently shared a hotel room, they never slept with each other. Dating, she says, means 'kissing and hugging', nothing more. 'My parents always told me not to have sex before marrying,' she explains, 'but I am sure some women do.' And she tells me the story of a woman she knows who did indeed sleep with her boyfriend. Their families didn't even mind. There is also her cousin, who is 22 and has just graduated. 'She is dating a married man from her company. She says, "I know he is 40 and will never marry me, but for the moment, it is so good." I feel like I am standing on the edge of something. China is not like it was before. People have their own thinking. Sometimes even I am confused about the way the younger generations are thinking.'

Chan Li, at 23, is only five years younger than Catherine but a social chasm separates them. She is dating an American guy who was her

French teacher. Li, who likes to use the Japanese name Miki, works in marketing for Disney Asia, is conspicuously financially independent and is absolutely the master of her dating transactions. She chose a foreign man, she says, 'because he thinks like me, and doesn't try to control me'. I tentatively ask Miki about the nature of her relationship with her boyfriend; she juts out her chin as if insulted that it should be questioned. 'Of course if I like a guy enough I'll sleep with him!' Her four girlfriends, all aged between 22 and 25, noisily agree. Solvent, attractive and intimidatingly confident, none of these women admits to any enormous desire to get married or, if they did, to have their allotted child. 'I will get married if I find a guy I really love,' says Miki. 'Or if I don't – why get married?' She'll think about having a child, 'if I have enough money'. For a moment it is hard to imagine a young woman anywhere in the world more assured of her own sexual power.

Last month, in a poll of 200 students from Fujian province in the south-east, 92 per cent of the respondents said they thought that premarital sex was acceptable. Virginity was not listed among the top 20 factors – including personality, appearance and income potential – that the students said they looked for in a partner. That is remarkable if you consider this: in 1990, just 14 years ago, a study by the Chinese Academy of Social Sciences found that 80 per cent of Shanghai residents believed that a woman's chastity was more important than her life.

If China's economic and social development in the past decade has been remarkable, the revolution in sexual mores that is taking place among sections of its society is simply dazzling. A 2003 survey found that nearly 70 per cent of young Chinese were not virgins when they married; only 15 years earlier, that figure was 16 per cent. (Even homosexuality – removed in April 2001 from the register of psychiatric disorders – has become almost acceptable; Shanghai now has a flourishing, if discreet, gay scene. 'They don't even close the bars down the way they used to,' notes one gay man wryly.)

A society that, perhaps more than any other in history, has been obsessed with regulating sex and its reproductive consequences now finds itself having created the conditions in which for many, actually doing it, whenever and with whomever, has become acceptable. But if sexual liberation has hit Shanghai with something of a bump, its impact is restricted to a tightly limited demographic, leaving those on the outside not a little bewildered.

I am having coffee with Miki and her friends in a Starbucks near the heart of Shanghai. They like it because it's the kind of place where foreign guys hang out – Chinese men, Miki notes with a little sneer, all want to go to karaoke bars and watch girlie dancers. It has always been more acceptable for Chinese guys not to wait until marriage, they all agree, but the men, too, are benefiting from the new sexual openness. (The huge boom in car ownership, offering previously undreamed of locations, has played its part.)

So how does this group think they differ from girls ten years older than them? 'Our lives are totally different,' says Gia, who works for an Icelandic-owned fashion company in the city. 'Girls ten years older are like another generation to us.' Angie, a quantity surveyor who will soon be moving to Australia for two years, says: 'Just three years is an incredible gap in the way people live.' Yet they are quite happy to talk to their mothers about their sexual adventures, pregnancy scares and all. 'My mother has learned a bit from me,' says Vanessa. 'I feel lucky she is willing to change.'

Shanghai's sexual history is so colourful, and so strange, that perhaps the fuel-injected sexual fizz of recent years should not seem so remarkable. The foreign influence on the bustling port has meant that its reputation has always been a curious mélange of the sophisticated and the slutty. James Farrer, a sociologist who has written a book on the city's recent sexual awakening, cites one claim that before 1949 Shanghai had more prostitutes per capita than any city on earth; in 1930, the sex industry was the biggest employer of women in the city.

But the draconian restrictions on personal, social and sexual behaviour imposed with the arrival of Communist rule in 1949, and the introduction of the one-child policy in 1979, mean that for half a century young people have undergone very curious sexual awakenings indeed. Dating was generally forbidden by high-school authorities – of the many students and young adults I spoke to, just one had had a relationship at school. Sex education, too, has until recently been minimal or non-existent, so many youngish Chinese still find themselves ignorant about basic sexual biology. A European journalist describes visiting a Beijing delivery ward with her translator, a streetwise, educated woman in her early thirties. 'She was very upset by what she saw there. She really had no idea how babies were born.' In the Jing'an district of Shanghai, it is only in the past month that a project to teach contraceptive methods to 'new couples' has been launched. 'Previously, we started education on family planning after people had a baby,' said a spokesman.

Not that any new sliver of openness about sex education can be attributed to a sweeping climate of social liberalism among the powers that be. Concern about Aids is finally activating China's public-health authorities – the UN has predicted that the country could have 10 million Aids cases by 2010 – resulting in a belated push on education about safe sex, and the beginnings of a programme to distribute condoms. But the unintended consequence of such huge-scale social engineering will be to give sexually active young people even greater sexual independence. The great irony of China's strictly controlled social programmes is that in Shanghai at least, they have created a subculture that has found the space to be remarkably socially liberated. A generation of girls, for instance, has grown up remarkably relaxed about abortion due to its widespread use in population control.

No one represents more acutely the complexities of Shanghai's new sexual climate than Zhou Wei Hui, a 30-year-old novelist whose 1999 bodice-ripper *Shanghai Baby* has become a samizdat Internet download in Shanghai, and an uncomfortable touchstone for the city's young. The novel, about a Shanghainese writer who, bored with her Chinese lover, embarks on a passionate sexual affair with a mysterious German, was a huge success in China when it came out in 1999. Soon after, it was banned, and 40,000 copies were publicly burned in 2000; Wei Hui was forced to flee Shanghai and denounced as 'debauched and a slave to western culture'. This helped to shoot the book to the top of bestseller lists around the world.

The novel is a fairly crude piece of erotica, but its whip-fast rattle through illicit open-air couplings and frenzied ruts in disco toilets clearly pressed manifold buttons in Shanghai. China's authorities, Wei Hui says, don't appreciate the extent to which people of her age have felt bereft of cultural voices. 'The pace at which China is moving now is really amazing. On the one hand this is good, but on the other, people are experiencing real anxiety they have nothing on which to attach their memories. Meanwhile, the new generation don't believe in the Communist thing, the way my mother and father did. The only thing you can believe in is money. Or, of course, sex.' It is important, she says, not to imagine that Shanghai's sexual revolution is more significant, or more widespread, than it really is. 'Western people, I think, have a kind of fantasy; they are very keen to see some huge change happen in this amazingly old, big country. But daily life is still boring in China, and people are still very conservative. Mothers will not allow their girls to go out late, to live with a boy before marriage. And if a girl gets pregnant by accident most will just go to the hospital, deal with that themselves, and not even tell their mother. It is true that things have changed a lot in China, but you can't compare the situation here to other countries.'

And indeed, while the change in the general acceptability of sexual behaviour among Shanghai's youth has been staggering in its speed and scale, this remains at heart a deeply conservative society. David Li, a 21-year-old student, says he and his four roommates in his university dorm do sometimes talk about 'girls and kissing' after they switch off the light and before they go to sleep, 'and sometimes sex, because we are very good friends'. David has never had a girlfriend; he says many of his friends are the same. 'I think I will give my first time to my wife. I'm quite traditional. I think it's not acceptable for me to have sex with anyone when my future is not guaranteed. At university I think we are more interested in finding pure love.'

Miki and her friends, meanwhile, are making plans for the weekend: which clubs they will go to, whether there will be lots of foreign guys there, whether there might be a lot of drugs around. 'I think Shanghai is very unusual,' says Gia. 'I think it must be a bit like New York City.' And are they very unusual? 'Maybe we represent a small group,' says Vanessa, 'but we are growing very quickly.'

THE MOST FASCINATING PERSON I HAVE EVER MET

Brian Whitaker

Tony Blair paid tribute to 'a huge icon for the Palestinian people' yesterday, while suggesting that the death of Yasser Arafat had created an opportunity. 'The most important thing is to make sure we reinvigorate the peace process. Because there is misery for Palestinians and there is misery for Israelis who suffer terrorist activity,' the prime minister told GMTV before leaving for talks with George Bush in Washington. Jack Straw, the foreign secretary, said Mr Arafat had played such a dominant role for so long that it was hard to imagine the Middle East without him. 'As the leader of his people, he created an international awareness of, and concern about, the plight of the Palestinian people. He displayed unquestionable devotion to his work.'

Britain's view was echoed by other European leaders, who focused on the more positive aspects of Mr Arafat's career while hoping for an end to the Israeli–Palestinian conflict. 'The Palestinian people have lost a symbol of the aspiration to assert their own national identity,' said the Italian prime minister, Silvio Berlusconi. 'We hope that all Palestinians will peacefully commit themselves to bringing about the objective of two states, their own and Israel, living side by side in safety, freedom and social development.' In a last show of respect, Jacques Chirac, the French president, spent ten minutes beside Mr Arafat's body at the Paris hospital where he died. 'With him disappears a man of courage and conviction who embodied for 40 years the Palestinians' fight for the recognition of their national rights,' he said in a statement. 'France, like its partners in the European Union, will maintain, firmly and with conviction, its commitment to two states . . . living side by side in peace and security.' Vladimir Putin, the Russian president, said Mr Arafat had dedicated his life to the Palestinians' fight for 'an independent state, which would coexist with Israel within recognised and secure borders'.

US reactions were guarded. George Bush ambiguously described the death as 'a significant moment in Palestinian history', while the secretary of state, Colin Powell, appealed for calm in the region.

Mr Arafat's Israeli detractors have said that he never missed an opportunity to miss an opportunity. Bill Clinton said that the prime opportunity missed was four years ago when Mr Arafat turned his back on the Camp David peace deal. 'I regret that in 2000 he missed the opportunity to bring that nation into being, and pray for the day when the dreams of the Palestinian people for a state and a better life will be realized in a just and lasting peace,' said the former US president. Nelson Mandela called Mr Arafat 'one of the outstanding freedom fighters of this generation', while a papal spokesman praised his 'great charisma'.

The UN flag flew at half-mast in New York, though Terje Roed-Larsen, the UN's veteran Middle East envoy, offered a blunt view of Mr Arafat's achievements. 'One of the reasons his credibility as a leader was undermined on the Palestinian side was an increasing agreement among the leadership and the Palestinian people that Arafat had led them in the wrong direction over the past four years,' he told Norwegian state radio. 'He was like a surrealistic painting, full of contradictions, full of mystery, full of inconsistencies. He was complex, deep, superficial, rational, irrational, cold, warm. He may be the most fascinating person I have ever met.'

14 November 2004

EID DIARY

Rory McCarthy

This morning an editor at the BBC asked their television reporter in Baghdad, on air, how Iraqis felt about the current situation. The reporter replied: 'I haven't really spoken to many people because we are unable to show our faces on the streets. It is too dangerous.' It used to be that journalists, seeing each other again in Baghdad for the first time, would ask: 'How long are you staying?' Now they ask: 'Are you going out much?' While 27 million Iraqis are trying to come to terms with the wrench from dictatorship into ugly occupation, foreign reporters can barely walk the streets in safety.

It was different in the months immediately after the war. We (myself and other *Guardian* journalists) took a house, a comfortable, whitewashed, cube-shaped home owned by the Khudairi family, a pillar of the rich elite. The building had been empty since they fled the country in 1991 during the first Gulf war, so the electrics and plumbing were in need of constant repair. Next door, in a much larger house also owned by the Khudairis, lived Sharif Ali, the pretender to the Iraqi throne. He kept sheep in his vast garden, next to the empty swimming pool, and entertained tribal sheikhs from across Iraq with lavish banquets.

We had two or three indolent guards who offered a minimum of protection, often slept through their shifts and started up the generator when the power went down every two or three hours. Yet we felt generally safe in our quiet backstreet. In April 2004, however, when the US military first attacked Falluja and a wave of kidnapping began, we moved out for a month and retreated to a hotel. It was better guarded but still outside the Green Zone, the Baghdad headquarters for the US, British and Iraqi governments on the site of Saddam's former palace and now heavily fortified with rows of blast walls, razor wire and tank positions.

I grew a beard, tried to dress more like a young Iraqi man might, and we returned to the house for the summer. We finally left for good in September, the morning after four carloads of gunmen kidnapped two Italian aid workers from their offices, in broad daylight, a few minutes' drive from our house. Returning to the hotel, which was by now surrounded by 12ft-high concrete blast walls and patrolled by Iraqi guards, felt like a deep personal defeat. After a year of trying to live among Iraqis, we'd had to hide behind our concrete walls. I was completely cut off from the people I was supposed to be writing about. The talk was constantly and exhaustingly of security.

A week after we left the house, Ken Bigley and two of his American colleagues were kidnapped from a house not unlike ours in Mansour, a wealthy district of western Baghdad. All three were later decapitated. Several journalists stayed in the hotel for days at a time. Our landlord's agent was eager for us to sign up for another year's rent, but there was no going back.

It was Eid today, the end of Ramadan, but it was excruciatingly quiet. No sign of the usual celebration.

MARGARET HASSAN

David Pallister

Margaret Hassan had devoted 30 years of her life to the health and welfare of the Iraqi people. She was a convert to Islam, fluent in Arabic, with an Iraqi husband. She was a well-known, respected and accepted figure in Baghdad and vocal critic of the US-led war on her adopted country. But last night it appeared that not even those credentials could save her from death at the hands of her kidnappers.

Over more than four weeks in which her frightened image was broadcast around the world, Mrs Hassan was revealed to be an intensely private person. Few people outside her immediate family and friends knew her well, but all who talked about her in the ensuing trauma of her captivity agreed her work was her passion. Felicity Arbuthnot, an Irish freelance journalist, testified to the affection Mrs Hassan received on her travels around the country for the charity Care International: 'She could go anywhere and didn't need a minder, even if she was going to a place that made Sadr City look like Knightsbridge.' Niall Andrews, the Irish former MEP who visited Iraq several times and met her twice, said: 'She struck me as a very powerful woman, a very strong person and a good person. She was apolitical, but very opposed to the sanctions. She was a very driven woman. She was very energetic, very committed, very compassionate.'

Born in Dublin, Mrs Hassan, 59, held joint British, Irish and Iraqi citizenship. She first moved to Iraq in 1972 after meeting her engineer husband, Tahseen Ali Hassan, in London. At first she worked for the British Council, teaching English. She became an assistant director of studies, then director of the Baghdad office. The council closed in 1990 after the Iraqi invasion of Kuwait, but after the 1991 Gulf war she found a new job as director of Care, one of the charities which remained in Iraq during the war. It specialises in projects involving health, nutrition, water supplies and sanitation. Mrs Hassan was a tireless opponent of the sanctions regime against Iraq, which she believed was responsible for the inadequate food and medical provisions for ordinary people.

In an interview with the *Guardian* in October 2002, almost exactly two years before she was kidnapped, she spoke of her concern that Iraqis were much more vulnerable to a conflict than before 1991. She predicted accurately that the limited electricity supply would almost certainly grind to a halt and would in turn badly affect water and sanitation plants. For months after the war her team was involved in tackling just that problem, trying to restart water treatment plants and replace rusting water pipes. 'Immunity levels are very low,' she said at the time. 'There is no cushion for the Iraqi population . . . It will take at least a generation to get back what they have lost.' Last year she warned of the humanitarian consequences of another war. 'The Iraqi people do not have the resources to withstand an additional crisis.'

Mrs Hassan's ordeal began on 19 October when she was seized by unknown militants as she was leaving for work from home in the Khadra district of western Baghdad. A series of ever more harrowing videos, the first released hours after her capture, came out. The videos contained specific threats that the kidnappers would kill her unless Britain withdrew troops from Baghdad and all women prisoners in Iraq were freed. In the first video footage she looked drawn, with her hands tied behind her back. She appeared to be talking, but no sound could be heard. Unlike most of the previous videos of kidnappings in Iraq, no militants or banners appeared. In the next video on 23 October, grainy footage was released on the Arab TV station al-Jazeera of Mrs Hassan pleading, 'I beg of you, the British people, to help me. I don't want to die like [Kenneth] Bigley. This might be my last hour.' It was the day after Britain announced a troop deployment to support the US military gathering around Falluja. She was seen calling on Tony Blair to withdraw troops from Iraq 'and not bring them to Baghdad. That's why people like Mr Bigley and myself are being caught. And maybe we will die like Mr Bigley.'

In the third video, on 27 October, Mrs Hassan looked close to tears. She asked for British troops to be withdrawn, for Care International to close its office in Baghdad and again for Iraqi women prisoners to be freed. Care responded by closing its Iraqi offices.

On 2 November, as Mrs Hassan's sister made a plea for her release in Dublin, a final video surfaced, which al-Jazeera decided not to broadcast on humanitarian grounds. Mrs Hassan reportedly pleaded for her life directly to the camera before fainting. It is believed a bucket of water was then thrown over her head and she was filmed wet and helpless on the ground before getting up and crying.

20 November 2004

PIT STOP

Michael Hann

There is an easy way to experience time travel. Stop for a meal when travelling on a motorway or a trunk road and be transported back to the 1970s (I swear that the last time I visited Leicester Forest East the ghost of Harold Wilson hovered at my shoulder, muttering about the value of the pound in my pocket as I surveyed the array of hot foods on offer). Our motorway services, we are often reminded, are the worst in Europe. This year's survey by the EuroTest group of motoring organisations, which includes the AA, rated Sandbach in Cheshire the single worst service station in Europe. But I'm an optimist. I don't like to think that way. I prefer to think of our services as traditional – as in 'traditional English fayre' – and visiting them as a return to the simpler days of English cuisine, when we could still believe radicchio was just a misspelling of radish.

When I visit motorway services, it doesn't matter to me that the tables are unwiped, the ashtrays unemptied or the food inedible. I get the same thrill I did as a child: for this meal, and this meal only, I can eat rubbish with a clear conscience, because nothing else is available. I've been heartbroken to discover perfectly functional chicken-sausage-and-pie places the length and breadth of Britain try to appeal to our better instincts by selling salads and paninis. Listen, Moto and Welcome Break and the rest of you, with your fancy ideas about going continental: in the land of the Little Chef, Panini will always be the manufacturer of sticker albums commemorating footballers, and nothing else. If you want to go continental, go to the continent. That's what it's there for. I don't resent the French having the best service station food in Europe (although the same surveys that damn the quality of our food note that the French have unhygienic facilities), but until we can replicate those standards (of cooking, not hygiene), we shouldn't bother with shoddy imitations. Sticking a vowel on the end of a franchise's name does not make it sophisticated.

The best service-station food I've tasted was at a stop high in the Massif Central. We pulled in not long after noon, having left Languedoc early that morning. In our desperate bid to make it from Castres to Kentish Town in as little time as possible, we had not been bothering with such niceties as minor roads. We were simply bombing up the deserted autoroutes, stopping only when the wailing of the child, the pressure on the bladder or the rumbling of the stomach became too much to ignore.

We ran through the rain into the pine lodge (Pine lodge? Eat your heart out, Heston), and on into the restaurant. Behold! A fresh, sizzling roasted ham, its juices trickling down the carved cliff of meat like tiny avalanches tumbling down a mountain face. I didn't get beyond the ham to look at the other main courses. I tried, but I was drawn back to the ham's elemental pinkness. And the fact that you got three slices, carved as you waited. Then, for pudding, a crème brûlée with the right balance of crunchy, sugary brûlée to soft, yielding crème. Is there any deficiency in the French service-station experience? Just, perhaps, one: is it entirely necessary (or, indeed, wise) to offer an extensive wine list? These are French motorways, remember. People are inclined to drive very fast on them even when sober.

Italian service stations, too, are reputed to offer food beyond the wildest dreams of a travelling salesman trapped at Toddington with only a Ginsters slice for company. But I wouldn't know. I find Italian motorways so terrifying that once on them I daren't stop until I'm long off the autostrada. Pulling in to the services would only pose the difficulty of how to safely get back into traffic moving at twice the speed of sound from a standing start.

We shouldn't blame our service stations for failing to meet the culinary standards of our European brethren. We regulate our services in a way they don't. Which doesn't mean Moto is legally compelled to turn the half-roast chicken with French fries and vegetable of the day into something made of pure carbon. It means our services have to provide a full range of facilities for free, and pay for them from the money they make on the concessions, without any help from road tolls or government subsidies.

That said, some of the excuses the station owners offer for the high prices they charge are risible. When the 2000 EuroTest survey results were published, a representative of the service stations appeared on the *Today* programme to offer a defence. The reason you end up paying the cost of a flat in Manchester for sausage and chips, he said (well, he didn't use those exact words), was the high transport costs of getting the ingredients to the restaurants. Eh? They're on motorways, pal. How hard to reach is that?

Nevertheless I won't join the chorus of knocking our services. At their best (or worst) they return you to the Britain of *Get Carter* (with less shooting), Alvin Stardust (with less silver lamé) and Dave Lee Travis (with less facial hair). If you want the quintessential services experience, avoid the modern chains and look for the names that spell classic. As long as classic is spelt G-R-E-A-S-Y. It was a comforting reminder of childhood to stop a while back at a Little Chef on the A1 and order a cheeseburger. 'One cheeseburger?' That's right. 'We don't have any cheese. Are you all right to have the cheeseburger without cheese? And we're out of buns. So that'll be one cheeseburger, no cheese, no bun.' All delivered with a smile, as if there is nothing more natural or joyful than a cheeseless, bunless (but not cheerless) cheeseburger.

TITTER YE NOT

Simon Callow

Conversation with Frankie Howerd was peculiarly disorientating. There he stood, in his usual stage uniform of brown suit and crumpled shirt, his toupee going up and down like a pedal-bin (as Barry Cryer memorably remarked), his eyebrows soaring up to join it, the face getting longer, the eyes looking wildly askance in horror or disbelief, the vowels extending and distending – being, in fact, in every particular the Frankie Howerd we all knew and loved. Except that he was not at all, not even remotely, for a single second, funny. What he was saying was almost identical to what he had said on stage the night before and the night before that to such side-splitting effect – a list of complaints, paranoias and resentments – but for some reason, while on stage it was the acme of hilarity, off it the laughter froze on your lips.

We had a little bit of an histoire, Frankie and I. One night, after the Olivier awards, where he had made his traditional superb speech – 'This afternoon I spoke to my agent, who thinks I'm dead,' it had begun – I was chatting to someone in the foyer and suddenly there he was, gloomily alone, half-listening to us. He said: 'Are you going to this party?' and of course I laughed, because to hear him was to laugh. He didn't laugh back, so I quickly said that I was, with my partner Aziz. He said, 'D'you want a lift?' I said that would be lovely, and off we went. He sensed we were a couple. 'Do you love each other?' he asked, without preamble. 'Yes, sir,' said Aziz. 'Very much,' said I. 'That must be nice,' he said sourly. 'Give me your hands.' In the dark of the back of his car he peered at our respective palms and rattled off some somewhat sobering – and not entirely inaccurate – observations about our personalities and what we had to offer each other. By now we were at the party, which consisted predominantly of playwrights. Having downed most of a bottle of vodka in about ten minutes, he announced:

'Why don't any of you lot write something for me?' Out of the babel of writers' voices offering their services, one dominated, that of Peter Nichols. 'But I have, Frankie. You turned it down.' 'What play was that, then?' '*The National Health.*' 'Oh, that. That was an awful play, a terrible play. It was all about death. You don't make fun of death. Write me a proper play, a funny play.'

Soon afterwards he said: 'Let's get out of here. I'll give you a lift. Where do you live?' When we arrived, he said: 'Aren't you going to ask me in?' I was thrilled, of course, at the idea of having Frankie Howerd on my sofa. The same thought had obviously occurred to him, but in a slightly more literal sense, because after a few minutes of rather strained chat, he said: 'Why don't we have an orgy? Just the three of us.' I laughed, but it was terribly, terribly clear that he wasn't joking. 'Well?' he said, implacably. 'I don't think so, Frankie,' I said, 'I mean, it'd be so embarrassing afterwards.' 'What d'you mean?' 'We're so tired. It'd be hopeless.' 'I'm not fussy.' 'No, Frankie, no, really, I have an early call tomorrow.' 'All right, all right, I get the message.' He headed crossly for the door, then paused for a moment. 'Not a word about this to anyone,' he said. 'There's a Person Back Home who would be very upset.'

The Person Back Home was Dennis Heymer, who now, in Graham McCann's fine new study *Frankie Howerd: Stand-Up Comic*, emerges from the shadows – but only just. Heymer is described as the love of his life, whom Howerd met when he was beginning to despair about his career and his physical attractiveness. Heymer had unshakeable faith in Howerd's talent, and spent his life extending his support in every way imaginable, most importantly by providing a domestic framework that reproduced the cosy and nurturing environment of his childhood home. Beyond these bare facts, however, we learn nothing of him. In fact, we learn little about Howerd, the man, either.

There are occasional tantalising glimpses of his friendships (with, for example, Rebecca West), but for all McCann's memorably ghastly anecdotes about him descending on chums such as Cilla Black and Barry Took with his sister and a bag of supermarket food, demanding that his reluctant hosts cook it for them while the visitors watched television, the sense of what he was actually like remains elusive. In a chapter entitled 'The Closeted Life', McCann gamely attempts to sketch the broad outlines of Howerd's sex-life, but beyond giving examples of the unattractive impatience of the sexual late starter – Frankie bellowing 'you don't know what you're missing!' at the rapidly escaping object of his unwanted advances – he refuses to add to what he considers to be the prurient and unfounded speculations of the tabloid press; sensibly, he regards Howerd's homosexuality as extrinsic to his comic persona, which, camp though it was, was no more gay than that of his deeply heterosexual and equally effete hero, Jack Benny.

Filth was, of course, at the heart of his comedy, part of the same great British tradition as the *Carry On* series, which enabled him occasionally to join the team. But unlike Sid and Ken and Babs and co, he was a great comic innovator, and it is in describing the evolution of young Frank Howard from Eltham into 'Frankie Howerd' that McCann comes into his own, guided by his subject, whose brilliantly titled autobiography, *On the Way I Lost It*, reveals an exceptionally acute and articulate self-awareness. This is partially the result of his many encounters with psychiatrists and analysts – including one who used LSD extensively – in his continuing struggle to find meaning in his life. McCann describes his agonisingly slow start (he was 29 before he got his first professional job), followed by his commensurately quick rise, which made him a national star within ten weeks of that first job. 'A completely new art form,' his first producer told him after his successful audition for radio's *Variety Bandbox*. Thanks largely to his performances, the show had a radio audience of nearly half of the total adult population. This was achieved not without enormous effort, accompanied by tension, rows and dread.

His initially successful style of 'anti-patter' had soon begun to stagnate; thinking hard, he realised that he was giving a stage and not a radio performance. He taught himself mastery of the microphone, painstakingly acquiring his characteristically wide vocal range, squeezing hilarious nuance out of a vast array of intonations. He discovered in Eric Sykes the first of many fine writers, commissioning from him the scripts which, building on his persona, invented the 'one-man situational comedy' ('I've had a shocking day') that stood him in such good stead for the rest of his career. He thought about every detail of his act, even changing the spelling of his name to make people look twice, thinking it must be a misprint. Ordinariness was the key. He eschewed the flashiness of Max Miller or Tommy Cooper's exotic troglodytism, creating the impression that 'I wasn't one of the cast, but had just wandered in from the street . . .' He had turned his perceived disadvantages as a performer – the unconventional appearance, the stammering, the forgetfulness – into comedic triumph, the stand-up comic as a paradigm of the oppressed little man. 'I played against the show,' Howerd wrote, 'as though its faults were all part of a deliberate conspiracy against me: I was being sabotaged by them – the cast, scriptwriters, management – and was striving to rise above it all.' Michael Billington, writing in the *Guardian*, was moved to describe him as 'arguably the most Brechtian actor in Britain', though Pirandello would surely have been equally delighted by the act.

His restless intellect (Aristotle and Aquinas were bedtime reading), and a profound conviction that the public could never be satisfied for long with what he was giving them, drew him to explore new forms and even new *métiers*, resulting in extreme vicissitudes in his popularity. Audiences were no longer sure who or what he was; for a while he was convinced that his real destiny was as an actor, a view shared by neither critics nor public. Peter Cook rescued him when he persuaded him to appear at the Establishment club, which resulted in appearances on *That Was the Week That Was* and a wholly unexpected new reputation as a satirist. The last few years were a sort of golden summer, in which he was finally reassured of the public's love. 'Can you believe I've been doing the same old rubbish for years?' he cheerfully asked Barbara Windsor during his last tour.

He was not easy to work with, and he seems only rarely to have experienced what most of us would call happiness, except when performing. McCann records Howerd's own (otherwise unsubstantiated) conviction that he was physically and sexually abused by his father, which would certainly be consistent with his eternal sense of self-rejection. The book's extensive transcripts from the act, with

Dog fight
The Countryside Alliance protest against the hunting bill in Parliament
Square (DAN CHUNG/GUARDIAN)

Devastation *(Overleaf)*
In Indonesia, a man stands amid the devastation left behind by the tsunami
(DAN CHUNG/GUARDIAN)

Holy father
Incense is cast over the coffin of Pope John Paul II in the Vatican, Italy
(DAN CHUNG/GUARDIAN)

Hoodies
Boys off school in Bromley, London (MARTIN GODWIN/GUARDIAN)

every um, yes, ah, liss-en, you see and no missus! in place, instantly evoke his unique comic creation, making one laugh out loud. However unloved Frank Howard may have felt, Frankie Howerd, this book clearly demonstrates, remains forever ensconced in British hearts, a quintessential part of us, in the presence of whom it remains impossible to be titterless.

27 November 2004

DEAR DIARY

Katharine Viner

When you think of 1988, you think of high Thatcherism. The third term of unfettered monetarist economics, the destruction of manufacturing industry, the rise of the entrepreneur, of City braggadocio, of conspicuous consumption and loadsamoney, soaring house prices and power suits. And what was I doing? Thrilling over a black-and-white photograph of a man holding a baby, sitting around moaning about boys, drinking cider and wondering if SH would ever notice me.

The year that launched *Guardian Weekend* may have seen the floodtide of 1980s materialism, but I can't say that the red braces ever made it to Yorkshire. Reading my detailed and excruciating diary of 1988, and scouring my memory, I've been trying to work out how much of being 16 was about the times, how much was about where I grew up and the people I grew up with and how much was universal, the stuff that's not changed since the teenager was invented.

In a way, the typical-teenager elements of my diary are the least surprising: the emotions in turmoil, the agitated hormones, the growing pains and agony of being noticed too much or, worse, too little. 'I BLOODY HATE HER AND THAT IS IT,' I wrote. And, 'Why can't they see I'm in PAIN?' Crushes were sometimes enduring, sometimes fleeting, but always, in my diary, baffling: 'I wonder if SH has noticed me at all?' 'God I wish I could stop thinking about AT.' 'SL smiled at me in badminton so that's good. Felt better.' There was also a JH, a CH and a TG, their identities forgotten for ever, obscured in case the diary got into enemy hands. (James Hill, JH was definitely *not* you.) One day I wrote, gloomily: 'Suddenly realised who I fancy. It is not good.'

The teenager's obsession with appearance is similarly evident. I thought Miss Selfridge was the absolute apotheosis of style;

otherwise it was Just In at Debenhams, Clockhouse at C&A and local chains. We bought earrings and nasty belts from the market, and went to Boots for hair dye, gold hairspray, blue mascara and eyeshadows with names such as 'Coppa Toppa' and 'Moonshadow' in shimmery shades. It was also a big year for crimpers; we'd backcomb our hair and then crimp for longer than it said and wonder whether that was smoke or steam. There is not one reference to my weight in the diary, nor do I ever seem to have weighed myself. Eating disorders have boomed since 1988, although I had several schoolfriends with bulimia, all girls.

Youth crime is an obsession for today's politicians, but in a small town in the 1980s there didn't seem to be much about. I came across drugs only when I met some wild boys from the exotic metropolis that is Thirsk. The violent crime I heard about, meanwhile, was largely distant and always terrifying: at primary school I was petrified of the Yorkshire Ripper until he was caught in 1981; later I was deeply troubled by the disappearance of Suzy Lamplugh in 1986. The crimes the young people I knew were committing were the taping of the Top 20 from the radio (which was made especially glamorous because of the urban myth that someone from Leeds had gone to jail for it), underage drinking and smoking dope. No one I knew was arrested.

However, my diary held a pleasing reminder that even a goody-two-shoes high-achiever like me got into trouble with the law. Our school, a Yorkshire state school, had made it to the London finals of a debating competition, previously the preserve of top public schools. The team was Simon, my political enemy (he was Tory, I was Labour; today he is a New Labour councillor), and me. We won, and to celebrate Simon and I and our supporters took over a flat in Fleet Street to which someone had the key, drank until the sun came up and were visited by the police at 5 a.m., just as a fellow pupil was demonstrating how to wear an elephant-trunk thong he had bought earlier. Who could complain about the youth of today?

I was quite surprised to read in my diary how much I went out drinking. There are quotes such as 'drank cider till midnight' and 'brilliant night, loads of booze, ended up in Darren's caravan'. (No ideas as to the identity of Darren.) I would list the nightspots visited: 'Unicorn, good, Gio's, annoying, Brontes, too many squaddies.' I was surprised to read all this, and it puts the current binge-drinking crisis into context: it had firm foundations to build upon.

Young people can be obsessive, and I was no exception. At 16 those obsessions were with the Smiths and books. The Smiths had split up in 1987, but that had only fuelled my passion. 'Why did they end before I could be even more enveloped by them?' I wailed one day. I quite liked U2, the Housemartins and the Daintees, but it was Smiths fanzines I wrote for, rare Smiths 12-inches I ordered through the post, obscure slogans in the run-off grooves of Smiths vinyl that I discovered. (If you've never noticed these, dig out your old Smiths records and take a look. 'Romantic and square is hip and aware' is my favourite.)

When I wasn't listening to records, I was reading, and found particular joy in Sylvia Plath (for whom I lit candles on 11 February, the anniversary of her death), Oscar Wilde, the Brontës, T. S. Eliot, Jean-Paul Sartre (hell was naturally all other people, all of the time) and D. H. Lawrence, especially *The Virgin and the Gipsy*. The title alone! In fact, like Morrissey, I think I was more obsessed with Plath and Wilde than most living celebrities. In my early teens, I had registered a celebrity-crush each month in my journal: it was usually John Taylor of Duran Duran. But celebrities are barely mentioned in my 1988 diary, beyond the occasional reference to 'sexy Imran Khan' or the intriguing, 'wrote to Barry Norman asking for Daniel Day-Lewis's address, I doubt I'll get it.' For love-objects, I was far more focused on blokes in the sixth form, or the occasional teacher.

Nobody I knew actually went out with a member of staff, although one friend did get to slow-dance with the exciting biology teacher at a school disco. Some of my friends had had sex by the age of 16, but most had not. Those who were having sex were either in long-term, winsome, across-the-classroom affairs, or were going out with local cable-pullers with second-hand Alfa Romeos. We were gripped by every detail. But there was also a great fear of Aids: 1987's iceberg advert, which has been much derided, I remember as terrifying – perhaps for teenagers, the looming, menacing iceberg represented our sexuality, with its unspoken desires, and we were scared enough of those already. We knew no one with HIV, and yet we were part of the Aids generation.

When we weren't avoiding or courting sex, we were watching films and TV. For one friend's sixteenth birthday we hired a video of *Straw Dogs* – although it had been banned since 1984. At the cinema we saw *A Fish Called Wanda* and *Crocodile Dundee 2*, but my favourite film of 1988 was *The Unbearable Lightness of Being*. I went to see this with my mother, who was single, our friend Mary, whose husband was away, and her hard-of-hearing mother-in-law, Flo. At the end of the steamy film, Flo turned to us all and bellowed in her broad Leeds accent, 'Well, here we all are feeling fruity and we haven't got a fella between us!'

Television, according to my diary, was mainly comedy shows (favourites were *The New Statesman* and Victoria Wood), *Brookside, 40 Minutes* and sport; my only entry on the Seoul Olympics is: 'Ben Johnson won gold in the 100m. He is SO fast!' I was very disdainful, meanwhile, of most No 1 hits, especially Bros ('I Owe You Nothing'), Kylie Minogue ('I Should Be So Lucky') and Cliff Richard, whose 'Mistletoe and Wine' was the Christmas No 1. We would wake up to the Radio 1 breakfast show, hosted in 1988 by Mike Smith and then Simon Mayo, although we would also moan about the records they played. My much cooler younger brother Patrick was appalled; he had been starting the day with the Stooges, MC5 and the Velvet Underground since the age of eight.

Like many teenagers, I couldn't see far beyond my own boundaries and the outside world had limited influence. In many ways, teenagers' lives happen outside of a political context; a government's decisions will affect them, but how much do they notice? My parents worked in the public sector, so we weren't affected by Thatcherism to anything like the same extent as those working in manufacturing or mining, nor, indeed, as those working in business. And yet I was obsessed with the Cold War and terrified that we would be a target because the Menwith

Hill US spy station was close by. I joined Youth CND and Anti-Apartheid, but there were no groups active within 25 miles. I went vegetarian at 16 (influenced by the Smiths' 'Meat Is Murder' and a first and last taste of chicken nuggets), bought *Spare Rib* feminist magazine every month, and sometimes read the papers. Nevertheless, political events are hardly ever mentioned in my diary, except in connection with school and those debates. 'Went to debate on terrorism. I was secretary. It went against terrorism.' And 'abortion debate cancelled because of hoo-hah about offensive posters. We all got bollocked.' Also, 'Gave talk in assembly about Bangladesh', which must have been about the floods. I was devastated by watching *Cry Freedom* at the local cinema in 1988, and noted: 'Cried and cried and cried but what good's that going to do?'

I met our local MP, David Curry, twice during the year as a still-serving MP. I must apologise to him for the lack of grace with which I wrote: 'Had a talk by David Curry about the EEC. Tory tit.' Having mentioned the world very rarely during the year, suddenly in my 'end of year summary' I have an unbelievable rant: 'Disaster followed disaster, Piper Alpha, Lockerbie, Armenia, Clapham, Jamaica, Bangladesh, Sudan, Northern Ireland still, and Thatcher. But there have been a few good things: Zia dead, Chile says no to Pinochet, Edwina Currie out (for now).' Not to deny my nascent political leanings, I don't really think the quality of Pakistan's president was something I knew much about. I can only think that I copied it out of *Spare Rib* or, perhaps, the *Guardian*.

As for the world of work, I clearly viewed it as a mug's game. After a week's work experience at the *Ripon Gazette*, I wrote, 'Came home at 5.45, absolutely knackered. You can keep your regular job crap.' I know that 16-year-olds think like this still, because my 16-year-old friend Beth told me she's been working in an old people's home and can't believe how much like hard work it is.

I was 17 by the time *Weekend* launched, on 3 December 1988. My diary entry for that day is: 'Amazing day. Bummed around in morning – bath, hairwash, records, town in afternoon. Read Woolf's *A Room of One's Own*, utterly amazing and spiritually influential! Then went out with Vix and Li Owen and I went to West Tanfield played a joke on G&G ha ha ha came back saw Sar lots of Merrydown back to Tanfield Owen, Dave and G came back for coffee. Amazing!' Which reminds me of something else about teenagers. Where do they get all that energy?

WINTER

BLUNKETT:
THE END OF THE ROAD

Leading article

In the end, in politics, it is the support of those around you that counts more than anything else. When the allegations against David Blunkett first surfaced in public last month, his party and his ministerial colleagues stood solidly by him. But, in the ensuing weeks, that initial support has steadily ebbed away, slowly at first but with gathering speed this week. Last night the emergence of a clear paper trail over the visa application for his lover's nanny hastened the collapse of his own political credibility. Support for Mr Blunkett had drained away for several reasons: because of the thin but steady trickle of further allegations that continued to drip into the public domain right up to yesterday morning, because of the repercussions of the unguarded contempt for his cabinet colleagues revealed in Stephen Pollard's new biography, and finally – the straw that perhaps broke the camel's back – because of Mr Blunkett's misjudged levity about his situation at a gathering of Labour MPs this week.

In the final analysis, Mr Blunkett presumed too much on the patience of those around him. His cabinet colleagues and his party had become too twitchy about where it would all end. A difficult general election is massively on all their minds, and Mr Blunkett was beginning to be part of the problem not the solution. Notoriously sentimental the Labour Party may be, but it handed Mr Blunkett the ivory-handled revolver last night with as little emotion as the Tory Party did to Margaret Thatcher 14 winters ago.

The hard reality is that, whatever sympathies many of us will always have for this very remarkable man, his departure will be widely welcomed, and not solely for the hard-nosed political reasons that brought it about. Many people sincerely believe that Mr Blunkett was one of the most destructive and dangerous home secretaries of modern times. No politician of modern times has had greater contempt for the rule of law or been readier to express it in public. None has been less in awe of the independence of the judiciary. Few have been as cavalier in their disregard of civil liberties or appeared to play faster and looser with the language of liberty and rights. Mr Blunkett's counter to this view is deeply held and serious. He believes that a progressive party must be tough and decisive about the threats that stalk everyday life – terrorism, violent crime, antisocial behaviour and the rest – so that it can do the things that must be done to create a more humane society, like reducing the prison population and encouraging multiracialism. Very few senior figures in the Labour Party would disagree with him on that, certainly not Charles Clarke, who was named as his successor last night and who is extremely well qualified for this latest, unlooked-for, promotion.

As the events of the past month have shown, though, it was not Mr Blunkett's policies that brought him down, nor his political acumen. It was, in the end, what the elder George Bush famously called 'the judgement thing' that scuppered him. Mr Blunkett put his judgement on the line, and was found wanting. The bitter disintegration of a relationship involving children was personal. The blurring of the personal and the political was, in the end, fatal. Mr Blunkett is a man of prodigious talents, and no one, however critical they may be of his policies, can ever fail to respect his huge personal achievement. But there was something missing. There was and is something about Mr Blunkett that is too arrogant, reckless and egotistical – and that was embodied in the book which finally caused his colleagues' patience to snap. It was still there in the angry resignation interviews last night. It was this which caused the great and tragic political fall of a flawed and remarkable public figure. And it is why, for all that he and we have lost by his departure, there is also a real sense of relief that he has gone.

OUT OF THE BLUE, A DEADLY WALL OF WATER

John Aglionby, Rory McCarthy, Jonathan Steele, Maseeh Rahman and Andrew Meldrum

Indonesia. Shock hits at 7.58 a.m. local time: 4,400 dead in Aceh and North Sumatra

The earth began to move 25 miles below the seabed, a massive rupturing of the earth's crust off the north-western tip of Sumatra. A section of seabed, 625 miles long, rose to 30 metres at a spot approximately 155 miles south-east of the city of Banda Aceh and 1,000 miles north-west of the Indonesian capital of Jakarta. Millions of people were living, fishing and holidaying around the Bay of Bengal and on the coast of Thailand and Malaysia, hundreds of miles from the epicentre. They were not to know that the gentle shaking that caused skyscrapers in Singapore and Chiang Mai in northern Thailand to sway would unleash a devastating tsunami, bringing a wall of water crashing down on their shores.

Mohammed Firdus, 36, a telephone operator from Bireuen, Aceh province, was sitting on the porch of his house, about 200 metres from the sea, when the earthquake struck. Then he heard a rumbling, but this time the ground was not shaking. Someone came running fast from the beach, shouting, 'Huge wave! Huge wave!' Mr Firdus said: 'And then I saw the water. It was a wall at least a metre high coming down the track towards us all. We all immediately turned and ran towards the main road with the water following us.'

Officials said it was impossible to say how many people were killed by the earthquake because it was quickly followed by tsunamis striking Aceh province and also the smaller islands, like the popular surfing resort of Nias, where an entire hotel, the Wismata Indah, was washed out to sea. 'The wall of water which came ashore was between five and ten metres high in many places,' said Ari Meridal, a provincial government official in Banda Aceh. 'It swept almost everything away for hundreds of metres inland.' Severed communications meant that estimates of casualty figures were imprecise. 'We have heard very little from west Aceh, which is the nearest point to the epicentre,' said Raifa Sistani of the Indonesian Red Cross. 'This is a major concern to us because logic says this area should have suffered the most.'

Thailand. Shock hits at 8 a.m.: 400 dead, dozens of foreign tourists feared missing, more than 5,000 injured

The packed Thai tourist resorts on Phuket and Phi Phi islands were the next to be hit with a succession of tsunamis ten metres high. Montri Charnvichai, a resident of Phuket, was on the beach at 10 a.m. when suddenly the sea water disappeared and the beach dried. He said: 'Then the first wave hit. It must have been travelling at about 70 kilometres [45 miles] per hour, it was very fast. It swept up the beach, carrying everything with it. There were many, many people in the sea at this time, and many of them were tourists. I have no idea what happened to them.' Then the second wave hit, about two minutes later. It was three metres high, and crashed into the buildings lining the shore. Simon Clark, a British photographer holidaying on Koh Ngai, described a huge wave crashing on to the beach, destroying everything in its wake. 'People who were snorkelling were dragged along the coral and washed up on the beach, and people who were sunbathing got washed into the sea,' he said.

The tsunami struck Phuket just after 10 a.m., when Christmas revellers were just starting to surface. 'It was like a really, really bad dream,' said Dawn Taylor from Stockport, who was on Kamala beach. 'It was a glorious day and a group of us were enjoying the beach when suddenly we saw this wall of water coming towards us. We just ran. The scale of the devastation is just enormous.' About 70 divers, many of them foreign tourists, who were exploring the famed Emerald Cave were plucked to safety after the first waves struck. The more remote Phi Phi islands, where the film *The Beach* was filmed, were hit even more badly. Heavy seas, however, prevented people from being evacuated.

Malaysia. Tsunami hits soon after 8 a.m.: 42 dead

Most of the fatalities in Malaysia were people swimming and jet skiing off beaches on the island of Penang who were struck by the tsunami. Other deaths were reported on the mainland, in Perak and Kedah states, from both tsunamis and the original quake as thousands of buildings were damaged or destroyed. 'It was crazy,' said Lin Wei Song, a restaurant owner on Batu Ferringhi. 'One minute I was preparing for the lunchtime rush and then the next thing I knew was that my tables were floating off down the street.'

Jasper Bintner, from Saskatchewan, Canada, was staying at Ali's guest house at Batu Ferringhi, north-west of Penang island. 'At first you could just see a wall of waves in the distance with the white tops crashing down. Luckily we had a lot of visual warning so we could get out of the water and the locals made sure we did. Around the corner, where the people were washed out to sea, they didn't have any warning. [The tsunami] just swept them off the beach and out to sea.'

India. Tremors at 6.30 a.m. Tsunami hits at 9 a.m.: at least 3,000 dead, including 1,625 in Tamil Nadu

The fishermen along India's southern Coromandel coast had just brought in the night's catch. Kalai Arasan in Kalapet, near Pondicherry, was crouched on the beach when he saw the ocean rise up before him. 'Suddenly I heard people from the village shouting: "Run! Run for your lives!" I saw the water coming and I tried to run back to my house to find my children, but as I got close I was washed away.' In just a few minutes, more than 1,800 villagers were killed along the eastern Indian coastline and thousands more were left homeless.

As the ocean raced inland, Mr Arasan, 30, clung to a coconut palm near his village at Kanaga Chettkuluan, one of the worst-hit areas along the coastline south of Madras. Although his wife had climbed on to a roof to safety, two of his daughters, Desika, aged just 20 days, and Dhia, 13, were killed. The house just crumbled. 'The girls were swept away,' he said at the Pondicherry Institute of Medical Sciences. Minutes later, the water receded almost as quickly as it had come in. At least 63 dead were brought to the hospital, all drowned. Another 140 injured were brought in, several critically ill.

Sri Lanka. Tsunami hits at 9 a.m.: 4,500 dead

Standing blankly beside the pile of thin timber and corrugated roofing which were all that remained of his flimsy wooden house, Ugatsiri Vidanage said: 'The first big wave came up the beach well beyond the treeline. It gave us a kind of warning. Half an hour later we saw a huge one, much bigger than the first. It smashed into the houses, destroying everything.' Ten miles south of Colombo, the poverty-stricken community of Moratuwa was one of Sri Lanka's worst-hit areas. Hundreds of shacks built alongside the railway which runs parallel to the island's west coast, 100 metres from the sea, were smashed by the water.

At the nearest hospital in Panadura, 29 bodies had been brought to the morgue, according to Roshan de Silva, Moratuwa's assistant police superintendent. The town's main temple was sheltering about 3,000 people. One person was brought in dead after being electrocuted as he stood in water in his home, said a doctor. Another man was in intensive care after seeing his wife and two children swept into the sea.

The island-wide death toll in what officials were calling Sri Lanka's worst natural disaster had reached 4,500 last night. More than a million people, about 5 per cent of the island's population, were homeless, injured, or otherwise affected. The president, Chandrika Kumaratunga, who was on holiday in London, declared it a national disaster and was flying home immediately. In Trincomalee, on the east coast, cars floated out to sea and corpses bobbed around in the floodwaters.

Maldives. Tsunami hits at 9 a.m.: 32 dead

The Maldives, a cluster of 1,192 coral islands in the Indian Ocean, off the south-western coast of India, was badly hit because much of its landmass is barely above water. Two-thirds of the capital island, Male, was flooded, and outlying atolls were completely submerged. A British tourist died of a heart attack after seeing the huge wave heading towards him at White Sand resort on South Ari atoll. An Italian tourist was seriously injured. Their identities were not released. Some 285 tourists were on the beach at the time. The Government confirmed at least 32 people had died.

Nazim Sattar, who was in the capital, said: 'The whole sea just lifted up. It swelled up. There was no sound. The sea just poured on to the island. Small boats were dropped on to the street. The people said that they did not know what had hit them.'

MANY STORIES

Jeremy Seabrook

The number of fishing boats from Sumatra, Sri Lanka and Tamil Nadu at sea when the Boxing Day tsunami hit will never be known. There is scarcely any population tally of the crowded coasts. Nameless people are consigned to unmarked graves in mosques and temples, makeshift mortuaries; people pull aside a cloth, a piece of sacking, to see if those they loved lie beneath. As in all natural disasters, the victims are overwhelmingly the poorest.

This time there was something different. The tsunami struck resorts where westerners were on holiday. For the western media, it was clear that their lives have a different order of importance from those that have died in thousands, but have no known biography and, apparently, no intelligible tongue in which to express their feelings. This is not to diminish the trauma of loss of life, whether of tourist or fisherman. But when we distinguish between 'locals' who have died and westerners, 'locals' all too easily becomes a euphemism for what were once referred to as natives. Whatever tourism's merits, it risks reinforcing the imperial sensibility. For this sensibility has already been reawakened by all the human-made, preventable catastrophes. The ruins of Galle and Banda Aceh called forth images of Falluja, Mosul and Gaza. Imperial powers, it seems, anticipate the destructive capacity of nature. A report on ITN news made this explicit, by referring to 'nature's shock and awe'. But while the tsunami death toll rises in anonymous thousands, in Iraq disdainful American authorities don't do body counts.

One of the most poignant sights of the past few days was that of westerners overcome with gratitude that they had been helped by the grace and mercy of those who had lost everything, but still regarded them as guests. When these same people appear in the West, they become the interloper, the unwanted migrant, the asylum seeker, who should go back to where they belong. A globalisation that permits the wealthy to pass effortlessly through borders confines the poor to eroded subsistence, overfished waters and an impoverishment that seems to have no end. People rarely say that poor countries are swamped by visitors, even though their money power pre-empts the best produce, the clean water and amenities unknown to the indigenous population.

In death, there should be no hierarchy. But even as Sri Lankans wandered in numb disbelief through the corpses, British TV viewers were being warned that scenes they were about to witness might distress them. Poor people have no consoling elsewhere to which they can be repatriated. The annals of the poor remain short and simple, and can be effaced without inquiry as to how they contrive an existence on these fragile coasts. What are the daily visitations of grief and loss in places where people earn less in a year than the price that privilege pays for a night's stay in a five-star hotel? Western governments, which can disburse so lavishly in the art of war, offer a few million as if it were exceptional largesse. Fortunately the people are wiser and the spontaneous outpourings of humanity have been as unstoppable as the waves that broke on south Asia's coasts: donations rapidly exceeded the amount offered by government. Selflessness and sacrifice, people working away at rubble with bare hands, suggest immediate human solidarities. But these are undermined by the structures of inequality. Promises solemnly made at times of immediate sorrow are overtaken by other urgencies; money donated for the Orissa cyclone, for hurricane Mitch in Central America, the floods in Bangladesh, the Bam earthquake – as for the reconstruction of Afghanistan and Iraq – turns out to be a fraction of what is pledged.

Such events remind us of the sameness of our human destiny, the fragility of our existence. They place in perspective the meaning of security. Life is always at the mercy of nature – whether from such overwhelming events as this, or the natural processes that exempt no one from paying back to earth the life it gave us. Yet we inhabit systems of social and economic injustice that exacerbate the insecurity of the poor, while the West is prepared to lay waste distant towns and cities in the name of a security that, in the end, eludes us all. Assertions of our common humanity occur only at times of great loss. To retrieve and hold on to it at all other times – that would be something of worth to salvage from these scenes of desolation.

SOME LESSER RUPTURE

Joan Bakewell

It will be a dull soul who does not raise a glass tonight. Whether it's among a motley crowd of strangers or sitting alone before the television, surely the ritual of New Year's Eve deserves acknowledgement. In my memory, the image that lingers is one of clocks: carriage clocks, Victorian railway clocks, the face of Big Ben, strong Roman numerals, neat plain numbers, even the blinking of the digital. Shut your eyes, and they emerge from the past, seared on the retina year after year marking the man-made calendar. 'No different from any other day,' says the New Year's equivalent of Scrooge, the wet blanket who goes to bed early with cocoa and no companions. But that is to miss the entire point. Rituals define us.

We have to have rituals: indeed, we live our lives by them. The feeding rituals of three meals a day, coffee and tea breaks, an evening drink, the final nightcap, the annual rituals of birthdays and anniversaries. Rituals are but the grand forms, habits the daily fodder. Both are the repeating routines by which we count our hours and days. Rites of passage mark the shift from one set of rituals to another. Students give up on the three meals a day, the retired give up the 8.15 to Paddington. Religions have built virtually impregnable rituals to back up implausible stories. That's why so many of us who have given up on the Creed still go for the carol service and the Easter hymns. There is nothing bogus about this. The stories themselves carry for the agnostic the message of hope, renewal and salvation, which for Christians is vested in the figure of Christ. Non-believers need that message and its rituals too.

The more multicultural we become, the more rituals we have. Schoolchildren in Britain now celebrate Diwali, the Jewish and Chinese new years and probably others I haven't heard of. Western tourists to Madurai throw lumps of butter at giant Hindu gods, the Queen covers her head in a Sikh temple in London. We are on a colossal ritual-sharing around the world. Currently, we are all caught up in the rituals of grief, moving with those personally involved in the tsunami along the pathway grief slowly takes towards some acceptance of loss. No doubt our shared feeling will express itself in services of remembrance, memorial ceremonies and such. Rituals offer comfort, in the bleak world of such random cruelties.

Getting older involves a radical shift in rituals. The higher ones remain, of course, although at Christmas we sit in the corner nursing a glass of mulled wine, rather than ricocheting round the kitchen in a panic of unfamiliar recipes and too many mince pies. Daily behaviours that are no more than entrenched habits somehow refuse to budge. How am I to persuade myself that I no longer need the alarm clock to go off at 7 a.m.? When am I to realise that I don't have to work five days and then enjoy the weekend off? I can work and play just as I like. But try telling that to my inner self. I am only slowly coming to realise that I don't need an August holiday, but can go when the costs are cheaper, the climate cooler, and the beach is not swarming with families.

New rituals arrive. Collecting the pension at the post office was once a comforting and regular excursion for loads of the old, snatched from them by the Government's wish for everyone to have bank accounts. Plenty of us don't have, and don't want, bank accounts. If you've never had one, 65 is no age to start.

The loss of post offices takes with it a whole host of other tiny rituals: applying for licences of all sorts, for currency of different varieties, posting parcels, all that stamping and registering. There was something comforting about those homely queues, with their gossip, thoughts on the weather, comments, sour and sweet, about the Government or neighbours. But good things happen too. Health is now transformed for the better by all the rituals of prevention: flu jabs, mammograms, annual check-ups. When were we so looked after even before we're ill?

As the year closes, the one ritual that itself endorses change comes around: the New Year's resolution. For a shared moment we can turn out the attic of old customs and redundant habits, and try to usher in new ways of doing things. Only the Scrooge who refuses the glass of wine thinks nothing can change. Even the old don't need to be stuck in their ways. I shall start by giving up that 7 a.m. alarm call.

BEGINNING WITH £1 MILLION

Jonathan Freedland

Most television programmers like to aim for a balance of light and shade, but the editors of the news bulletins over the holiday period have not really had that option. Instead, and for each evening since Boxing Day, the TV news has been a glimpse of hell. Report after report, from Indonesia or Sri Lanka or some flyspeck island in the middle of the Indian Ocean, has brought some new horror. Not the pictures of the mangled buildings and upended ships – it is surprising how quickly we have become inured to those. But the stories – of orphaned children, of babies snatched from their mothers' arms, of fathers washed out to sea – seem only to get worse, taking us ever deeper into the calamity.

All that the bulletins have had to lighten the gloom is a related story: the British reaction to the disaster. On this the media have spoken with one voice, lauding the great British public for a generosity that has made us among the most open-handed nations in the world.

The scale of British giving has been moving, especially acts of kindness by those with least to spare: cleaners or pensioners or the unemployed donating sums that either took a week to earn or were a week's keep. People have drawn a legitimate pride in this and in the public's outpacing of government, whose earliest pledge of £1 million looked so paltry. Ministers increased that to £50 million and yesterday hinted there would be more if needed. That is welcome, but hardly overwhelming. Others have pointed out the contrast between that contribution, even if it rises to, say, £100 million, and the £6 billion the UK government found so readily for the war on Iraq. But one need not look so far. The cost of the new national identity card scheme, for example, bringing food and shelter to no one, is estimated at £3.1 billion. Next to sums like that, £50 million or £100 million is, to use a grimly appropriate phrase, a drop in the ocean.

But the Government is doing plenty of other things: lending military assistance to stricken countries as well as deploying staff in London and around the world. No, anger, if we feel it, should be directed at the third lead player in public life: not citizens or government, but big business. Corporate Britain was quick to realise it needed to stand with the public mood and publicise its concern. The major companies doubtless feel proud of their generosity. They shouldn't. They should be ashamed.

Vodafone announced it would be giving £1 million and matching all staff donations. A million pounds is a lot of money to you and me, but not to Vodafone, to which it is pocket change. The company's annual profit, registered last May, was £10 billion. That means the company made substantially more than a million pounds an hour. Yet that is all they gave – less than an hour's profit. It is less than they gave their new boss, Arun Sarin, for his annual bonus. Put another way, Vodafone has given a mere one ten-thousandth of its annual profit. (Not its total revenue, mind, which would be a larger figure, just its profit.) Think of your own annual income, after you've paid off all your expenses. Now work out what one ten-thousandth of that sum would be. If you had given just that amount to the tsunami appeal, would that be enough? Would you announce it with pride?

Or look at one of the early givers and publicity seekers: the Premiership. It gave the same Vodafone figure, £1 million. The Premiership is made up of 20 clubs, so that would have set back each team a grand total of £50,000. That is what Manchester United pays Wayne Rooney for four and a half days' work. That club alone is worth £700 million. Its annual profit is £47 million. Maybe the Man U players did the maths and felt guilty, but, if they did, it was not nearly guilty enough. Between them they raised another £50,000. When you think that Rio Ferdinand earns £80,000 a week, that is scarcely an impressive total from an entire squad. They could each have sold off a couple of diamond ear studs and raised more than that.

The roll-call of shame continues. BP gave a healthy-looking £1.6 million: fine, until you realise the oil giant's expected profits for 2004 weigh in at £9 billion.* Abbey National's trading profit from its core businesses topped

*In fact they were £8.7 billion.

the billion-pound mark in 2004, even if the company made an overall loss. Times must be tough, though, because when it dipped in its corporate pocket it found just £25,000. I've done the sums: on my comfortable *Guardian* salary, that's the equivalent of me giving less than two quid. Tesco is proud that it has sent food, water and hygiene products to Thailand and Sri Lanka – but it's still a shock that, with annual profits of £1.7 billion, it only managed to give an anaemic £100,000. Philip Green, the BHS boss, is a famously generous man, giving serious sums to charity. But even his £100,000 in cash and £1 million-worth of clothes looks like less of a sacrifice when one notes that his Arcadia group paid him a dividend of £460 million last year – and that he spent £5 million on a toga party to mark his 50th birthday two years ago.

None of this should really come as a surprise. Battle-hardened viewers of *Children in Need* and *Comic Relief* will have noted the corporate givers' eagerness to grab free publicity – handing over a cheque on TV – combined with their stunning levels of stinginess. The sums they give are the coppers down their sofa, the lint in their pockets – and we are expected to be grateful. The problem is not just rich companies, but rich individuals. According to the Charities Aid Foundation, the wealthiest 10 per cent of UK income earners give just 0.7 per cent of their household expenditure to charity, while the poorest 10 per cent allocate 3 per cent of theirs.

What explains this institutional miserliness at the very top of Britain's wealth tree? Historically, the argument was always that Britain was so heavily taxed, the rich did their bit by paying whacking sums into the national exchequer. In the US, by contrast, the ultra-affluent knew they were barely taxed so they made up for it with personal and dynastic philanthropy: think Carnegie, Mellon and Rockefeller. But that logic no longer applies. Today's British companies enjoy some of the lowest tax rates outside America. Now they have the best of both worlds: low tax and no guilty expectation of philanthropy. They can keep almost all their money to themselves.

Unless we, their customers, say otherwise. This last week has seen a rare and stirring demonstration of people power. Maybe we ought to turn to the big companies and say: you can no longer have it both ways. Either you give as generously as we do – or we will take it off you in tax. Either way, it's time to start paying.

A LOST WORLD

Ian Jack

One day last month I was lucky enough to sit in a small cinema at the British Film Institute in London and watch a series of short films, none more than a few minutes long and all of them about 100 years old. Only one of them contained people who might have been actors. Most of them showed the industrial working class of northern England, with occasional forays north to Scotland, west to Wales and Ireland, and south to the Midlands. This was working Britain at its apogee as the world's supreme imperial and industrial power, brought alive in black and white pictures that were wonderfully clear and sharp, unscratched and unfogged. Watching them was to see generations of people, known to us mainly through still and stiff family photographs, become more fully human. They walked, they ran, they clowned at the camera or self-consciously ignored it. There was a lot of humour and confidence in them. Some of these people – the old woman weaver or a white-bearded mechanic – must have been born before 1850. They might remember the Crimean war. Now they were walking towards me, sometimes staring boldly at me, on a screen in central London in late 2004.

These pictures were moving in another sense. It is hard to put a finger on why, though when a selection of them is shown later this month on BBC2 and at the National Film Theatre I am certain that their audience will be as affected as everyone else who has seen them so far. It isn't as though we don't know that our Victorian and Edwardian ancestors walked and ran and laughed, or worked in mills, or took the tram, or bled when pricked. Some of us thought we knew these things quite vividly. In my own case, I briefly shared a bedroom (and, come to think of it, a bed) with a grandfather who was born in 1874 and could recall the storm in Glasgow that, further east, blew down the Tay Bridge. I remember his long underwear and his pipe, which was tapped out only before he made the decision to sleep. But even though I knew this man, and as a child literally rubbed up against him, he was for me a relic. In one of these films, he would be different: a young man among other young men and women, a lively part of the age that shaped him, working in a bleachworks, stepping out into the twentieth century, innocent of all the wonder and horror it would eventually contain. Sitting in the BFI's cinema, I felt that history had suddenly been enlarged and one of its divisions abolished, that between the living and the long dead.

Why has this feeling been so delayed? Where have the films been until now? The answers lie in a remarkable story of preservation, discovery and restoration that to British film history is a near (if not parallel) equivalent to the finding of Tutankhamen's tomb or the Dead Sea Scrolls. In 1994, workmen stripping out an empty shop at 40 Northgate, Blackburn, Lancashire, went down to the cellar and discovered three large metal drums, like big rusting milk churns, which turned out to contain more than 800 rolls of nitrate film. A cinephile and film historian, Peter Worden, knew of the site as the old studios of two Blackburn men, Sagar Mitchell and James Kenyon, who had made and processed films there until 1913.

Worden had kept a watchful eye on the shop in case anything was discovered inside it. He arranged for the metal drums to be delivered to him – the alternative destination was the skip – and transferred their contents to 17 plastic food containers, the size of family ice-cream tubs, and stored them in a chest freezer. To preserve and restore the films proved beyond Worden's means. The BFI took them over as the Mitchell and Kenyon collection in 2000 and then began their painstaking restoration at its laboratories in Berkhamsted.

Most were made between 1900 and 1907, but the age of the films is not in itself the most significant thing. The Lumière brothers, generally accepted as the founders of cinema, showed their first film to a paying audience in Paris in 1895 and in London the next year. By the late 1890s several British film-makers were at work and several of their films survive – short bursts of sea breaking on rocks, trains at speed, the procession at Queen Victoria's diamond jubilee in 1898. Nor, when their hoard was discovered in 1994, were Sagar Mitchell and James Kenyon unknown. Their films of the Boer War, depicting British bravery and Boer depravity, had a minor celebrity as early examples of cinematic propaganda and fakery (they were shot entirely in the Lancashire countryside). To the film historian, what was exciting about the discovery was its size – translated to DVD or video, the films take up to 28 hours of viewing time – and its technical quality. The reels were the original negatives, kept in good condition for most of the century in the cool of the cellar. Their positives, the film actually projected on to the screen, would have been damaged by the wear and tear of machinery, the heat of the electrics, the carelessness of the operator.

The images, then, have a freshness and clarity, but that (to the film historian or otherwise) is only part of their appeal. What they show is a world now lost to us: the busy world of northern Britain in its manufacturing, mining heyday; the world that, among other things, created and sustained this newspaper as the *Manchester Guardian*. Not until the 1930s and the British documentary movement did film-makers pay it so much attention again, this time as a subject for moral concern because it had then begun its slow collapse.

In Mitchell and Kenyon's films you can see it as an independent civilisation, glorying in its new recreations and enjoyments such as electric trams, professional sport, street parades and pageants, and seaside holidays. There are films of 32 northern soccer matches, and of 18 rugby games played by professional teams in the newly founded Northern Union (later the Rugby League) which broke from the amateur Rugby Football Union in 1895. You can see the new electric trams in Halifax, Lytham and Accrington, Catholic and temperance processions in the streets of Manchester, a flotilla of destroyers moving up the Manchester Ship Canal, the crowded piers at Blackpool and Morecambe. You see horses pulling people and goods – stables in British towns then contained 1.7 million of them. You see many factory chimneys, smoking.

Most of all, you see people. Very few of them, no matter how poor, are bareheaded: the men wear flat caps, bowlers, straw boaters, trilbies, toppers, the women shawls or floral hats. Waistcoats are everywhere, as are moustaches and mufflers, pipes and cigarettes. Tobacco smoke drifts close to the camera, coal smoke further off. Nobody is fat. Many have bad teeth; people have a way of smiling which manages not to reveal them. Perhaps this technique has been forgotten; a particular male stance afforded by the waistcoat – the thumbs in its pockets – has also disappeared.

The streets of Lancashire look impossibly crowded and surging, and probably they were much more so then than now. But there is another reason for this vibrancy: the film-maker's presence. Mitchell and Kenyon were businessmen and only by accident social documentarists. They made three kinds of film: the fake (as in their Boer War films), the fictional (as in *Diving Lucy* of 1903, billed in the US, improbably for a film made in a Lancashire public park, as 'the hit British comedy of the year') and 'actualities'. The last, also known as 'local topicals', were their bread and butter, and worked on the principle then (and still) well-known to local newspapers: the more names of local citizens that appeared in the paper – as prize-winning scholars, Sunday school excursionists, speech-making councillors – the more the paper sold to people who liked to see they had been noticed.

So it was with the local topicals, which were mainly commissioned from Mitchell and Kenyon by showmen and fairground owners who had begun to see the potential of cinema shows in tents and civic halls (there were as yet no cinemas). People would come to watch the huge novelty of their appearance on film; the more people Mitchell and Kenyon could capture in the frame, the larger the showman's audience, the more handsome the profit. The countryside and the market town were no good for this. A large and dense population such as industrial Lancashire's was ideal. But where could the largest press of people be found – people moving quickly, one face replaced by another, streaming through a space no wider than the lens on a fixed camera could accommodate, as many people within a one-minute film as would, with their friends and relations, make a decent audience at the screening a few nights later? The solution was the factory gate, but not the factory gate at clocking-on time, when workers arrived too randomly and at the wrong angle, but when their shift was over and they surged out, free and quick, and straight towards a camera being hand-turned by a man behind a tripod, against which a sign might be mounted: COME AND SEE YOURSELF AS OTHERS SEE YOU, SEVEN O'CLOCK P.M. AT THE DRILL HALL IN JESSOP STREET. And there they would go and, according to contemporary accounts, point to themselves on the screen and shout out, tickled by the strangeness of it all.

Mitchell and Kenyon didn't invent this genre, 'the factory-gate film', which is as old as film itself. The film shown by the Lumière brothers to their first paying audience in 1895 was called *Sortie de l'Usine*, one of three shot outside their factory gates in Lyon, not to make money from their workforce but to demonstrate to a Paris audience how a film could capture human movement. Nor were Mitchell and Kenyon its only British practitioners. In southern England, the pioneering film-maker, Cecil Hepworth, announced in his promotional literature that: 'A film showing workers leaving a factory will gain far greater popularity in the town where it was taken than the most exciting picture ever produced. The workers come in hundreds, with all their friends and relations, and the film more than pays for itself the first night.'

The Blackburn men, however, were in the right place at the right time. In 1900, Lancashire employed 600,000 men, women, and children in its cotton spinning and weaving factories and another 100,000 in the cloth finishing trades. More than 60 per cent of cotton goods traded internationally were made in Lancashire, and they accounted for a quarter of British exports by value. Blackburn's own speciality was the dhoti, the traditional Indian loincloth, many millions of which were shipped over to Bombay and Calcutta. The mills were on the film-makers' doorstep, and if these mills were ever exhausted as audience providers, then it was easy to move on to collieries, engineering shops and ironworks, or to take the train across to the worsted factories of Yorkshire, or further afield to the great shipyards on the Tyne, or in Barrow or Greenock. In an office at the BFI they have a map of Britain on the wall, with pins to mark the hundreds of Mitchell and Kenyon's known locations; very few pins south of

Birmingham and then a dense spread across the Pennines to the north: Darwen, Chorley, Ormerod's Mill in Bolton, Pendlebury Colliery, Parkgate Ironworks, Platts of Oldham, Haslam's Ltd of Colne.

In the Parkgate film, a young man does a rather modern thing and gives a V-sign to the cameraman. In another film entitled *20,000 Employees entering Lord Armstrong's Elswick Works*, made on Tyneside in 1900, we see a grave crowd of men moving steadily down a slope towards the camera, ready to begin a day's work in the yard that built battleships for the Japanese. It lasts for two minutes and 34 seconds, the camera angle unchanged: a sea of faces moving forward, replenished from behind, like something out of Eisenstein. Many other films have the crowd controller in shot, sometimes James Kenyon and sometimes the showman who commissioned the film. Their good suits separate them from the crowd and they can be seen gesticulating, urging their subjects to move past the camera rather than stand and stare at it, or staging a mock fight or teasing a woman – anything to give the film animation and interest. In this way, and unlike many documentaries since, their version of reality is strikingly honest. You can see the human intervention in it.

The people leaving their factories in these films look happy enough and yet, despite the wealth they created, many of them lived in ill health and poverty – a scandal that was beginning to rumble through Britain in the same years that the films were made. The Boer War had brought certain facts to light. Four out of ten young men offering themselves as recruits to the British army had to be rejected because their bodies weren't up to the job. They had bad teeth, weak hearts, poor sight and hearing, physical deformities of all kinds. Most obviously, they were too short: in 1901, the infantry had to reduce the minimum height for recruits to 5ft from 5ft 3in (it had already been lowered from 5ft 6in in 1883).

A government committee (the frankly named Inter-Departmental Committee on Physical Deterioration) was set up and reported in 1904. It found that boys of ten to twelve at council schools were, on average, five inches shorter than those at private schools; that working-class girls, according to the evidence of a factory inspector, exhibited 'the same shortness of stature, the same miserable development, the same sallow cheeks and [decayed] teeth'. It was established that breast-feeding was rapidly declining, partly because increasing numbers of new mothers went out to work in the factories, but also because many mothers were simply not healthy enough to provide milk. Chronic digestive troubles, bad teeth, anaemia, and 'general debility' were almost universal among working-class women. Instead of milk from the breast, mothers gave their infants the cheapest food they could buy, which was usually sweetened condensed skimmed milk – high in sugar and devoid of fats and thus an excellent diet to promote rickets. The very poorest mothers substituted a mixture of flour and water, which was milk-like only in appearance. In the county of London – and the same was surely true in the northern cities – more than one in every five children did not live beyond infancy.

All this began to change well before the First World War, but too late for the boys and girls leaving Ormerod's mill in 1900. Think of them when you see these films and of what that war held for them. Think also of the fate of Blackburn and its dependence on the imperial dhoti trade. India imposed cotton tariffs in the early 1920s. J. B. Priestley visited Blackburn early in the next decade, and wrote: 'The tragic word around [Blackburn], I soon discovered, is dhootie [*sic*]. It is the forgotten Open Sesame . . . This fabric was manufactured in the town and the surrounding district on a scale equal to the needs of the gigantic Indian population. So colossal was the output that Blackburn was the greatest weaving town in the world. It clothed the whole vast mad peninsula. Millions and millions of yards of dhootie cloth went streaming out of this valley. That trade is almost finished.'

The terms of international trade were to blame. Lancashire, Priestley concluded, was 'learning a lot about this queer interdependence of things'. Every factory town in the Mitchell and Kenyon films has since learned the same lesson. The people who appear in them, however poor and unhealthy, held the key to Britain's industrial importance to the world. Which among them could have realised that that superb position was as temporary as life itself?

GREER DIARY

Libby Brooks

Diaries – of the non-appointment variety – are the home of self-conscious over-statement. So it was that on Thursday night I wrote in mine: 'Germaine Greer is on *Celebrity Big Brother*. Nothing is allowed to mean anything any more.' I woke yesterday morning from dreams of tilting trains feeling gloomier still.

For all her ego and opportunism and inconsistency, I've always been grateful for Greer, which is why this latest act of contrarian bravura has made me just a wee bit sad. For me, Germaine Greer's persona – the peaks and plains of which can be charted over the next 17 days of incarceration – has always been a secondary, if undeniably gripping, aspect of the whole woman. The primary force was her words, bold, brilliant, and not occasionally bonkers, which I started reading as a teenager because I thought it made me more interesting, and have since challenged and changed the way that I see the world. It was because of those polemics: shouted over the airwaves or across the page, they always contained at least one thought so zizzling with energy and newness that it would stand your own thinking on its inadequate head. Most of all, I loved her for the gentle, generous wisdom that she brought to bear as she tramped bravely across the most painful territories of women's experience – rape, abortion, childlessness. Her words in these areas have often been interpreted as wanton self-exposure, but her writings about her absent father, or her regrets about not having children of her own, are among her most honest. And, at times in my life when I've had to make sore journeys, her words have felt like a gift.

Sure, it's only *Celebrity Big Brother*. It's not meant to be taken seriously. It's the perfect place for a 'clever fool', as Angela Carter described her. And won't it be fun to watch her berating Caprice for her boob job and bullying a 19-year-old boy-bander into submission?

I should hardly be surprised that she's decided to take part. Greer has always been an individualist and a skilled media player. She's also long relished taking a highbrow stance on lowbrow culture, and perhaps she will pass off her *Big Brother* diary as a piece of academic research (serial rights to the *Daily Mail*, massive fee TBA). But I am sorry that one of my greatest heroines has fallen foul of our ghastly witness culture, which dictates that nothing has any validity unless it is viewed contemporaneously by several thousand others. As the tabloids laid out the odds for the eight contestants yesterday, Greer was said to be determined to show that older women could still be sexy, confessing to a love of 'going commando'. I'd dearly like to think that, radical to the last, she'll subvert her inclusion as the ancient lady eccentric and bring home the revolution on a damp January evening. But even if she plays the iconoclast in the *Big Brother* house, she has already been willingly neutered.

Celebrity is now her main moniker – attention-seeking, money-grabbing, evacuated of any meaning beyond herself. She is no longer a woman with a gorgeous and exciting brain, who has made a contribution to our intellectual life. It's not that she's lost credibility, it's that she's lost her core. When I'm feeling especially dismal I imagine what it must have been like to have been born before the days of triangulation, irony, multiple referencing and every other post-post-blah that empties out the truth and replaces it with a terribly handsome void. Germaine Greer was one of the few people who always reminded me of why passion doesn't have to be postmodern.

12 January 2005

MEDIA STUDIES

Owen Gibson

Germaine Greer launched a withering attack on the Channel 4 reality show *Big Brother* last night, hours after walking out on a celebrity version of the series. The writer, broadcaster and feminist icon, who had surprised commentators by agreeing to take part in the show, compared conditions in the house to a 'fascist prison'. She said she was 'appalled' at the psychological pressure put on her fellow housemates. The 65-year-old calmly packed her bags and left at lunchtime yesterday. 'I woke up in the middle of the night and thought, I have more to lose than I have to gain.' She said she was frustrated at having to leave but that she had been forced out by the 'bullying' of Channel 4 racing pundit John McCririck and actor Brigitte Nielsen.

'I would like to look at the epidemiology of bullying to see if the rise and rise of bullying and the rise and rise of *Big Brother* have anything to do with each other.' She said that *Big Brother* had behaved like a 'child rather than a parent'. 'It was demonstrating the role of taunting in the playground and there are so many children whose lives have been ruined by taunting in the playground. I was worried about the object lesson in bullying I have participated in.' Greer said she was particularly concerned about the treatment of Nielsen, after her former mother-in-law Jackie Stallone was introduced to the house without warning. The pair had not seen each other for 17 years. 'She [Nielsen] could see the tabloids turning it into the kind of sludge that could ruin her access to her children.'

The author of *The Female Eunuch* said that her friends had been surprised that she decided to enter the house but that she was willing to do anything to help save her 50-hectare (125-acre) rainforest in Queensland. She is planning to invest her estimated £40,000 appearance fee in conserving the area, but was still in negotiations with

Channel 4 and the producer, Endemol, over whether she would receive her full fee.

On leaving the house she said it was noticeable that the other housemates all had their own agenda. Model Caprice was there to push her lingerie line, boy-band member Kenzie wanted to publicise his group and the others all had products to promote, she said. Greer said she felt 'slightly humiliated' that she had not persuaded the other housemates to stand up to *Big Brother*. 'Persecution is what happens, holocausts are what happens when good people do nothing. [But] I am an anarchist, we can disrupt situations, we don't take them over.'

Greer also said she feared that reality TV would only get 'dirtier and dirtier'. 'I can only hope and pray that people's appetites will turn, that they will sicken of this fare and you and I know what the likelihood of that really is because we all live in the real world.' She did not care what the public thought of her but she wanted former Happy Mondays dancer Bez to win the series⋆ because he had had a hard life and would make the most of it.

⋆ He did.

25 January 2005

CAMPAIGN DIARY

Ghaith Abdul-Ahad

A large sandstorm has covered Baghdad in a yellow shroud for the past five hours. The streets are still flooded with water and sewage from the morning's rain. The sky is shaking with explosive thuds every few minutes – or are those rumbles of thunder? Hopping between sewage pools is a man in his early fifties wearing an old blue jacket and a pair of torn brown trousers. His shirt is buttoned up and his grizzled hair laid flat on his head. Thick glasses rest on his nose. His hand is clutching a bundle of papers. 'Vote for the People's Alliance,' he says to people as he hands them the flyers. On one side of the paper there is a drawing of a circle with sunrays coming out of it and giving instructions on how to vote, on the other side there is a calendar.

The man is a Communist, walking the streets of a conservative Shia district where old man Sistani is watching from every street corner. I follow, keeping a good distance. Every time he approaches someone I close my eyes, expecting a gunshot or at least some sharp object to find its way to his head. It doesn't happen. Instead, people appear happy to stick the leaflets in their pockets. 'Look, it has a calendar,' one woman tells her friend as they admire the little leaflet. A couple of children follow the man for a few blocks and every time he hands out a leaflet they run in front of him asking for more.

'Do we have to vote for you if we take some of these?' asks one of the kids.

'No, no,' says the man, waving his hands. 'It is up to you to choose who you vote for.'

The man – brave enough to hand out Communist leaflets in the middle of bomb-torn Baghdad, but not brave enough to agree to have his name published in the *Guardian* – was trained as a teacher but lost his job after spending long periods in Saddam's prisons. For him, elections are the way to undo the miseries of his past.

'It doesn't matter who wins, it is the election that counts. When people go out and vote they will never allow a new Saddam to emerge again,' he says cheerfully.

Election fever is picking up. Almost every single wall in the city is covered by hundreds of posters, some pasted over others, giving a sense that Baghdad is itself one big collage of big heads, white beards and moustaches mingled with the Samsung phone ads. Some posters show the face of an old man, Adnan Pachachi, who was a minister more than 35 years ago. He gives a warm smile from underneath a poster of Allawi which has been partly ripped off. Allawi, for some weird reason, has decided to use a photo of his eyes to represent his campaign motto: 'strong leadership'. I think the original plan was to have fierce-looking eyes chasing you wherever you go. Instead, Allawi has the weasely look of Tony Soprano. By far the most distributed poster is that of the Shia list. The old man Sistani is again posted over walls, bus stations and restaurants. There are also hundreds of posters of men with big moustaches.

The Shias are handing out their leaflets after Friday sermons and in mosques. Christian liquor shops are handing Christian posters to anyone who buys two cans of beer. The reds are crazy enough to give out leaflets in the streets. Every new Iraqi army vehicle is covered with posters of the minister of defence and Saddam's big old murals are covered with one or another of the Shia clerics running for a seat. But for most of the candidates, the voters will only see their names for the first time on election day. People don't know where to vote or how to do it. People are scared to vote, but a considerable number think it is like Saddam's good old referendums, when the Government cut the food rations of those who didn't vote.

The posters and murals are the only safe way of campaigning in these elections, because of the car bombs and assassinations. With less than a week to go, the war has intensified and every day's violence becomes the best material for the campaigners. To defeat Allawi's 'strong leadership', the Shias are putting up huge street murals showing the faces of two children, one a happy little infant and the other covered in blood and burns, a victim of one of the car bombs. 'We will do what they failed to do,' says the mural.

27 January 2005

FIRST KNOW YOUR DONKEY

Timothy Garton Ash

This global stocktaking week of the World Economic Forum in Davos began with the inauguration of a new, democratically elected Ukrainian president and will end with elections in Iraq. Ukraine and Iraq represent two radically different ways – shall we call them the right way and the wrong way? – of attempting to expand freedom, a goal which Europeans and leftists should support, even though it is George Bush who proclaims it.

Ukraine is the right way. What President Yushchenko in his inaugural address justly called 'a victory of freedom over tyranny, of law over lawlessness' was the latest in a long series of velvet revolutions which have helped spread democracy around the world over the last 30 years. Ukrainians did it for themselves. With a little help from their friends, to be sure. But whatever the role of western support, this was the Ukrainians' own idea, and the people I met on the ground taking risks for democracy, in the freezing camps of Kiev's tent city and on Independence Square, were Ukrainians.

This nation-building orange revolution was entirely peaceful. No one was killed, although Mr Yushchenko nearly died as a result of what was almost certainly an attempt to poison him by senior representatives of the secret police with close ties to the Russian-backed candidate. What follows will be messy, but the chances are that it will be better for the people who live there than what went before. In 15 years' time, if all goes well, Ukraine could yet be a democratic nation-state of both Ukrainian- and Russian-speaking citizens, and a member of Europe's commonwealth of democracies, the European Union.

Iraq is the wrong way. It began with a war, on what turned out to be a false prospectus about weapons of mass destruction. The justification for democracy-building only rose to its present, unique salience as the evidence for WMD and direct terrorist links evaporated. Most Iraqis were glad to be rid of Saddam Hussein, but this was not their initiative. Granted, in a totalitarian dictatorship such as Saddam's, unlike in a *democratura* such as post-Soviet Ukraine, people can't say what they want. But many who were against Saddam turned out to be even more against foreign occupation. In such circumstances, it is right to listen to political exiles, but foolish to believe that they can tell you how their compatriots back home feel and will react.

The American occupation has been carried through with gross incompetence and insensitivity, not to mention the human rights abuses of Abu Ghraib. Its financial cost has been staggering. With Bush's latest funding request, I make the total cost of war and occupation more than $250 billion. How many lives around the world could have been saved for $250 billion? And what is the result? Probably most Iraqis feel more free than they did under Saddam. They also feel more insecure. Despite the efforts of many brave Iraqis who, even more than the Ukrainians did, are risking their own lives for democracy, this is a country in a state of lawlessness and on the edge of civil war. It has become both a playground and a new breeding ground for terrorists – the very opposite of the effect intended by the Bush administration. Next to Palestine, it's now the main rallying cause for all the anti-western and anti-liberal forces in the Islamic world.

A single election does not make a democracy. Shias, led by the Grand Ayatollah Ali Sistani, call for participation in the elections in the hope of achieving majority rule. Their rule, that is. But democracy is not a tyranny of the majority. Sunnis and Kurds will not accept this. At the very best, what comes out of Iraq's civil war will be a decentralised, unstable federal state, something like Yugoslavia before its civil war. At best. In Ukraine, disparate ethno-linguistic groups are slowly coming together in a process of nation-building from below. In Iraq, outside occupiers' attempts at nation-building from above are catalysing fragmentation along ethnic and religious lines.

Meanwhile, the serious foreign policy debate in Washington now concerns how to get out of this mess. Two major articles in the latest issue of *Foreign Affairs* discuss strategies of disengagement, starting from the premise that the United States cannot win the war in Iraq. Two veteran heavyweights, Henry Kissinger and George Shultz, have just laid out their guidelines for what they call 'a realistic exit strategy'. Kissinger, we recall, was the architect of American withdrawal from Vietnam.

The *New York Times* columnist Thomas Friedman, who really does care about democracy in the Middle East, fairly complains about the European refrain of 'we told you so'. 'What,' he asks, 'happens the morning after "we told you so"?' Good question. If Osama Bin Laden can declare victory in Iraq against the West and its godless democracy, that will be at least as dangerous for Europeans as it is for Americans. So what does Friedman think the European Union should be doing at this juncture? Answer: 'Actively urging Iraqis to vote, and using its own moral legitimacy in the Arab world to delegitimise the insurgents.' Right, let's do it. But will that save Iraq?

It's tempting for Europeans to say that Ukraine represents the European way to democracy, and Iraq the American one. Venus pats herself on the back, Mars buries his head in his hands. But Europe has not earned the right to such self-congratulation. The magnetism of the European Union was a significant factor in Ukraine's orange revolution and EU diplomacy played an important part in its success. But Americans – governmental, non-governmental, and quasi-non-governmental – have for years been more active than Europeans in supporting the democrats there. To the limited extent that what happened in Ukraine was a victory for external actors at all, it was a joint victory for Europeans and Americans.

The comparison between Ukraine and Iraq – that is, between the beginning and the end of this Davos week in world politics – is by no means just about the past. It's about what Europe and America can do together over the next four years, and what they might end up quarrelling over. The biggest, most obvious test case is Iran. If we had done for Iran over the last five years what we did for Ukraine, and not invaded Iraq, there was a chance that Iran could have been the Ukraine of the wider Middle East. The country, that is, where a peaceful democratic revolution from below, made at home with some discreet help from outside, could have set in motion a different dynamic in the region.

Now Iran's Islamic regime is more firmly entrenched than it was before the Iraq war, with the democratic elements of that country's own *democratura* further weakened. The mullahs feel themselves fully entitled to push ahead with a nuclear energy programme (probably with weapons potential on the side) and many of their democratic critics agree. If another crisis of the West is to be avoided, Europe and America have to agree a joint approach, with more European sticks and more American carrots. Neither the Ukraine nor the Iraq options are available. But we can learn one crucial lesson from both Ukraine and Iraq: everything depends on a correct analysis of the likely domestic consequences, in the country concerned, of our actions from outside. In short: before waving either carrots or sticks, know your donkey.

31 January 2005

AFTER YOUSSEF

Michael Howard

Sabria Sharif Mohammed rose at dawn and prepared for the day that she and her family had been dreaming of. Like several hundred thousand others who voted yesterday in Kirkuk, this historic city of Kurds, Arabs, Turkomans and Christians, Sabria was hoping to use her vote to right past wrongs. She believed that taking part in the first elections in her life would help win back the house and land seized from them under the regime of Saddam Hussein. Before making the three-mile walk to the polling station with her husband and two oldest sons, Sabria sent her youngest, Youssef, 16, to fill the urn at the communal pump. Within minutes he lay dead, the victim of a mortar bomb.

Sabria washed her son's body, covered it with a white burial shroud and arranged for it to be taken to the nearby cemetery. Then, remarkably, she went off to vote. Holding a Kurdish flag and wailing in grief, she entered the polling station in the northern Shorjah district, crying: 'I will never put this flag down. Saddam threw me out of my house and home and now he's killed my son. Voting won't bring my Youssef back, but it must stop Saddam from coming back.'

During its Arabisation programme, the Ba'athist regime had systematically widened the ethnic and sectarian fissures coursing through this oil-rich, but neglected city of 750,000. Thousands of Kurds and Turkomans were expelled or murdered. Land and homes were given to Arab settlers from the south. With Kurds, Turkomans and Arabs vying for control of the city and province, US and Iraqi leaders have looked nervously to Kirkuk as a potential flashpoint for a civil war. Meanwhile, regional neighbours such as Turkey have warned they will not tolerate Kirkuk falling into Kurdish hands.

Election monitors described turnout in the predominantly Kurdish and Turkoman areas of the city as brisk. Arab districts to the south-east of the city were reported to be less enthusiastic. 'In some Kurdish districts, they ran out of ballot boxes, and new ones failed to arrive in time,' said one election official. The mood was one of celebration, not defiance. But the crumbling Ottoman-era buildings are a sad reminder of the shocking state of disrepair into which this city had fallen under Saddam's rule.

'The oil has been a curse on Kirkuk,' said Herro Talabani, the wife of Jalal Talabani, the leader of the Patriotic Union of Kurdistan (PUK), as she returned to vote in the city where she went to school. The PUK and its rival, the Kurdistan Democratic Party, want Kirkuk to be the future capital of their federal Kurdish region. For them it is a symbol of years of repression by the Arab-dominated government in Baghdad. But their designs are resisted by many in the Arab and Turkoman communities who live here.

In post-war Kirkuk there is one thing many of the original residents of the city agreed on yesterday: the Kurds, the Turkomans, the Arabs and the Christians mostly get along quite well. It is the outsiders, they say, who are causing the problems.

18 February 2005

THE LAST HURRAH

Sandra Laville

As the stanzas of a little-known poem echoed across a Sussex valley even the hounds fell silent, brought to heel by the huntsman underneath an ancient chestnut tree. Observed by hundreds of foot followers, many with tears in their eyes, it was a scene that marked the end of centuries of rural tradition. Across the country from Cumbria to Cornwall, 150 of Britain's 250 hunts performed their own final rituals yesterday as they rode out in their thousands for the last time before fox-hunting with dogs was made illegal at midnight. After months of direct action, marches and legal wrangles it was the moment they had been dreading.

At Petworth Park in West Sussex, where around 500 foot followers and 100 riders met before the chase, Rikki Bennett, the master of the Chiddingfold, Leconfield and Cowdray Hunt, had asked: 'Do I dare to read a poem?' The cries of 'Yes' resounded around the park from the gathered crowd, many wrapped against the cold in the uniform of hunting folk: Barbour jackets, green wellies and for the old men, well-worn flat caps. Mr Bennett hesitated before flawlessly reciting the words he believed best fitted the hour.

We have no wish to exaggerate
The worth of the sports we prize . . .
Yet if once we efface the joys of the chase
From the land, and outroot the Stud,
Good-bye to the Anglo-Saxon race!
Farewell to the Norman blood!

A few miles away, across country, the hunt saboteurs could not hear the verses of Adam Lindsay Gordon's 'Ye Wearie Wayfarer'. Sitting in a white van, they had walkie-talkies at the ready as they waited patiently to play their part in a choreographed cat-and-mouse chase which has taken place for the last 15 years in this part of West Sussex. They had neither champagne for each other nor words of sympathy for their defeated foe. 'This is the end of the war,' said one, 'but only the beginning of the battle.' But Mr Bennett, his huntsman Adrian 'Sage' Thompson, the 100 mounted followers and the ten-deep crowd of supporters on foot, were not about to hurry to a confrontation which happens more regularly in this area than the killing of a fox. If this moment marked the last time they could hunt foxes with hounds, members of the Chiddingfold, a hunt with a 330-year history, were going to savour it.

In solemn silence the riders followed two by two as the huntsman and his hounds paraded before the foot followers. As they passed, the children were hushed and the men on foot doffed their caps to the 30-strong pack of hounds. Then the 100 riders moved up towards Holland Wood where they hoped to draw their first prey. Nearing the crest of the hill, they were halted by the master, his scarlet coat distinctive on the grey horizon, and the riders stopped and looked back. At that moment Mr Bennett lifted himself from the saddle and raised his riding hat in a final salute. In the valley below 500 men, women and children roared the last hurrah.

'Is this the last hunt we are going to have ever?' a girl asked her mother. 'Well, it's the last legal one,' she replied.

Half an hour later the motorised pack were forced to a standstill as they converged at a remote crossroads beside arable fields outside Holland Wood. Diesel fumes choked the air as they waited for the hunt to approach and waved at a police van full of officers, who responded in a similar fashion to locals they would meet later at the pub.

'I feel like I am in a daydream,' said Louie Eze, a regular foot follower. 'I feel most sorry for the children who are only just getting into it and for the huntsman, it's his life. He lives and breathes it.'

After several blows of the hunting horn, a trot across countryside, a short gallop, a lot of standing around but no sign of a fox, the hunt paused for lunch at The Stag, which has played host to riders and hounds for more than 300 years. The more affluent jumped off steaming horses to be handed a second mount for the afternoon's chase ahead.

'We will all be criminals tomorrow,' said Hamish Hiddlestone, the landlord. 'When was the last time a sport was banned? Imagine if you said to Manchester United you can't play football any more. It is the same thing for all these people.'

But despite the legislation now weighed against him, the master of the Chiddingfold was a long way from surrendering as he knocked back a mulled wine and rolled a half-time cigarette. From now on, Mr Bennett made clear, the poetry would remain on the bookshelves. 'It seemed poignant today. But there won't be any poetry again. We'll be out on Saturday and then it will be time to turn the emotion of today into action, action to bring about a change.'

19 February 2005

WHITE NILE FEVER

Nils Pratley

Phil Edmonds's test match bowling average of 34 was hardly distinguished, but the former England cricketer is now producing mind-boggling numbers. His £15,000 investment in White Nile, a company looking for oil in Sudan, has been transformed in a fortnight into a stake worth £20 million. It's a theoretical price, because trading in the shares was suspended on Wednesday. But, given that one of his other African mining companies also invested, Mr Edmonds can claim to have boosted his net worth by an average of about £1.5 million a day this month.

After just four days trading on the Alternative Investment Market, White Nile is already a legend. The surge in the shares from 10p to 137p took the company's valuation to £212 million, despite its sole asset being £9 million of cash. It was an absurd over-valuation and proved White Nile fever is as dangerous and inexplicable as the speculative madness of the dotcom years. Just as then, Internet bulletin boards, where small investors swap rumours and opinions in the hope of quick profits, played a part. Nobody knew what deal White Nile had secured in Sudan, but the rising share price was interpreted as proof that it must be lucrative. Yesterday was meant to be the day that White Nile revealed all. On Wednesday, the company said it had agreed to buy a 60 per cent interest in a 67,500 sq km block in part of the Mugland basin in south Sudan and would elaborate further. It waited until 5.10 p.m. yesterday to announce that it had 'not yet been able to prepare such information'. Wait until next week, it said.

White Nile may have something interesting. The problem is its £200 million valuation. The political risks look real. The autonomous government of south Sudan was established only last month after 20 years of civil war. Even if the seismic results from the field are promising, more cash will be needed to build roads and other infrastructure in the area, notably a pipeline to carry the oil.

Even before the suspension of trading, such facts of life had not escaped another breed of investor from the dotcom days – the short-sellers. Betting that a share price will fall used to be the preserve of market professionals, but spread-betting companies made the process simple. Anybody can do it on the Internet or by telephone. The granddaddy of the shorters is Simon Cawkwell, who enjoys the nickname Evil Knievil and established his reputation long ago by shorting Robert Maxwell's companies. Mr Cawkwell announced his scepticism about White Nile from the outset, vowing in his Internet diary not to be deterred by the rising share price. He made the reasonable point that another Sudanese oilfield, called Heglig, had just changed hands for $750 million (£400 million) but had a major advantage over White Nile's: it is actually producing oil – 220,000 barrels a day. 'So, 60 per cent of Heglig is worth £246 million and is throwing off cash like billy-o,' he wrote. 'Sixty per cent of an area where all we have is seismic data and which is miles away from any infrastructure is worth £197 million? Give me a break.'

Other shorters took their cue. Angus Campbell, head of sales and marketing at spread better Finspreads, said shorting White Nile has been 'the trade of the year so far' for his clients. IG Index, unable to get hold of White Nile shares to cover its position, refused to take bets. 'It's extraordinary, it's almost like the tech bubble revisited,' said senior dealer Will Armitage. Indeed, a classic bubble had developed. White Nile's shares are tightly held by the directors and the handful of investors who were invited into the £9 million pre-float placing. The harder the shares became to buy, the more the price rose. As it passed 100p, some even bought on the theory that the shorters would panic and start buying to cut their losses. Hardly anybody paid attention to the prices paid by the directors and the initial investors. Mr Edmonds and his business partner Andrew Groves got their 9.7 per cent stakes at 0.1p soon after the company was founded last December. The outsiders in the placing, who include George Robinson, co-founder of Sloane Robinson, one of London's most successful hedge funds, paid 10p a share. All these prices were disclosed in the flotation document.

Mr Robinson, a multimillionaire, invested £800,000 of his own cash and describes as 'bizarre' what has happened. He regards the 10p level for the placing as 'fair' given that White Nile was a cash shell company. 'We were paying 1.6 times book value, so there was a premium there,' he says. Mr Robinson also has a tentative answer to the question that has been bothering many: if south Sudan is really so lucrative, why is its government negotiating with an ex-cricketer and the 36-year-old Mr Groves? The pair have been successful in Africa in the past, but they are not BP. 'I think the oil majors are there,' says Mr Robinson, 'but this route – through a London-listed company that can raise money and get things going – may mean that they [the south Sudan authorities] get their oil revenues quicker. If you ask most people about south Sudan, they think of the Janjaweed [the militia] and throw their hands up in horror, and I think that applies to most corporates as well.'

And, of course, small mining stocks can be highly profitable investments. Quoted hedge fund RAB Capital, which has invested £1 million in White Nile, has generated spectacular returns from mining stocks in the past. Asia Energy, for example, has produced a 50-fold return, says RAB chief executive Philip Richards. 'It's a bit like the nineteenth century – the world is opening up and you can invest in places that 15 years ago it would not have been possible,' he says. 'With Asia Energy, there was just a big field in Bangladesh with, we hoped, a large coal resource underneath. You can look at these things as a glass either half-empty or half-full. On the half-full view we were well on the way to proving there were a billion tonnes of coal there. It is the same with White Nile. It is just a patch of ground in war-torn Africa but, if you can get the oil out of it, it could be worth a lot of money.'

It could be. For sophisticated investors such as RAB and Mr Robinson, it makes sense to invest at 10p a share in management they trust. They are running portfolios of such investments. The bulletin board speculators, however, are playing a very different game. Their strategy tends to be quick-in, quick-out and trade on rumour. The more sophisticated may make money by exploiting wishful thinking, and the law of averages dictates that some will just get lucky. Many more will not. Bubbles are bubbles, and whether they inflate dotcom wannabes or oil explorers, they still pop.

24 February 2005

WHEN THE CHIPS ARE DOWN

Sam Wollaston

Jamie Oliver has a dream. Smiley happy children eat tomato focaccia, butternut squash and bean chilli with mixed leaves. So he hops in the Maserati (remember when it used to be a scooter?), and heads down to Kidbrooke School in Greenwich, where the revolution will begin. And the revolution will be televised, of course – in *Jamie's School Dinners* (Channel 4). Starting here in south-east London, Jamie's going to get Britain's kids eating properly. He wants us to have a 'fucking better, cooler, healthier nation', he says.

He does swear a lot, does Jamie (what is it about chefs?). But they seem to have over-prepared for this when he addresses the whole school at assembly – everything he utters into the microphone comes out as a loud beep. It looks as if it's been programmed to recognise his voice and beep out every word he says. But it turns out to be an electronic problem, and he eventually manages to say 'nice one' a few times, which goes down well.

There are three obstacles to Jamie's dream. The first is money – the food in one school dinner costs just 37p, and you don't get many sun-dried tomatoes for that. The second is called Nora. Lovely Nora. She's head dinner lady at Kidbrooke, and as rubbish at cooking as she is wonderful at being Nora. Until Jamie's arrival, dinner at Kidbrooke meant opening boxes of prepared burgers, pizzas and mountains of chips, then heating them up. Jamie has to work with Nora because he's not going to be around for ever, he'll hand the helm back to her when he's done sorting the place out. The third problem is the kids themselves. They don't like Jamie's fancy chicken stews and Thai curries, they prefer Nora's food. Or, as Jamie calls it, 'those fucking horrible scrotum burgers, reconstituted, mechanically reclaimed sacks of old shit pressed into shapes of drumsticks and fish'.

They're a funny pair, Jamie and Nora. She tries to go along with it all, but half the time she has no idea what he's talking about. Focaccia? 'Po . . . well, I ain't even going to be able to say it.' And as for the mozzarella? 'Monster ella?' says Nora. 'I never saw no monster ella.'

Jamie, meanwhile, burns the focaccia, goes way over budget, loses his temper, has hissy fits and generally behaves like a spoilt foul-mouthed child. And he has a very high opinion of himself. Of the conditions and restraints he's working under he says: 'It's a bit like taking away David Beckham's football boots and giving him a pair of Jesus sandals.'

I'm sure he'll turn it around, and sort out not just Kidbrooke's and South London's bad food problems, but have all the kids in the country eating healthily. And he's to be applauded for that. But that doesn't mean I have to like him. When he goes hungry and exhausted back to his restaurant and says to the chef there, 'I'll eat a dog's arse if you give it to me,' I couldn't help wishing the guy would actually produce a dog's arse – I'd like to have seen Jamie tucking in to one of them. It's terrific television, by the way.

Ah, *Ellen MacArthur: Taking on the World* (BBC1). Maybe this will settle an argument that has been raging on the pages of this newspaper. Is she a national hero, to be applauded for a remarkable achievement? Or an unlovable little whinger? Well, I've watched it now, and though I don't like to sit on whatever the nautical equivalent of a fence is (a gunwhale?),★ I think both crews could be right. To suggest it wasn't an amazing achievement seems harsh. She went through extreme physical hardship and sleep deprivation to break that record. But she also seemed to hate every minute of it – I'm so tired I don't know what to do, I've had enough now, I'm exhausted, I'm disappointed, I'm frustrated, I'm just empty. Why do it if it makes you so miserable?

And I'm not sure about your diet, Ellen: packets of freeze-dried food into which you're pouring hot water – 72 days of what are essentially *Pot Noodles*. Not much better than scrotum burgers, surely. So here's a thought: why don't you take Jamie Oliver with you next time? You can do the very fast sailing, and he can make you lovely tomato focaccia. We can appreciate the brilliance of both of you from afar, celebrate you as national heroes, and the two of you can swear and shout and moan and whinge all you want. And you'll be in the middle of the ocean so it needn't bother anyone.

* Corrections & Clarifications (26 February 2005): The nautical equivalent of a fence might be a gunwale or gunnel but not gunwhale.

SPRING

A WEDDING POSTPONED

Stephen Bates and Steven Morris

Prince Charles headed off a budding royal controversy yesterday by agreeing to postpone his wedding to Camilla Parker Bowles in deference to the Vatican's plans to hold the funeral of Pope John Paul II in Rome on Friday. Even before the formal announcement by Clarence House, diplomatic sources had made it clear that the prime minister would be attending the funeral instead of the royal wedding. The decision by Downing Street means that for the first time a serving prime minister, as well as the Archbishop of Canterbury, will attend the funeral of a pontiff. Instead of celebrating his wedding, Prince Charles will fly to Rome to represent the Queen. The wedding will take place on Saturday morning.

Downing Street had told the British embassy in Rome that the prime minister would give precedence to the funeral of the Pope. British officials spoke to the Vatican about the funeral arrangements – but did not feel the need to mention that there was a possible clash with the nuptials. The Archbishop of Canterbury, Dr Rowan Williams, who was due to bless the Prince's wedding in a service at St George's Chapel in Windsor Castle on Friday, also made it clear he wished to go to Rome.

The Prince's acceptance of the inevitable came as the sheer scale of the Vatican obsequies became clear. More than 200 world leaders, including 100 heads of state, are expected to be present. The extraordinary nature of the event is manifested in the determination of Mr Blair and Dr Williams to be there: the archbishop will be the first primate of the Church of England ever to attend a papal funeral. The late Lord Callaghan did not attend the funerals of John Paul II's two immediate predecessors when he was prime minister. Prince Charles's press secretary, Paddy Harverson, said that Mr Blair's decision to go to Rome had no bearing on the postponement of the wedding. 'That's absolutely not the case. The decision was made by the Prince and Mrs Parker Bowles and by them alone,' he said. 'There was no communication between No 10 Downing Street before or after.'

Last night, the authorities of the Holy See in Rome were braced for hundreds of thousands to line up and file past the Pope's body over the next three days. St Peter's Basilica will remain open throughout most of the night to accommodate the crush. Up to 2 million people are expected to pour into the city between now and Friday to view the lying in state and the funeral, with the authorities laying on tented villages in the suburbs for accommodation. The corpse of Pope John Paul II, who died on Saturday evening at the age of 84 of septic shock and heart failure, was moved from the papal apartments for the last time to St Peter's Basilica yesterday for the lying in state. A meeting of 65 cardinals at the Vatican also established the form of the ceremony, and that the pontiff would be buried with his predecessors in the vaults of the Vatican, rather than in his native country, Poland.

The Prince's plans were finally set aside after the prospect dawned of him sipping champagne at Windsor while huge parts of the rest of the world – including much of the Commonwealth – were focused on Rome. Britain's tabloids, still smarting from last week's bruising, if trivial, encounter with Prince Charles during a photocall at the start of his skiing holiday in Klosters, Switzerland, were already circling yesterday. Assorted MPs were also calling on the royals to acknowledge proprieties. A statement from Clarence House said that the Prince would attend the funeral instead. 'As a mark of respect, His Royal Highness and Mrs Parker Bowles have decided to postpone their wedding until Saturday,' it added. Palace sources said the Prince had made the decision immediately after his early return from Klosters yesterday, after a brief consultation with Mrs Parker Bowles. The wedding could neither be brought forward, nor postponed beyond the weekend because Windsor Guildhall, where the civil ceremony will take place, is licensed only on Fridays, Saturdays and Sundays.

It is historically remarkable, however, that the royal family should defer to the Vatican in changing its plans, given the long and tense history between the two institutions. A Buckingham Palace spokeswoman said that the Pope's funeral must take priority. The Prince was said to have been very keen to be sensitive. Diplomatic sources made clear that although the British embassy to the Vatican had been in touch with officials about high-level attendances at the funeral, they had not thought to mention the wedding. It is inconceivable that the cardinals would have altered their plans, even had they been aware of it: Vatican rules state the Pope must be buried within a week of death.

Rumours were circulating at Westminster yesterday that Downing Street had had to put pressure on the Prince to postpone the wedding. But Mr Blair's official spokesman said: 'I think Clarence House was very well aware of the significance of the Pope's funeral . . . The decision was for them and them alone to reach. But the prime minister is now very glad he is able to go to both events.'

The Prince and Mrs Parker Bowles attended a Mass for the Pope at Westminster Cathedral, together with Mr Blair and Catholic members of his cabinet, including John Reid, the health secretary, Ruth Kelly, the education secretary, and other political leaders. They heard Cardinal Cormac Murphy-O'Connor add his name to the growing number of senior figures in the church calling for John Paul II to become only the fourth pontiff in history, and the first in modern times, to be awarded the soubriquet of 'the Great', a preliminary to canonisation. Describing an 'epic' papacy, the Cardinal added: 'If one man's dying can evoke such an outpouring of love and gratitude, it is true we are all in God's hands. That is why, dear friends, he has been described as one of history's greatest Christians and why he shall surely be called Pope John Paul the Great.'

5 April 2005

CATAFALQUE

John Hooper

In the end, popes go back to the beginning, to the grottoes beneath St Peter's that hold what is held to be the apostle's own tomb. Even this Polish pope yesterday began the return journey. Under a clear sky, on a crimson catafalque, John Paul II travelled the first stage of his last journey. Earlier, and despite some predictions to the contrary, it had been announced that he had decreed that his body would not return to Poland, but remain here in the city of which all Romans agree he was an outstanding bishop.

Since Sunday it had lain in the Sala Clementina, the papal antechamber where even the very great and the very good can be made to cool their heels before being ushered into the pontifical presence. Yesterday, it was borne aloft by twelve ushers in grey tailcoats down the frescoed Scala Nobile. Flanked by Swiss Guards in their Renaissance uniforms of orange and blue, the catafalque bearing the dead Pope made its way along the Prime Loggia of the Apostolic Palace, through its Sala Ducale and Sala Regia to the Scala Regia, the Regal Staircase, one of the most extraordinary architectural features in a city of illusions. Built in the 1660s, in the days when the papacy was first trying to overwhelm the world with lavish and ingenious art, it is almost 200 feet long. But it looks even longer because of the progressive narrowing of its width and the reduction of the distance between the columns at the top.

The procession reached the great Bronze Door, which tradition has it must be kept shut from the death of one pope to the election of his successor, and emerged into the clear, spring light of St Peter's square. The curving porticoes were designed by Bernini 'to give an open-armed welcome to all Catholics'. John Paul II, the leader of all the world's Catholics for more than a quarter of a century, was greeted with restrained applause. His body continued its journey across the square, under the gaze of television cameras and the carved saints on the portico balustrades, past the ancient Egyptian obelisk that has served as a sundial since it was brought here by Sixtus V in 1585.

To those few of us admitted to the basilica, the applause came as a first indication of the arrival of the Pope's body. Then we saw a cloud of incense swirling up from the censor being swung by a deacon.*
Behind him came a line of more priests, bishops, archbishops, cardinals and patriarchs than any of us is likely to see again, almost 1,000. As they entered, the choir was invoking the saints on Pope John Paul's behalf, more than 100 of them – from the universally honoured to the barely remembered, from Saints Peter and Paul to Saint Ignatius of Antioch. As the name of each was chanted, the approaching clerics chanted back, '*Orate pro eo*' (Pray for him), and as they grew in number, so the volume of their chant swelled till it filled the cavernous basilica.

Outside, the catafalque bearers halted in front of the central door of St Peter's, directly below the window from where John Paul's successor will be proclaimed. They turned so that the face of the late pontiff looked out at the great crowd in the square. The rows of priests were followed into the basilica by phalanxes of purple-robed bishops and archbishops, and by the cardinals in red. Earlier in the day, the cardinals had heard their late pontiff's will and fixed the date of his funeral in a way that, no doubt unintentionally, snookered the wedding of a divorced English heretic.

At the end of the procession, just in front of the catafalque, walked the man who presides over the interregnum between popes, the chamberlain of the Holy Roman church, Cardinal Eduardo Martinez Somalo. The Pope was carried to the end of the aisle and lowered on to a tilted, draped, trestle. Two more Swiss Guard halberdiers stood to either side, legs akimbo, their black helmets topped with vermilion plumes. Behind the catafalque, stood a vast candleholder, taller than the guards, and bearing a candle of the same height. Beyond it was the glittering gold and white altar at which only a pope may say Mass, and above the altar Bernini's vast baldachin, 100ft high, its helical columns spiralling up towards Michelangelo's giant cupola and the presumed location of heaven beyond. As the choir and the congregation continued their prayers, Cardinal Martinez slowly circled the body, sprinkling it with holy water.

What a strange place the Vatican is. No wonder it excites awe and mistrust in equal measure. Eduardo Martinez and Karol Wojtyla were top executives of a global organisation. They had worked closely with one another for more than a decade. And here was the one flicking holy water at the other's corpse as he lay there in crimson robes and slippers. The body will lie like that now until Friday, while the crowds file past to pay their last respects: hundreds of thousands, certainly, maybe even millions. Then, amid further pomp it will be taken down into the bowels of the basilica for interment alongside the bodies of the other pontiffs.

Today, the assembled clerics had little time to reflect on the vagaries of time and mortality, so vividly symbolised by the giant sundial and the marble saints outside. The prayers over the Pope's dead body lasted less than half an hour. They came to an end with the Cardinal chanting '*Requiescat in pace*' ('Let him rest in peace'), to which the congregation replied 'Amen', John Paul II's reported final word.

★ Corrections & Clarifications (7 April 2005): In our coverage of the death of the Pope on 5 April, we reported: 'Then we saw a cloud of incense swirling up from the censor being swung by a deacon.' That would have been a censer, or to move even further from the land of the homophone, a thurible. We also said that the Swiss Guard halberdiers stood beside the catafalque bearing the body of the Pope, their 'legs akimbo'. Only arms can be akimbo.

No to EU
Badges urge rejection of the vote on the European constitution in Lille,
France (SEAN SMITH/GUARDIAN)

Babyshambler
Pete Doherty performs at the Live 8 concert in Hyde Park, London
(DAN CHUNG/GUARDIAN)

The games come to London
Confetti at a party to celebrate the capital being awarded the 2012 Olympics
(HENRY BROWNE)

Out of hell
An injured tube passenger is evacuated from Edgware Road station after
another of the London bombs (MARTIN ARGLES/GUARDIAN)

CROWNING NONSENSE

Leading article

About two out of five weddings now involve second marriages. So today's events in Windsor are very much of our times. In this respect, though in few others, the Prince of Wales and Mrs Camilla Parker Bowles are at one with the millions of remarried people over whom they will one day reign as king and queen. However, in other respects the Prince, in particular, is not at all as others are. He is the heir to a throne that is the keystone of the constitution. He will be the head of a faith that unconditionally condemns adultery and does not permit remarriage in church. Until very recently, the ceremony in which he and his new bride are about to participate – a royal adulterer marrying a divorcee with the church's blessing – would have been constitutionally inconceivable.

Today the old rules and precedents on royal weddings will be set aside – for unanswerably good human reasons. The Prince and his bride will be married in a civil ceremony, before making an act of repentance for their 'manifold sins and wickedness' and being blessed by the Archbishop of Canterbury. At which point, the Prince and his supporters clearly hope, we can all move on and behave as though nothing has changed. One day, the Prince hopes, he will stand in Westminster Abbey and be anointed with holy oil before swearing the 1689 coronation oath to maintain 'the laws of God and the true profession of the Gospel' and to 'maintain and preserve inviolably the settlement of the Church of England, and the doctrine, worship, discipline, and government thereof, as by law established in England'. If he does, the oath will have become a nonsense.

The importance of today is that it marks a point of irrevocable disjunction between the supposed mysteries of the monarchy and its modern reality. In one sense, that is all fine; a remarried king may not be inappropriate in a modern society. But ours is not in any way a modern monarchy. It is one that retains, largely unchanged, most of the trappings and privileges – many of them now deeply offensive and inappropriate – of the late-seventeenth-century settlement. From today, the gulf between the two becomes insuperable. As we said yesterday, the case for antidisestablishmentarianism has never been more threadbare. And if the case for the sovereign as head of a meaningful faith has gone, then the case for the sovereign has changed too.

At some stage we must decide as a nation if we are content to live with this nonsense. Some will say, as we do, that we should not. Others will say, with the Prince, that we should muddle along as though none of it matters. One day, however, maybe in his lifetime, we will discover that it does matter. Those who want the monarchy to be sustainable in the modern world need to grasp that, as from today, the gap between the fantasy of monarchy and the reality has never been wider or more in need of reform.

CAMPAIGN DIARY

Simon Schama

It was when Michael Howard shifted into the conditional mood that I knew which side of the Atlantic I was really on. 'On Friday,' he said, 'Britain could wake up to a brighter future.' COULD? You mean . . . it might not happen? If this had been Detroit or San Diego or Dubuque, incredulous staffers would have rushed the candidate off podium for emergency reprogramming. 'Will, Michael,' they would chant patiently at him until he Got It. 'Never, ever so much as breathe a possibility of defeat.' But this wasn't Dubuque, it was the Ashford Holiday Inn, and the Somewhat Beloved Leader was addressing the Party faithful on how, probably, all things considered, he might, with any luck, and showery periods on Thursday, even the score by full time.

Howard's vision of a briskly spring-cleaned Albion was meant as a rousing clarion call, but it had all the resonance of a tinkling bicycle bell in a country lane. I was just a few hours off the jumbo from Newark, New Jersey, but it felt like dropping down the rabbit hole and emerging into parish-pump politics. Compared with the engorged rapture, the fully orchestrated Hollywood production numbers, the serried ranks of Raybanned Secret Service Men, the ululating good 'ole boys, the big-hair hoopla, the bra-popping, pompom-waggling cheerleaders, the Spandex high kicks, the tossing ocean of flags, the relentlessly inspirational gospel songs, the banners as big as a wall, the parade of uniforms (any uniform will do – firemen, police, marines, traffic wardens, apartment-house doormen), the descending chopper blades, the eventual appearance of the Awaited One to swoons of joy and exultant whoops of messianic acclaim – compared to the whole delirious cornball razzmatazz that passes for democratic politics in the great American empire, Ashford on a bank holiday weekend was utter Ambridge. Thank God. Except He, too, was mercifully missing from the general election.

After the stifling incense-choked sanctimoniousness of American politics, getting back to Britain was like coming up for air. Or was I just nostalgic, childishly elated to be on the electoral roll for the first time, after 20 years of residential disenfranchisement? Maybe I was succumbing to antiquated memories of campaigns past: traipsing house to house for Harold Wilson in the brickier zones of Cambridge in 1964, exhilarated that we were at last on the threshold of seeing off the Tories, who'd been Her Majesty's government ever since I'd become aware of politics. (Many years on, I'd seen The Enemy close up. Tripping over a rug in the Christ's College senior common room, I rose to find myself face to face with Harold Macmillan's whiskers. 'There there,' Supermac drawled, not missing a beat, 'gratitude understandable, prostration quite unnecessary.') Little did he know. In 1964 we were the New Model Army in Morris Minors, interrupting Housewives' Choice to drive aproned grannies to the polls, transforming, as we thought, a forelock-tugging squirearchical Britain into the bracing social democracy of George Brown, Barbara Castle and Roy Jenkins.

There had always been a streak of political feistiness in our family. Living in Margaret Thatcher's Finchley, my father had been so furious at the presumption of whomever it was that had put up a Conservative sign in front of his block of flats, suggesting collective allegiance, that he'd hung from the window balcony of Number 26 the biggest Labour Party banner he could find. No one spoke to him in synagogue for months after that. So, yes, coming home politically probably meant returning to unrealistic expectations of face-to-face, high street, argy-bargy oxygenated polemics. But even if it fell short, it would still feel like red meat compared to the white-bread pap I'd had to consume in the last election I'd covered for this paper: Bush v Kerry 2004, primetime-ready brand marketing, punctuated only by sleazebag character assassination.

I'd heard reports that British politics had been invaded by focus-group, market-tested campaigning. That, between Lynton Crosby and Maurice Saatchi, the Tories were playing the American game, eavesdropping on Basil Fawlty in the snug and turning his pet peeves into electoral policy. Are you drinking what I'm drinking, squire? But if slick persuasiveness was the idea, Howard's performance at Ashford suggested there was more work to be done. After a sly warm-up speech by Damian Green, the local MP, the Somewhat Beloved Leader entered to the stirring chords of *Victory at Sea*, composed for television in the early 1960s by the true-blue American Richard Rodgers. Was this a good idea? Tory Party as HMS *Victory*, fine. Pity about the 'At Sea' bit, though.

There then followed what in America would be called the Stump Speech, except that 'stump', with its evocation of cigar-pulling, down-home wisdom, cookie-bake homilies and a feverish orgy of babykissing, isn't really mid-Kent. To rapt silence, broken only by aldermanic murmurs of assent, the SBL painted an apocalyptic picture of a New Labour Britain – *Blade Runner* with tea – in which pensioners no longer feel free to go to the shops in safety, where MRSA pullulates in hospitals unchecked by Matron, where a critical swab shortage holds up urgent surgery, a Britain where the police are doomed to standing around on street corners sucking on pencils as they complete interminable questionnaires while platoons of drunken yobs, Shauns of the Undead, run amok in the high street, pillaging Starbucks and sacking Boots. Under his government, Howard pledged, the police would be liberated from pencil duty and set free to 'invade the personal physical space' of the yobs (protected, presumably, by rubber gloves obtained from Matron). SWABS not YOBS: who could possibly disagree? And on and on in this vein until his uncanny resemblance to the goldfish from *Cat in the Hat* became not just physical.

Several times we were promised a government which would roll up its sleeves (though those of Howard's blue shirt remained elegantly buttoned). Then came the really worrying bit. SBL's voice dropped, the eyes moistened, the smile widened. Acute observers could instantly recognise the onset of a Sincerity Attack. 'I love my country.' Then he told us how he truly feels. About himself. About Britain. Proud. Immigrant roots. State school. Really proud. Work hard. Do well. What Britain's all about. Not layabout. This sort of thing is of course obligatory for American campaigns where the 'story' of the candidate –

a combination of autobiographical confession and patriotic profession
– is the sine qua non of 'making a connection with the voters'. But in
Ashford, among the flowery frocks and jackets flecked with doghair,
the narrative seemed wetly embarrassing. Then exit to reprise of *Victory
at Sea* and sustained (if not exactly deafening) applause. The faithful
were giddy with excitement. Well, almost all of them. One loyalist with
a bottle-green, flying-ducks tie, was still barking over the State of the
Country. 'Are you optimistic about Thursday?' I asked tentatively. 'I
TRY to be,' he conceded, 'though I was going to desert the sinking
ship.' 'Where to?' 'Montenegro.' 'Montenegro?' 'Yes, Montenegro.
Not many people know this, but the wine is wonderful and –' (he
whispered confidentially) '– they have the most beautiful women in the
world. Though, of course they do tend to be a bit hairy.'

As indeed do the campaigns in these endgame days. Not that you'd
guess it watching Howard taking a walkabout on his own patch. For
once the sun shone benevolently on his progress. ('We arrive, it rains.
It always rains,' said one campaign Eeyore on the battle bus.) Howard
was bouncily affable as he trotted Folkestone high street, a place
inexplicably bereft of the roaming hordes of ruffians and mendicant
asylum seekers he says infest New Labour's derelict Britain. Surely he
can't mean the ubiquitous Ecuadorian pan-pipers (are there any left in
the Andes?) who warbled away while the SBL closed in on
constituents, for an economical handpump (pensioners got a
concerned left hand on their arm too) adroitly avoiding, in short order,
the Green Party table overstocked with belligerently pacifist eco-
literature, giggly girls stuffed into jeans shouting their resolution to
vote for the Official Monster Raving Loony Party and burps and hoots
from acne-stricken yoofs dressed, bafflingly, in Boston Celtics kit.

As the Leader ducked into Celeste ('A Taste of Heaven on Earth') for
lunch I was left marvelling at the village green cosiness of it all –
unthinkable in the United States where the candidate would be flanked
by a wall of myrmidons with imperfectly concealed shoulder holsters,
and would never ever be unplugged from the earpiece through which
staff would prompt his every reply. ('Remember, Michael, WHEN we
win, not IF!') As for the Monster Raving Loony Party, they would be

in a Secure Holding Facility, not munching on ham sandwiches 10ft away from the Leader. But in Folkestone, the sun glinted off the sea, vagrant scavenging gulls wheeled around the battle bus (send 'em home) and the violent grunge-hole of Howard's Albion seemed a long way away.

What is it that draws British politicians down to the sea? Conferences in Blackpool and Brighton, a rally for the Labour Party in Hove? In America they go to the major markets: conventions, then, in Chicago, Los Angeles, New York, not Cape Cod or Virginia Beach. I was at the only exception, 40 years ago: Lyndon Johnson's coronation in Atlantic City, where, amidst the toffee vendors on the boardwalk, porky pink straw-boatered men from Mississippi with wilting bowties pretended not to notice the civil rights demonstrators. At the moment of apotheosis, LBJ, the Hidden One, rose majestically on to the stage on a hydraulic platform as thousands of minute plastic cowboys descended on parachutes from the convention hall roof. 'All the Way with LBJ!' the Democrats roared. And they did go all the way to Hue and Saigon and the helicopters on the roof.

But whatever's wrong with this election it isn't hubris. No one was shouting 'If you care, vote for Blair!' in Hove last Sunday. In fact, they weren't shouting at all. Everything and everyone, except David Blunkett, who gave new meaning to the word unrepentant, was a tad defensive, beginning with the lighting of the stage – not exactly shameless red, more softly fuschia, the kind of ambient glow that lap dancers use to juice the tips (an observation based, I assure you, on cinematic evidence only).

The audience in Hove town hall resembled an almost ideological parade of domesticity: babies had tantrums, toddlers toddled, primary schoolers kicked balls around the back with New Labour dads. Blunkett eschewed altogether the much-vaunted masochism strategy in favour of unapologetic balls-of-brass: 'You know why they're attacking Tony Blair?' No, go on, on tell us. 'Because Tony Blair is the greatest asset the Labour Party has.' He even told a story against himself involving blindness and flirting, which somehow managed to make him endearing.

The comedian Jo Brand, warming up for Blair, was rather more equivocal. She gave him just one stick-on star for achievement, but two for effort. She would vote Labour, she conceded, but there were some, well, a lot really, of things, she wasn't too keen on – the small matter of a dodgy war for instance. But you know, you wouldn't want Michael Howard, would you?

Stateside, this less than ringing endorsement would be a cue for loud music and dimming of stage lights, while Brand was swiftly escorted from the podium and conveyed to a long and richly deserved vacation. Instead we got – by way of reminding us that someone in this outfit (Darth Campbell?) could play electoral hardball – a video evoking the Dark Side of the Tory leader: a brilliantly mixed little cocktail of malice (take one part Poll Tax and one part record unemployment, top with ice and shake) that could have had the campaign heavies in New York and Washington beaming with satisfaction that at last the limeys have learned something about negative campaigning.

But what would they have made of the prime minister, next up, irradiated with the fuschia glow, in full The Passion of the Tony go-on-give-it-to-me mode. Look, he understands the three Disses: as in -enchantment -agreement and -illusion. But really, come on, that's real life, not just politics. And there's so much to be proud of. The faithful agreed. Two rather small 'If you value it, vote for it' banners waved back in puppyish salutation. But whatever elixir had been downed that night did the trick. By the Monday morning press conference at – yes, a primary school – Blair was back in punchy, shoot-from-the-hip form, as he did what he likes doing best, pouring ridicule on Tory capacity to do the sums, Howard's and Oliver Letwin's fitness to be CEOs of Britannia Inc. The prime minister and the chancellor then went into their alto and tenor sax riffs, the bright and the baggy, Blair at his most engaging, the chancellor at his most solidly Gladstonian. As Brown upbraided the Tories for being insufficiently faithful to Margaret Thatcher's fiscal prudence, the map of Cuba on the classroom wall with its slogan of 'Socialismo o Muerte' drawn in the Caribbean seemed to turn redder by the minute. Or perhaps I just imagined it.

Then followed questions from the press, the only feature of which that might have been recognisable to American reporters would have been the well-practised habit of leaders to disarm questioners by remembering their first names. In the White House press room (a calculatedly dismal prefab in the grounds) it might have the effect of defanging the journalists with mock camaraderie, but not in Wimbledon at nine in the morning. Even in the dress code of the press conference – jackets and ties for both party leaders (who'd suited up from the calculated, open-necked, informality of the walkabouts) – there was the unspoken recognition of the ritualised, gladiatorial nature of the exchange. 'Right, James (or Brendan or Andrew).' 'Yes, well, going on about the danger of letting the Tories in if you vote Lib-Dem, isn't that the wife-beater sneering, "You'll stay, you've got nowhere else to go"?' To this kind of question it's safe to say, the famous Dubya lightness would not have responded well. Instead: the tell-tale dilation of nostrils, the giveaway smirk behind which plans for No Future Admission would already be being finalised. Instead, both Brown and Blair laughed and, *mirabile dictu*, it was not at all the laugh of someone about to be sick.

The ability to take this kind of take-no-prisoners irreverence on the chin – indeed, to expect it – is breathtaking to visiting reporters from the US, where oppositional politics (such as it is) is mired in a tar pool of tepid glutinous reverence, where Democratic fury has been frightened into milquetoast bleating by pre-emptive Republican accusations of 'divisiveness'. If John Humphrys is thinking of a late career move across the pond he should forget it. But then again, what must American observers make of the fact that it's Blair and Brown who are given to evoking the New Deal (albeit vintage 1997, not 1932) rather than Democrats who, with Bush prosecuting a deeply unpopular 'reform' (gutting) of social security, ought to be rallying to defend what little is left of it with their last breath? The spectacle of all three parties (for Howard, pledged to abolish student fees, would be identified as well to the American left of centre) campaigning on their own particular approaches to fine tuning the welfare state is enough to fill the neutered American opposition with envious despair. They look at a government standing on a record of economic success, committed to defend public services – the mere mention of which, in the US, would likely trigger the opening of a File in the Department of Homeland Security – and, even with the long trail of muck leading from dubious intelligence reports and suspiciously altered legal advice about Iraq, they listen to the ferocity of Blairophobia and scratch their heads. (At which point, perhaps, they should remember LBJ, for whom no amount of virtue prosecuting the Great Society exonerated the sins of Vietnam.) But if Blair wakes one morning and feels one prick of the pincushion too many, he might well consider a career move across the pond, where he'd be a shoo-in for the next governor of New York. We're already assuming Mayor Clinton. The dynamic duo, then, reborn on the Hudson! Can't wait.

Most wondrous of all, perhaps, is the conspicuous absence in British hustings rhetoric of the one campaign helper without whose assistance no American candidate can possibly hope to prevail, namely God. But then the election is being held in a country where, unlike the US, it is assumed that Darwinian evolution is actually incontestable scientific fact, rather than just a wild hunch that has to compete with creationism for space in textbooks and lessons. The G-word finally got uttered in the Lib-Dems' last press conference before the election. 'So, Charles, do you think you'll be making another run as leader in 2009?' 'God – and my colleagues and constituents willing,' Kennedy cheerfully replied, invoking the deity with no more theological conviction than if someone had sneezed and he'd said, 'God bless you.' And he would, wouldn't he? On parade at the press conference were all the virtues of his party and leadership: disarming honesty, cornflake-crisp optimism, milk-of-human-kindness concern for, *inter alia*, pensioners, students, the landscape of Britain and doubtless the Scotties and red deer that roam it.

Was I – after only a few days impersonating a political reporter – becoming, perish the thought, a tad cynical? Or was Kennedy's niceness somehow worrying? Lust for power? Not a sniff. Killer instinct? I don't think so. Even an attempt to congratulate him on the decapitation strategy provoked a denial that he'd ever thought of any term so brutal. If he doesn't want to be confused with Robespierre, perhaps Kennedy ought to spend a little time with Machiavelli. At the press conference, I asked whether he was happy to go into the election positioned as the true centre-left party. He smiled and said well, yes, the Lib-Dems were indeed progressive. Progressive as in heirs to the great reforming post-war Labour government and the bitterly unrealised dreams of the Wilson years? Well, yes, he acknowledged, apparently quite happy to slip into history tutorial mode, but I should remember that those achievements were built on the foundation of the Liberal Party reforms of the people's budget, old-age pensions, the Lloyd George/Churchill years before the First World War. Back to the future, then, with the Lib-Dems!

It was fabulous, this sit-down chinwag as if we were both sipping pints. And perhaps that's what Kennedy likes doing in his crofter fastness. Jean-Jacques Rousseau would have endorsed this pastoral version of politics, for he warned that while popular democracy was the only right and just political system, it could only prosper in republics of 25,000 or less – the size of eighteenth-century Geneva. However low the turnout today, it will be rather more than that. But coming from America where the manipulation of the millions presupposes the priority of commodity marketing, massive up-front investment, saturation advertising, the reduction of politics to the soundbite and the photo-op, a British election looks rather closer to Rousseau's ideal. In these few days I've heard colleagues say they've never seen an election more remote from the people, to which I can only reply, try coming to Baltimore or Minneapolis.

There was, though, at least one big American-pie mob scene to sample: Howard's monster rally out in Docklands. There, I met America's most prolific and famous blogger, Markos Moulitsas, who has never seen British politics first-hand before. He marvelled at the absence from the proceedings, not just of the big campaigner in the sky but also flags, bands, the whole pumped-up operation of patriotic euphoria and snake-oil pitches without which the business of American politics is just so much grey newsprint and paid-for televenom.

Not that this event was low-key. Since Ashford, the SBL had had a slight but telling makeover. The shirt cuffs now were definitely open, the shirt itself was pink, the tie had been banished. He was ACTION MAN with the ACTION PLAN! He was ready to be ACCOUNTABLE and to prove it he announced a calendar of achievements, designed with wonderfully meaningless specificity. On 6 June 2006, mark my words and your diaries, the British Border Patrol WILL start patrolling! (What's wrong with 5 June?) But this heady vision of a new Britain got the crowd on its feet and, yes, they were cheering. For the new Britain turned out, in fact, to be the old Britain: cricket and courtesy, picnics and politeness, yob-free, swabs aplenty, and to prove it, as the SBL unburdened himself once more of a profession of love of country, there began the low rumble of unmistakably British Music. He ended unequivocally. The backroom boys had done their job. There will, after all, be a brighter tomorrow, starting Friday. The cheers got as riotous as English cheers can get. Elgar's *Nimrod* powered up and Howard drank in the glory, rode the crescendo all the way to the exit, for one sovereign moment, elated, omnipotent, and wholly unconditional.

14 May 2005

HOODIES

Patrick Barkham

Street rats, says Ainsley, 17. 'That's what they're called.' 'They sit on the street and drink,' explains Lauren, 16. 'They're everywhere,' adds Carly, 17. The teenagers from Bexleyheath describe the disrespectful youths of today as they glide along the Bluewater shopping centre in Kent. Street rats wear hooded tops and baseball caps. They are mainly boys, but girls tag along. They aren't into serious crime. It's graffiti or stealing garden gnomes, although Carly thinks they beat people up. When they see hoods up, the girls say they cross the road and hold on to their phones.

Happy-slapping, binge-drinking, hoodie-wearing feral yobs have been swearing and spitting their way across the country this week. Tube drivers said yesterday they would strike over intimidating behaviour by gangs of youths on the District Line. John Prescott recalled ten 'fellas with hoods' trying to beat him up and film it at a motorway service station. Tony Blair said people were 'rightly fed up with street corner and shopping centre thugs' and promised to make the restoration of respect a priority for his government. Both endorsed the approach taken by Bluewater, which has banned hoods and caps.

There is a moral panic over hooded teenagers. What's wrong with the kids? Are they worse than ever? 'Yes,' chorus the girls shopping at Bluewater. 'My 14-year-old sister acts so much more grown up than I did when I was that age,' says Carly. 'It's unbelievable how old she acts – she wants to go to the pub.' 'When we were 14 we went to the cinema,' says Lauren. 'Now they all sit on the streets drinking and smoking.' But none of the teachers, pensioners, mothers, employers and teenagers out shopping at Bluewater want to admit they are part of a society rearing a generation of hooded hoodlums.

Both government and shopping centre initiatives sprang from fearful focus groups. Voters told the prime minister of teens' loss of respect.

Shoppers told Bluewater they hated the young hooded gangs listlessly congregating in the brightly lit mall. Its ban was shrewd PR, helping the 330 chain stores identify shoplifters on CCTV and sending a message to shoppers: leave your hoodie-infested local shops and come to Bluewater. (Gamestation, the computer games retailer, opportunistically announced yesterday that it would welcome hooded top-wearing teens into its stores.) Now Kent's cavernous shopping centre seems to be where the hooded street rats come with their mums or girlfriends for a spot of down-time after skulking at the bus stop all day. From middle-aged women to teenage boys, all are wearing their hoods responsibly – down, not up. They come in their thousands to buy more hoodies: on sale in the windows of dozens of other shops yesterday.

Most of the teenage 'guests' hanging out at Bluewater say their schools – in Gillingham, Rochester, Sidcup and Bexley – have banned hooded tops. Newsagents, pubs and clubs in these ordinary towns and suburbs have also outlawed hats and hoods so they don't obscure troublemakers' faces on CCTV. Cameras are everywhere. It is not just hooded happy-slappers who flourish their phones to film attacks. 'I used to wear my hood up all the time when it was in fashion about a year ago,' says Craig Wilkshire, 20, with his Nike cap on and Reebok hoodie down. 'I was walking down the road once and a bus driver stuck his phone out of the window and took a photo and said, "Now I've got you." That's what it's like in Woolwich. Everyone wears hoods. It's really bad.' His girlfriend, Julie Hogben, 23, is angry about the stereotyping. 'The other side is people think you are causing trouble so you might as well go and cause trouble. It's labelling the youngsters. It's society pushing them to do it – "We've been given a bad name, we might as well carry it through."'

Violence, cameras, hoodie bans, more cameras. People seem bewildered by this spiral of fear and control. 'You can't wear hooded and caps in our school,' says John Halford, 34, a teacher at a secondary school in the Medway. 'I don't agree with the ban but the argument was crime could be committed in the school and they could remain anonymous on the CCTV cameras. The subtext is they are trying to stop all youths wearing things they consider offensive. It's a scare tactic.

Hoodies signify they are rough, tough kids but what you wear is not necessarily a signifier of who you are. They gave a whole assembly talking about former New York mayor Rudy Giuliani and that's seeped into many schools – sort out the small things and you sort out the big things. But if you quash freedom of expression that much you are going to make kids do other things.'

The Government is talking tough, but critics fear it lacks a coordinated approach to tackling the problem. David Miliband's appointment as minister of communities in Mr Prescott's office has created grounds for a turf war between it and the Home Office. There are also rumours that the much-hyped antisocial behaviour unit is to be closed. 'I'm not sure it is always a good idea to see youth as a problem. We want young people feeling wanted in society,' says Joanna Shapland, professor of criminal justice at Sheffield University. 'Hooded tops are a problem if you are relying on cameras and policing at a distance rather than face-to-face personal security.'

According to Richard Garside, the director of the Crime and Society Foundation think-tank, the Government's drive for respect has simply amplified perceptions of antisocial youths. West Midlands police has complained the force is being inundated with calls about innocuous antisocial behaviour. 'First it was squeegie merchants, then it was antisocial behaviour and now it's respect,' says Mr Garside. 'By creating this category of loutishness or kids hanging around, the Government can acknowledge anxieties without admitting there may be a problem with crime.' It is unhelpful, he adds, to place what young people wear on a continuum of antisocial behaviour that includes vandalism, noise pollution and crack dens. 'It is a collection of discrete problems,' he argues, which require specific solutions. Draughty village halls and games of ping-pong overseen by the vicar may not cure youth ennui any more but providing teenagers with greater mobility would stop them hanging around on street corners. 'There are generalised solutions too, like poverty reduction, but they are not the ones the Government is talking about.'

While more than 65 per cent of people consider youth crime is rising and experts agree there can be a connection between antisocial behaviour and serious youth crime, statistically, youth offending is falling. The number of 10- to 17-year-olds convicted or cautioned fell from 143,600 to 105,700 between 1992 and 2002, a drop of almost 26 per cent. Government research has found the most mentioned antisocial behaviour is speeding – an adult problem. 'We are not complacent, but anyone familiar with social history knows that teenagers have been complained about in every era,' says Rod Morgan, chairman of the Youth Justice Board. 'We mustn't attempt extreme responses. Would we be wise to exacerbate the problem by making certain forms of dress or behaviour even more attractive by damning them? We have to be careful we don't demonise them. Having said that, if young people are engaged in serious antisocial behaviour, destroying the quality of life in neighbourhoods, it needs to be dealt with.' Mr Morgan insists that projects such as voluntary work with parents of young children seen as at risk and providing local facilities for teens must be pursued. 'It will not be a solution if our response is to lock up many more children. All we will do is create adult career criminals.'

There is fear, but not terror, in Kent. 'We don't see too much of it [antisocial behaviour], but there isn't the respect now that there used to be,' says a pensioner, Wendy Wadeson, from leafy Pratt's Bottom, near Bromley. 'Kids used to stand up for you when you were on the bus or open doors.' Her husband Colin says: 'In the evening when you're out and there's a group of youngsters in a dark area it can be threatening. It's an impression. It doesn't mean that they are causing trouble. Historically there's always been this kind of thing. The teddy boys and the mods and rockers created fear.' Were they mods or rockers in their youth? 'Mods, I suppose. We had scooters. We did more sporty things with them – we'd drive to Italy,' says Mr Wadeson. Did he go to Brighton, where the mods and rockers famously clashed? 'Oh, there were those days too. People were drawn into it. It's easily done.'

NUMBERS UP

Janine Gibson

My favourite moment of last week was when the man from *Newsnight* asked if the sudden national newspaper Sudoku frenzy was because, in the lull after the election, there was no news to fill the papers. The overwhelming temptation was to reply: 'No, but I suspect that might be why you're covering it on *Newsnight*.'

Let's face it, the very idea that the election was a useful way of boosting circulation and filling newspapers is in itself a dark joke. The election? Anyone who doesn't now recognise that election coverage is to newspaper sales as religious broadcasting is to BBC ratings is deeply misguided. The fact that so much political coverage appeared during the election is a tribute to the well-hidden public-service soul of the newspaper industry. If it was just about giving the mass-market what it wants, then newspapers would be filled with celebrities and, er, number-based puzzles.

Last week it was all about the number-based puzzles, which seemed to just come out of nowhere. They didn't, of course: the first Sudoku puzzle hit the UK press in *The Times* six months ago. The *Daily Mail* launched one shortly thereafter, though it was called Codebreaker and everyone else ignored it. In fact the *Mail* was in danger of being written out of the collective history of the Sudoku Phenomenon as it emerged day by day last week, until it devoted half of its front page to a bold 'we was first' claim. It's possible the *Mail* may now be regretting eschewing the Japanese name, which we can only assume it did in case its readers got upset by the idea of it being foreign.

Anyway, between November and the middle of last week, pretty much everyone piled in and tried to think of a different way to distinguish their offering. Kudos, by the way, to *Sun* Doku which launched on Tuesday and distinguished itself immediately by being a puzzle that someone else has already half completed. The *Guardian* launched its own version on Monday, sprinting for the high ground with 'the original Japanese puzzles hand-crafted by its inventors' and gently putting the boot in to the computer versions run by other papers. The others responded with suitable outrage. 'We were first,' said *The Times*. 'We've got four!' shouted the *Independent*. Sighs from baffled readers everywhere.

This really isn't about the puzzle, though Sudoku is a very good puzzle with some addictive qualities which have been tested to their very limits in one highly charged week. It's not even about puzzles *per se* – the *Telegraph*, *Mail* and *Express* have long recognised that puzzles are a fantastic inducement to frequency of purchase, and help insinuate the paper into the rhythm of the readers' day, whether it's the quick crossword over tea, the cryptic on the train or the codebreaker at lunch. Mostly it's about the strange machismo that kicks in when newspapers try to outdo each other, which occasionally spills over into drunken violence (see the British Press Awards) or, at its best, into a competitive wit which results in *Sun* Doku or 'G2 – the section with Sudoku on every page!'. A late entrant to the race on Friday was the *Mirror*'s 'Can you conquer Carol?' (The Carol in question being *Countdown*'s resident maths mistress, Carol Vorderman.) This was almost my favourite, simply for the cod-oriental script in which 'Su-Doku' was written. Note the hyphen as well: a key innovation.

I had a small part in bringing Sudoku into the *Guardian*. From the cold chill of the first reader's letter claiming that the *Grauniad* had typically got its puzzle wrong (no, Mr Jones, I checked many times, I'm afraid you just went wrong) to the thrill of being dissed by the *Independent* on *Newsnight*, it has been a dizzying insight into the business end of newspapers as well as one sodding Sudoku too far.

So I propose a truce. We've all got one now, let's just leave it alone. Do the puzzle, don't do the puzzle, just don't talk about it.

MR GALLOWAY GOES TO WASHINGTON

Oliver Burkeman

Whatever else you made of him, when it came to delivering sustained barrages of political invective, you had to salute his indefatigability. George Galloway stormed up to Capitol Hill yesterday morning for the confrontation of his career, firing scatter-shot insults at the senators who had accused him of profiting illegally from Iraqi oil sales. They were 'neo-cons' and 'Zionists' and a 'pro-war lynch mob', he raged, who belonged to a 'lickspittle Republican committee' that was engaged in creating 'the mother of all smokescreens'.

Before the hearing began, the Respect MP for Bethnal Green and Bow even had some scorn left over to bestow generously upon the pro-war writer Christopher Hitchens. 'You're a drink-soaked former Trotskyist popinjay,' Mr Galloway informed him. 'Your hands are shaking. You badly need another drink,' he added later, ignoring Mr Hitchens's questions and staring intently ahead. 'And you're a drink-soaked . . .' Eventually Mr Hitchens gave up. 'You're a real thug, aren't you?' he hissed, stalking away.

It was a hint of what was to come: not so much political theatre as political blood sports – and with the senators, at least, it was Mr Galloway who emerged with the flesh between his teeth. 'I know that standards have slipped in Washington in recent years, but for a lawyer, you're remarkably cavalier with any idea of justice,' he told Norm Coleman, the Minnesota Republican who chairs the senate investigations committee, after taking his seat at the front of the high-ceilinged hearing room, and swearing an oath to tell the truth. 'I'm here today, but last week you already found me guilty. You traduced my name around the world without ever having asked me a single question.'

The culture clash between Mr Galloway's bruising style and the soporific gentility of senate proceedings could hardly have been more pronounced, and drew audible gasps and laughs of disbelief from the audience. 'I met Saddam Hussein exactly the same number of times as Donald Rumsfeld met him,' Mr Galloway went on. 'The difference is that Donald Rumsfeld met him to sell him guns, and to give him maps the better to target those guns.'

American reporters seemed as fascinated as the British media: at one point yesterday, before it was his turn to speak, Mr Galloway strode from the room, sending journalists of all nationalities rushing after him – only to discover that he was going to the lavatory.

By condemning him in their report without interviewing him, the senators had already given Mr Galloway the upper hand. But not everything was in his favour. For a start, only two senators were present, sabotaging Mr Galloway's efforts to attack the whole lickspittle lot of them – and one of the two, the Democrat Carl Levin, had spent much of his opening statement attacking the hypocrisy of the US government in allegedly allowing American firms to benefit from Iraqi oil corruption. Even so, Mr Galloway was in his element, playing the role he relishes the most: the little guy squaring up for a fight with the establishment.

For these purposes, Senator Coleman served symbolically to represent all the evil in the world – the entire Republican Party, the conscience of George Bush, the US government and the British government, too: no wonder his weak smile looked so nauseous. 'I gave my heart and soul to stop you committing the disaster that you did commit in invading Iraq . . . senator, in everything I said about Iraq, I turned out to be right and you turned out to be wrong,' Mr Galloway told him. And yet for all his anti-establishment credentials, Mr Galloway is as practised as any of his New Labour enemies at squirming away from awkward questions. Under scrutiny by Senator Levin, he deployed a classic example of the bait-and-switch technique that is the government minister's best defence in difficult questioning.

But Mr Galloway Goes To Washington had never really been an exercise in clarifying the facts. It was an exercise in giving Norm

Coleman, and, by extension, the Bush administration, a black eye – mere days after the bloody nose that the Respect MP took credit for having given Tony Blair. And it went as well as Mr Galloway could have wished.

SUMMER

3 June 2005

DEATH OF A TREATY

Martin Kettle

The people of France and the Netherlands have killed the EU constitution. It is an ex-treaty. But if we must respect what the voters have done, we must also respect the reasons they have given for doing it. Commentators who impose their own romantic or apocalyptic scenarios on facts that do not support them are just as culpable as EU leaders in denial.

So we cannot just ignore the fact that 52 per cent of French No voters told the exit pollsters on Sunday that the main reason they voted the way they did was that they were discontented with the current social and economic condition of France, while 35 per cent of them said it was a chance to oppose Turkish membership of the EU. Sure, 40 per cent of them said the constitution was too economically liberal for their taste. But any attempt to interpret the French vote as an intifada against globalisation is misleading.

Likewise with the vote in the Netherlands. There, Dutch No voters gave exit pollsters 20 different reasons for doing what they did on Wednesday. First on their list was a fear that the Netherlands would lose influence in an EU that would favour large countries. Next was the complaint that Dutch politicians had failed to consult sufficiently. More than a quarter said they were voting to oppose Turkish entry.

Let those who wish to interpret the two referendums as a great shout on behalf of the European social model – but which one? – or as the rejection of the euro that they would like to see rejected by British voters one day – do so. A more accurate analysis is that these No votes were made up of many strands. While one of these may well have been left-wing opposition to market economics, another, at least as strong, was right-wing opposition to immigrants, black minorities and Muslims. The No vote would not have won in France without the forces of Jean-Marie Le Pen. And the No vote would not have won in Holland without the supporters of Pim Fortuyn. Not one word of this is to belittle the results in France and the Netherlands or the crisis that now presents itself within the EU. It is merely to say that interpreting the mood among 450 million people is as complicated as it is necessary.

Here's my take. Many in Europe have not yet woken up to the changed, challenging but better world created by the end of the Cold War. This goes for western Europe's politicians as well as its voters. On Europe's Left and the Right, there is a yearning for a politics that will make the perceived problems of the post-Cold War era – market forces for some, black people for others – go away. Some of Europe's politicians occasionally imply that bits of this might be possible. But it is not.

In the aftermath of the death of Communism, referendums provide an ideal weapon for backlash politics of the sort that we have seen this week. But these referendums are not the foundations of a serious alternative or a new kind of politics. They are a warning that Europe's politicians have failed to give Europe's anxious citizens an overarching explanation of how governments can help to manage their place in the globalised market economy of the post-Cold War era. With the death of the EU constitution, they will simply have to go back and try again, because this is still the only game in town.

JACKSON AGONISTES

Dan Glaister and David Teather

Michael Jackson, one of the world's biggest pop stars, was acquitted yesterday on all counts of child molestation charges. The 46-year-old singer, who faced up to 18 years in prison had he been found guilty, reached for a tissue and wept as the clerk completed reading the succession of not guilty verdicts. In a packed courtroom in the small town of Santa Maria, north of Los Angeles, the clerk of the court began reading the verdicts at 2.12 p.m. As they were read, the prosecution slumped back in their chairs.

Jackson left the 20-minute session to be greeted by screams and cheers from 100 fans gathered outside the court. Accompanied by his family and holding his mother's arm, Jackson got straight into a waiting black SUV and left the court. He acknowledged the fans, but there was no repeat of the grandstanding that accompanied some his previous court appearances. Inside the courtroom the verdict was greeted with gasps and tears of relief from the public gallery as the 40 fans allowed inside took in the implications.

Jackson, dressed in a black suit, white shirt and black tie sat immobile, as he had been throughout most of the trial. After the clerk had completed reading the verdicts Jackson's attorney, Thomas Mesereau, gripped the singer's forearm. Once the jury had left the court, the judge said: 'Mr Jackson, your bail is exonerated and you are released.' Jackson embraced each member of his defence team and then stood alone in the court, looking bewildered and saying nothing. When asked his reaction, Mr Mesereau said: 'Justice was done.'

The judge also read out a statement from the jury: 'We the jury, feeling the weight of the world's eyes upon us, all thoroughly and meticulously studied the testimony, evidence and rules of procedure presented in this court since 31 January 2005. Following the jury instructions, we confidently came to our verdicts. It is our hope that this case is a testament to the belief in our justice system's integrity and the truth. We would like the public to allow us to return to our private lives as anonymously as we came.' In a statement last night Jackson's ex-wife Debbie Rowe said: 'I would never have married a paedophile. And the system works.'

The jury sent word that they had reached a verdict on the ten-count indictment at around 12.30 p.m., 8.30 p.m. in Britain. The eight women and four men had deliberated for seven days after listening to 14 weeks of testimony. The singer, who had been awaiting the verdict at his Neverland ranch, was given a little over one hour to make his way to the courthouse. When the cars pulled in, surrounded by a motorcycle police escort, emotions were running high, with supporters screaming 'Innocent!' Jackson looked apprehensive as he made his way into the court. He was flanked by members of his family, including sisters Janet and LaToya Jackson and met by the silver-haired Mr Mesereau. Due to intense media interest, the judge allowed an audio feed of the verdict to be read out, which was subsequently broadcast across the world.

The extraordinary course of events that led to the eventual acquittal of one of the world's biggest stars began when Jackson was arrested on charges of child molestation in November 2003. The charges arose from a British television documentary, *Living with Michael Jackson*, broadcast in February 2003. In the documentary, Jackson was shown holding hands with the then 13-year-old Gavin Arvizo. He also defended sharing his bedroom with children, describing it as an innocent, childlike practice. 'What could be more natural?' he asked his interviewer, Martin Bashir. However, he denied that he shared his bed with the children, saying that he would sleep on the floor.

In January 2004, Jackson appeared at the Santa Maria courthouse for his arraignment, and was admonished by Judge Rodney Melville for being late for court. Three months later, at a subsequent hearing, the details of the allegations facing the singer were revealed for the first time when the charges were read out. After a two-week jury selection process, which saw Jackson make the first of the many hospital visits that were to punctuate the trial, testimony began on 28 February. After 65 days of testimony spanning 14 weeks and involving 130 witnesses, the jury retired on 3 June to consider its verdict. In the seven days of deliberation, it had to consider not only the testimony of the witnesses and some 600 items of evidence, but 98 pages of often bewildering jury instructions from Judge Melville. The twelve-person jury consisted of eight women and four men. Described by analysts as a conservative jury that reflected the predominantly working-class area, eight of the jurors were parents, and eight over 40.

DAZED

Sam Wollaston

'The first thing you notice is the light,' says Geldof in Africa (BBC1). 'Light everywhere. Brightness. Everywhere.' Big pauses between words. Geldof speaks. On Africa. He's putting paid to the myth of Africa the Dark Continent, as so often described by writers from the gloomy northern skies of Europe. Well, actually Bob, in my experience, though it may be less insulting, it's as much of a tired old cliché for gloomy northern writers to go on about the light and the big African skies. I expect you'll mention the heat next and there'll be shimmering no doubt.

'This is the luminous continent, drenched in sun, pounded by heat.' Aha. See? 'And shimmering in its blinding glare.' Thought so.

For Geldof, though, heat is not just about temperature. 'Here, heat is a shape.' Eh? What shape is that? 'A form,' he continues. What, as opposed to a shape? 'Even a taste.' A taste? What are you on about? That's just bonkers. How hot is it? It's so hot it . . . it's triangular and tastes of almonds?

'Any movement has a purpose,' Bob continues. 'Even then it's done with economy, a captivating grace of elegance and of gesture.' Ah, yes, there are the graceful elegant people, moving sparingly because of the heat. But what about the ferocious intensity of the midday sun, surely you can't not mention that? 'During the daytime everything burns. Even the shade is hot. People, animals, even plants stop moving. At times it feels like I'm walking on the surface of the sun. Then noon arrives.' There it is! Noon, midday, it's all the same thing. And it's hotter than the surface of the sun. Churn them out, Bob.

It's a shame really because there's lots of interesting and important stuff in this six-part personal journey through the continent. It has everything – history, people, nature, Africa's troubled relationship with the rest of the world, Africa's troubled relationship with itself, reasons to be cheerful, reasons to be gloomy. But there's something about Bob's charmless, shouty, humourless and cliché-riddled, guff-heavy delivery that I don't like. At one point we even see him lecturing a bunch of unfortunate Africans under an acacia tree. Leave them alone – as you say, they've probably got enough to worry about already, without having you boring on to them about their own continent.

And he seems to be everywhere suddenly. How about if we all promise to listen, and give you the money, or the awareness or whatever you want this time, and risk our lives rowing rubber dinghies across the Channel to collect French people to bring back to the G8 summit, then will you promise to shut up and go away for another 20 years?

30 June 2005

GLAZED

Dominic Fifield, Nils Pratley and Matt Scott

The Glazer family's first visit to Old Trafford ended in ugly and violent scenes last night as police clashed with supporters who had effectively barricaded Manchester United's new owners inside the stadium. Malcolm Glazer's three sons, Joel, Avi and Bryan, were given first-hand experience of the vitriol generated by their controversial takeover as they had to be smuggled down the players' tunnel and out of the ground in two police tactical aid vans for their own safety. United fans then sat in the road, forcing the vehicles to stop. When some of the 400 supporters started hammering on the vans and pelting them with stones, police officers used dogs and batons to clear a path.

It provided a farcical if troubling finale to a chaotic day at Old Trafford. United officials had initially indicated that the Glazers – unaccompanied by their father – would not be visiting the stadium following their talks on Tuesday with the sports minister Richard Caborn and officials from the Premier League and the Football Association. That proved to be little more than a smokescreen and, with confirmation that the three brothers, the chief executive David Gill and the commercial director Andy Anson had arrived at the ground in three silver people carriers at around 6.15 last night, disgruntled fans began gathering. Their presence prompted a huge security operation. The club employed their own new 8ft-high steel gates to keep the increasingly frustrated crowds away from the directors' entrance, though the fans wasted little time in building their own makeshift barriers across roads, effectively laying the new owners under siege.

Supporters launched angry chants of 'Die, die Glazer!' and 'We'll be running round Old Trafford with his head!' while the Glazers themselves enjoyed a stroll around the pitch and met various members of staff. After more than four hours inside the stadium, and with their exit apparently barred, the Glazers were ushered into police vans, parked at pitchside, and whisked up the players' tunnel and, eventually, away from the ground.

United's new owners had planned to launch a charm offensive, starting with an interview with the club's in-house TV station. 'Joel Glazer will be recording a full interview with MUTV, broadcast at 6 p.m. on Friday,' said their spokesman. The Glazers are understood to have arrived in Britain on Monday. They dined at the House of Commons with the sports minister, having earlier met officials of the Football Association and the Premier League. The meetings, also attended by Gill, were a minor publicity coup for the Americans as they won a cautious welcome from the governing bodies. Richard Scudamore, the Premier League chief executive, said the Glazers had given 'an unequivocal commitment' to continue the league's agreement on the collective selling of TV rights. Fears that the Americans would try to opt out had been at the heart of the league's concern about the £790 million takeover. 'There was an open exchange. They detailed their motives and aspirations for the club and we shared our strategic objectives for the Premier League,' Scudamore said. 'There is a great deal of common ground between us.'

The Glazers then met the FA's chief executive Brian Barwick, executive director David Davies and chairman Geoff Thompson. Barwick said later: 'We enjoyed a very constructive meeting.' Caborn was most enthusiastic, saying he was 'delighted with the positive response' given by the Glazers and Gill on issues of support for the community. Joel Glazer said: 'There's been a lot in the UK press about us in the last 18 months and this has been an invaluable chance to tell the men who run the game what the truth is.'

PARTY POLITIC

Decca Aitkenhead

About ten years ago, a friend confided that he had something to ask. It was embarrassing, he admitted, but he thought it was time he should know – when people talked about 'politics', what did they actually mean? This wasn't a philosophical inquiry. Terms like left-wing and right-wing were meaningless to him. He didn't know what any of the parties stood for, how they got into power or what they did with the economy. He wasn't even sure what the economy was. We spent a long afternoon going over the groundwork, by the end of which we had covered most of the basics and he seemed much happier. (Oddly enough, he later had a relationship with Peter Mandelson, but I do not think the two things were related.)

I was quite shocked at the time. How had he reached his mid-20s without knowing any of this stuff? I think he was surprised, as well, by how simple it was to grasp. The conversation lived with me for years because it always made me smile, but I remember it today for a different reason. I couldn't say when everything changed, but if someone asked me the same question now, I wouldn't have a clue what to say.

From something you could summarise in an afternoon, politics has morphed into a kind of global infinity – more like the Internet, with little indication of how to apportion priority. I can be worrying away over how the World Bank works when someone says casually, 'You know, everything's down to China and Taiwan. If those two go to war, our economy's down the tube.' Hell, I think, I'd better read up on Chinese/Taiwanese diplomacy. Then someone else says the only thing worth thinking about is climate change. Or the Gaza Strip.

I used to blame home improvements for the confusion – if only I'd spent less time thinking about property prices, I'd know what was going on in the world. But I read more newspapers than I ever used to. I even subscribe to *The Economist* – an amazing state of affairs to me, and a measure of my anxiety about finding out what is going on. It hasn't helped a bit. One million people now read *The Economist*, apparently, from which all I can conclude is that nobody understands what is happening any more.

Last week Bob Geldof persuaded everyone at Glastonbury to hold hands and chant 'Make Poverty History'. Did any of them know what it meant? Probably not. There's no knowing what Live 8 audiences will be in for today, but it's a safe bet that whatever they chant will go clean over their heads. The bigger worry is whether the world leaders at Gleneagles next week will have a significantly better grasp. But how will any of us even be able to tell if they do or they don't?

When we talk about public political disengagement, the problem seems less like apathy than bewilderment about what it is we're supposed to be engaging with. Democracy relies on an assumption that we will be qualified to judge the performance of the people we elect. When those people speak a language that seems either beside the point ('Clamp down on bogus asylum seekers') or completely unintelligible ('Percentiles of foreign debt relief calculated by margins of aid'), the system breaks down.

A small number of people in the world probably do know whether it's Taiwan or climate change or Gaza we should be getting to grips with. But it's anyone's guess who those people are, and optimistic to hope they might be politicians. For all I know, Bono might be one of them – or just a jumped-up pop star who reads *The Economist*. All any of us can say for certain is that something is wrong.

You shouldn't be able to buy three T-shirts for under a fiver. There's clearly also something odd about an economy that reroutes a customer's call about a faulty washing machine to someone in Mumbai who trained to be a doctor. All of us can look at Africa and see that something is drastically wrong. I used to get annoyed with people like Geldof for muddling pop and politics. 'Awareness-raising' jamborees looked like a poor substitute for proper understanding, and Live Aid's reluctance to place Ethiopia's famine of 1985 in any kind of political context seemed to oversimplify the problem to the point of meaninglessness. If we weren't going to try to understand what was going on, what was the point?

I would have loved it if Noel Gallagher had been around back then. 'Are they hoping one of these guys from the G8 sees Annie Lennox singing "Sweet Dreams" and thinks, "Fuck me, she might have a point there, you know"?' he asked last month. 'It's not going to fucking happen, is it? Keane doing "Somewhere Only We Know" and some Japanese businessman going, "Aw, look at him . . . We should really fuckin' drop that debt, you know."' Gallagher is probably right. But it's hard to laugh when you don't know what you're talking about yourself any more. By now, a concert seems as good a place to start as any, while we wait for something to start making sense.

5 July 2005

AN AFRICAN CLEARANCE

Duncan Campbell

The giant prehistoric Balancing Rocks that stand ten miles from the centre of Harare are one of the great symbols of Zimbabwe, etched on to banknotes and pictured in every tourist guide. Immediately across the road from the rocks is a new symbol of the nation, one that is unlikely to feature in any guidebook or on the notes of the collapsing Zimbabwean dollar. It consists of piles of rubble, corrugated iron and random belongings – a basin, a single shoe, a coat-hanger – like the detritus left in the wake of an earthquake or a storm. This was home to hundreds of people in the suburb of Epworth until President Robert Mugabe announced last month that Operation Murambatsvina (Clear Out the Trash) was under way. He authorised the destruction of the homes of hundreds of thousands of people across the country as a way of removing what the police commissioner, Augustine Chihuri, described as 'this crawling mass of maggots' who had settled into makeshift townships on the fringes of cities. So far at least seven people have died in the clear-out, there have been six suicides reported and 22,000 people have been arrested or had their property confiscated. 'They stood there with their AKs [Kalashnikov rifles] and told us we must knock our own homes down,' said George, a bearded, middle-aged man who told his story as though recounting something utterly unfathomable. 'Last night, we all slept on the ground under a blanket with plastic bags over us. This is what the Government is doing to its people.'

The drive back into town has a surreal quality to it. On one side of the road, a group of apostolic worshippers dressed in immaculate white are conducting an open-air service as tsiri-tsiri birds hop beside them in the fields. On the other side, hundreds of people desperate to get into Harare to work or buy food try to flag down overloaded cars and lorries. 'We have to start walking at four in the morning now to get to work,' said Joyce, a young woman from Hatfield, another affected area. Most will end up walking the ten miles as petrol has almost run out, and drivers queue for up to seven days, sleeping in their cars as they wait for the pumps to open. 'Some of the petrol stations, they ask to see your Zanu-PF [Mr Mugabe's ruling party] card before they serve you,' George said. In the centre of the highway, armed police man roadblocks, waving down and searching cars. 'This country is upside down now,' said one young man. 'Once we had beef and tobacco and maize and now – look – we have to stand in line for petrol, for money, for mealie meal, for sugar. Soon there will be no country left at all.' A retired carpenter in his eighties said he had never seen Zimbabwe in such a state. 'You have to be careful what you say in public,' he said. 'You don't know who is listening and what may happen to you but even under the whites there was always work if you wanted it.'

Operation Murambatsvina was launched in the wake of Mr Mugabe's fiercely contested election victory earlier this year, which established him in power, with 108 of the 150 parliamentary seats, until 2008, at which stage he has indicated he will step down after 25 years as president. It also comes as he has increased from two years' imprisonment to 20 the penalty for 'publishing and communicating false statements prejudicial to the state'. But the law has not curbed his critics. 'Once he was our darling,' said Marcus, a young businessman in Harare. 'I remember when we were at school, we would all clap when we saw him on television and he did great things with education, with healthcare. But now the old man is ruining the country. He says that he will go in 2008, but even if he does, that will be too late. He needs to go tomorrow. He cannot go on treating people like this. He is not Pol Pot and he is not Hitler, like some of his enemies say, but he has been behaving brutally. It has never been this bad before. What you have here is a de facto state of emergency.'

Not only Harare has been affected. From the Victoria Falls to Bulawayo to Beitbridge, the bulldozers have gone in. Over the past week a transit camp has been opened at Caledonia Farm near the capital to house some of the homeless in single-sex units, but many now sleep in the open or erect shelters secretly at night and pull them down before dawn. No one knows exactly how many have lost their homes.

The government figure is 120,000 while opposition groups have claimed as many as a million. Aid agencies suggest the total is around 300,000. The Government remains bullish. Didymus Mutasa, minister for state security and head of the Central Intelligence Organisation, said on Zimbabwe state radio: 'Everyone in Zimbabwe is very happy about this clean-up. People are walking around Harare saying "We never knew we had such a beautiful city".'

Yesterday, the UN special envoy, Anna Kajumulo Tibaijuka, continued an inspection that started last week at the behest of the secretary general, Kofi Annan. According to the government newspaper the *Herald*, she applauded Mr Mugabe's 'vision', but the report was immediately dismissed by a UN spokesman as inaccurate.

Why has Mr Mugabe launched such an operation, which has brought him the attention of the UN and condemnation around the world at a time when he is already beleaguered? The Government's justification is threefold: that the settlements consist of illegal structures which create a health hazard and damage Harare's fragile infrastructure, that they breed crime and that the 'parallel market' of unauthorised businesses dealing in currency, goods and fuel constitute a serious threat to the country's economy. Inflation is at 144 per cent and unemployment is nearing 80 per cent. While the official exchange rate is around ZW$9,000 to the US dollar, the black-market rate on the street corner in Harare outside Meikles Hotel is ZW$25,000. Lack of foreign currency after the collapse of the tourist industry has caused the latest fuel shortage. The other shortages Mr Mugabe blames on droughts and what he portrays as a racist campaign waged against him by Tony Blair and George Bush.

Mr Mugabe's opponents see his motives very differently: to punish those from the settlements who voted so heavily against him and for the Movement for Democratic Change (MDC) in the elections, and to disperse people who might foment an uprising in an increasingly hostile political environment. 'Another reason he is doing this is because farming has collapsed since he took the farms away from the white farmers and gave them to the war veterans [who fought the white regime] – although many people think he just gave them to his supporters,' said a young technician in Harare. 'The people who had worked on the farms came to the cities because there was no work for them in the country. Now Mugabe wants to drive them back because the farms are producing nothing.' On the streets of Harare, people ask how much a flight to London costs, what an average wage is there, what work is available. An estimated 3 million Zimbabweans now live abroad, mainly in South Africa but also in Britain – as evidenced by the current hunger strike by asylum seekers – and the money they send back keeps the economy afloat.

Politically, the clean-up has already prompted fissures within the ruling party. Two days ago a Zanu-PF central committee member, Pearson Mbalekwa, resigned, declaring himself 'perturbed and disturbed' by what he saw. He is seen as testing the water for others to follow and there is talk of a 'third force', a grouping of disillusioned Zanu-PF members and some MDC politicians. The MDC's shadow justice minister, David Coltart, said yesterday that he thought that unlikely. 'I think it's a distinct possibility that Zanu will fragment,' he told the *Guardian*. 'I think an uprising is unlikely and the country will just literally grind to a halt. Sadly, when you go to some other African states, you will see that Zimbabwe has quite a way to go.'

Mr Mugabe remains unbowed. In an interview with the magazine *New African* he denounced Tony Blair, saying he 'wants to continue to maintain this headmaster type of attitude – you must submit, after all you are a black nigger'.

The new minister for information, Tichaona Jokonya, defended the laws governing the media and the prohibitions on foreign media operating in the country. He said the BBC, which is banned in Zimbabwe, had wanted 36 people accredited for the elections. 'Obviously, we knew what they were up to,' he told *New African*. 'They wanted journalists to come here with a pack of intelligence guys.' The *Guardian*'s former Zimbabwe correspondent, Andrew Meldrum, was deported two years ago, and in May two *Sunday Telegraph* journalists were jailed for two weeks after being detained for reporting without permission. This report was compiled on the same basis and the names of members of the public interviewed have been duly changed.

The one country in the region with the power to influence events is South Africa, but its president, Thabo Mbeki, has reiterated the position of the African Union: Zimbabwe is a sovereign country and what it does within its borders is its own affair. Mr Mbeki has also echoed Mr Mugabe's view that the West is only concerned about Zimbabwe because of its old colonial interests. This week, however, Mr Mbeki has held talks for the first time with the MDC leader, Morgan Tsvangirai, who yesterday called on G8 leaders to intervene in Zimbabwe. The only other South African with the personal and moral power to intervene is Nelson Mandela, and pressure is already being put on him by Zimbabweans to act. Mr Mandela has been invited as guest of honour at a party to celebrate the Mugabes' tenth wedding anniversary. In an open letter from 'concerned Zimbabweans' in the opposition newspaper the *Zimbabwean*, an appeal has been made to Mr Mandela to stay away. 'We, your admirers, are concerned that your attendance at this event will be construed as a blessing of the things that are occurring in Zimbabwe,' urges the anonymous letter writer. 'I do not think that you are able to eat and drink and make merry while Africans are being oppressed.'

Mr Coltart, the shadow justice minister, believes South Africa now has to engage in meaningful efforts to broker a way out of the crisis. 'When Zanu realises that they have to jettison Mugabe, then maybe something will happen, but the outlook is pretty gloomy.' The International Crisis Group, the Brussels-based body chaired by Lord Patten, said in its report on the elections last month that 'economic meltdown, food insecurity, political repression and tensions over land and ethnicity are all ongoing facts of life that the election has not changed for the better in any way'. It concluded: 'Robert Mugabe has been the father of Zimbabwe in many respects but he is now the single greatest impediment to pulling the country out of its precipitous social, economic and political decline.'

Out in Epworth, there is a plume of smoke from burning tyres. The Balancing Rocks of Chipenga may have survived for thousands of years, but modern Zimbabwe's balancing act seems more precarious by the day.

GLORY DAYS

Leading article

With perfect timing, the Red Arrows flew fast and low over London just minutes after the news from Singapore, leaving a bright red, white and blue vapour trail against the grey skies. On the ground, there was instant celebration too. In Trafalgar Square, there were hugs and kisses for the cameras in front of the banner that simply said *Thank You*. And the response was just as enthusiastic away from the limelight. On a Jubilee Line train, a carriage-full of normally taciturn Brits – and one Frenchwoman – burst into excited and friendly chatter as a lunchtime visitor from the surface broke the news. On a bus going down Farringdon Road, a Londoner loudly announced that this was an excellent day: George Bush seemed to be changing his tone on climate change and London had won the 2012 Olympics. Perhaps, he suggested, this means they have forgiven us for Iraq.

That may be a stretch too far, but London's famous victory is, quite simply, a brilliant achievement. Brilliant for British sport, which will never receive a greater boost than it will get over the next seven years – a legacy for the generations. Brilliant for East London, one of the poorest parts of urban Europe, which can at last look forward to the ambitious regeneration that it never properly got after the batterings of World War Two and the collapse of old industries like the docks. Brilliant for modern London as a whole, for which the Olympics will provide a thrilling validation and climax to its twenty-first-century re-emergence as an open, multiracial and dynamic world city. And brilliant too, we must ensure, for other cities and other parts of Britain. Many of them will play a role in 2012 and their interests must not be forgotten, even if in the end the focus inevitably concentrates on this extraordinary and wonderfully diverse capital city of ours.

London won this prize because of the excellence of its bid and the imaginative talent of its bid team. Not for the first time, admiration goes out to Sebastian Coe, one of the greatest sportsmen this country has ever produced, who led the team so well. But Tony Blair and Tessa Jowell played a blinder, too, and fortune favours the brave. David Beckham, as so often, supplied a decisive touch at a crucial time. But Lord Coe led a team of men and women, black and white, able-bodied and disabled (to say nothing of a princess) who presented a bid that emphasised investment in the future and openness to the world. That, more than anything, seems to have won the day. Nelson Mandela's accolade three months ago – 'There is no city like London. It is a wonderfully diverse and open city providing a home to hundreds of different nationalities. I can't think of a better place to hold an event that unites the world' – went to the heart of why the whole of Britain is entitled to feel both proud and delighted.

Getting the Olympics gives a thrilling boost to our too often fragile national morale. It is an unrivalled goal for London to build towards. Perhaps, in time, the 2012 Olympics may also be seen to symbolise the new and changed Britain emerging from the churnings of the Thatcher and Blair years. That, though, is a speculation for another day. For now, genuine delight should not turn into improper triumphalism towards any of the four great defeated cities. London won by 54 votes to 50 over a bid from Paris which, had it won instead, would have surprised no one. In the current state of British–French relations, London's victory obviously has political frissons, but it would neither be true nor neighbourly to pretend that it proves anything very conclusive about these wider disagreements – and neither Britain nor France should act as though it does. London is a great city. It will host a terrific games. The world has given us a wonderful opportunity. The words on the banner in Trafalgar Square say it all: *Thank You*.

8 July 2005

PARTY OVER

Oliver Burkeman

It was late on Wednesday night by the time the last revellers, giddy on Olympic victory, drifted away from Tim Harrold's bar, Masque, just behind King's Cross Station. Barely ten hours later, the first dazed and soot-blackened commuters stepped through the door. Then the emergency services arrived and explained that they needed to prepare the premises to receive the walking wounded.

Across London, the sense was the same: a barely comprehensible lurch from limitless jubilation to a very provisional emotion, mixing horror and bafflement in equal measure. Starved of information about what was happening, Londoners and out-of-towners alike spent much of the day in near-silence, pacing the streets and pounding the call buttons on their mobile phones in the hope of making a connection – or just to stay busy.

At Tavistock Square people stopped to peer over police lines at a scene through the trees that they couldn't quite make out. 'I can't see what I'm looking at,' one man said. Then it dawned on him: a double-decker bus with its top deck ripped off, nothing remaining except for a few orange handrails sticking up into the drizzly air. What looked like blood was splattered on the stone frontage of the British Medical Association building.

'I'll say it again,' a police officer shouted through a loudhailer at the onlookers. 'If you can see that bus, you are in danger from it, until it has been checked for secondary devices. Get behind the building lines.'

Of the celebrations the evening before few signs remained: London's night armies had long removed most of the bunting from Trafalgar Square, along with the boards saying *Thank You London!* from the foot of Nelson's column. Only the occasional *Back the Bid* banner flapped from a lamppost in the worsening rain, while copies of the first edition of yesterday's celebratory *Evening Standard*, already long out of date, lay abandoned in gutters.

'The party was just getting started, wasn't it?' said Dennis Bloor, who had arrived in the city on Wednesday night from a village outside Stoke-on-Trent, planning to visit the Hampton Court Palace flower show with his wife, Alma. 'We watched the Red Arrows, we watched all the singing.' Then, yesterday morning, they were evacuated from their hotel. 'As soon as I heard the bang, I knew it was a bomb. I've been in the army, so you know what they sound like,' said Mr Bloor. 'But without knowing it, we ended up walking as far as we could go towards where another of the blasts had happened. It was like we were walking from one bomb to another. You can't get your head around it, really.'

The Bloors had taken shelter at Friends House, the Quaker headquarters on Euston Road that provided hundreds of people yesterday with food, drink, telephones on which to call their families, and constant access to radio news. The broadcasts kept explaining that London was in chaos. And yet, even yards from the blast sites, it was a quiet kind of chaos. Only snippets of conversation revealed an undertone of panic:

'I'm never travelling on the Tube again.'

'Are there people still trapped underground?'

'I've got my family in Greece giving me more information than I'm getting here.'

Others passed the time making jokes, because, in the absence of any information, there seemed no obvious reason not to. 'You realise if we have to get hotel rooms tonight,' one male banker said to his male colleagues, laughing, 'we're going to have to share.'

With swathes of the capital cordoned off, the surrounding streets were eerily quiet where they should have been noisy and packed where they might otherwise have been quiet, as thousands of people sought out back routes from West London to the north and east. For those with longer journeys, there was little to do but wait, and to speculate about the future.

'These guys, they don't care who they kill – Muslim, Christian, black, white,' said an overground train manager from Manchester, who declined to give his name, but said that he came from a Muslim background. 'I was born and bred here, but when people in this country start feeling threatened, you don't know what's going to happen. Maybe they lash out. Maybe they start to look for people they can blame.'

Suzy and Michael Moore, from the tiny town of Alfred, in Maine, had been thrilled to be in London on the day the city won the Olympics. But now, at Friends House, Mrs Moore, wrapped in a foil blanket, and her husband seemed only happy to be at a distance from their hotel. 'First thing I did, I closed the curtains and told my daughter "Stay away from the window",' Mr Moore said. 'That was some explosion. I can't bear to think too hard about it.' They had called home to reassure their families that they were safe. But it seemed clear to them, as to almost everyone else, that there was little else to be done except to try to make travel plans, stay out of the rain, and wonder what the weeks ahead might hold.

At the height of the Olympic celebrations the night before, the talk had been of the Grand National triumphs in 2012. But yesterday it was the quiet virtues that were on display: the lending of telephones, the poring over street maps, the cars and pedestrians waiting for each other at junctions, and the making of small talk, to hasten the point at which the day would be over.

GLIMPSES OF A SMOKY HELL

Sam Wollaston

The Sky News ticker that moves along the bottom of the screen told the story as it unfolded: *At least one explosion on the London Underground – explosions on Underground thought to be have been caused by 'some kind of power surge' – two trains remain stuck in tunnel . . .* As the morning went on, the ticker began to tell a bleaker story: *Witnesses said some people in tube trains 'were covered in blood' – two fatalities confirmed – police have declared the emergency a 'major incident'.* And then, as if to remind us that this was a story about people, a human tragedy, the ticker started to offer a different kind of service: *Jamie Edwards and Bela OK and safe – Neil Davis is safe at home – please can Geoff Hook contact his daughter – Steve and Kate looking for Victoria Bull.*

Spelling mistakes added to the desperation and urgency of the situation: *Could Margaret Barr please ring home – Ben Davies from the Isle of White is OK.* There was even something tragic about the punctuation: *Will Edward McFadden please call his family? Can Allan Walkden phone home?* The question marks turned requests into uncertainties about the future. Will Edward McFadden call his family again, or not? Can Allan Walkden phone home or is he, for some terrible reason, unable to do so?

Above the ticker the pictures told a story of uncertainty: a police cordon, the entrance to an underground station, confused commuters unsure which way to walk. But the severity of the tragedy was evident from the sheer quantity of fluorescent yellow on the screen – on the dozens of ambulances, the jackets of the emergency services, the NOT IN SERVICE sign on the front of the Number 10 bus that was going to ferry the walking wounded to hospital, even the collars of the sniffer dogs. The more yellow, the greater the emergency.

And then the first people came up from under the ground, faces blackened, like miners at the end of the shift, but with eyes that told of the terrors they'd witnessed. Some were willing to speak to the cameras and described carriages full of smoke, flying glass, people screaming, waiting, and medics performing operations on the platform. Others just reached for their mobiles to phone home. The less fortunate were unable to walk out on their own, or at all. It all looked exactly like one of those speculative TV programmes: *Terror Alert: What If London Was Attacked?* – that kind of thing. But this time it was for real. There was no studio debate afterwards.

The most horrific picture was of the bus near Tavistock Square, its roof rudely ripped off to reveal the top-deck seats, all desperately empty. This photograph was taken a while after 9.50 a.m. when that blast went off, and the bodies were gone. Apparently, the windows of the BMA building next door were splattered with blood.

'Our determination to defend our values and our way of life will triumph over the terrorists' determination to cause death to the innocent,' said Tony Blair from Gleneagles. David Davis called it an act of almost unspeakable depravity and wickedness. And then the numbers started to come in – seven killed on the bus, more at Edgware Road, possibly 20 at King's Cross. Forty-five in all, thought Sky at half-past three. Pictures too: mobile-phone videos made by people escaping carriages. If 11 September was the first major tragedy that allowed us to listen in, then this one was the first that allowed us to watch, technology moving us ever closer to the event. But this was not a spectacular television tragedy like New York, because most of it happened in a smoky hell under the ground.

And still the ticker ticked on, reminding us that there were real people involved, with real families and friends. Some of the news was good: *Shelly and Lisa Levene are OK.* For others it was unsure: *Ben Edwards is looking for Catherine Pereira.* And for others still, the news will be very bad.

8 July 2005

SAVAGELY WOKEN

James Meek

All the shock was Wednesday's: London's Olympic day. All the horror belonged to Thursday: London's day of bombs. And the fact we were not surprised makes it no easier. No easier to know, now, that on that mild grey morning, among the millions moving through London's transport system, with their banal thoughts of delays and meetings and lunch and holidays and money, were a handful of people whose thoughts were not banal at all. Like many East Londoners, I went to bed last night astounded to find myself living within walking distance of the Olympic Games. Like many, I woke up not in the least surprised to find myself living within walking distance of a ruthlessly executed act of mass murder.

I take the 73 bus between Hackney and central London most days and, on Wednesday, for the first time ever, the driver made a news announcement over the PA. 'For those who are interested,' he said, 'London has been chosen to host the 2012 Olympic Games.' Nobody could quite believe it.

Next morning the same bus drew up at the stop outside my house, the doors opened, and for the second time ever the driver made a news announcement. A different sort of announcement. It was easy to believe. But did it have to be so soon? As I walked towards Newington Green, on my way to central London, I passed a delivery van from London's *Evening Standard* newspaper travelling in the opposite direction. THURSDAY'S BREAKING NEWS, proclaimed a poster stuck to the side. OLYMPIC TRIUMPH SPECIAL SUPPLEMENT. I stood in a doorway for a moment to shelter from the rain and call my wife, who was working not far from Russell Square. As we spoke a man passed me, one hand pushing a baby in a buggy, the other hand pressing his mobile to his ear. '. . . I was just worried . . .' I overheard him say.

Walking down Essex Road – which leads from the border of Hackney through Islington towards King's Cross and the western edge of the City – everybody was talking, sometimes to each other, mostly to their loved ones on their mobiles. The networks were strained but just about coping. You kept hearing snatches of conversation as the news spread and people confronted the sudden reduction of London to a pedestrian city: '. . . bus is blown up . . .' '. . . really nasty . . .' '. . . I'm just waitin' . . .' '. . . they've all got bastard attitudes . . .' Even those who weren't speaking on their mobiles were holding them in their hands, expecting them to ring, waiting for a signal, or just as talismans of the idea of order, of the idea that this last electronic totem of technology and civilisation would lead them through a rude intrusion of chaos.

Here, only 20 minutes' walk from the immense security cordon thrown around inner London, half the people you met were beginning to acquire the kind of set, dogged, suffering face you see in refugees, and half were going about their business. They were delivering mushrooms, they were drinking pints in the Green Man, they were looking in estate agents' windows at the Angel, Islington. A grand hearse led a funeral cortege away from W. G. Miller's the undertakers. Death, like life, went on.

It was only when you got to the shuttered gates of Angel tube station that the full sense of a capital in the grip of an emergency began to sink in. The Angel crossroads, leading to Clerkenwell, the City and King's Cross, was thick with pedestrians marching on unexpected journeys. It was the kind of weary crowd of clerks on foot that stimulated entrepreneurs into building the underground railway, the world's first, 142 years ago. In the last century, in two great wars, the Underground protected the people of London from bombs. One ad for the tube in the First World War read: *It is bomb-proof down below. Underground for safety; plenty of bright trains, business as usual.* In this century, in a war without clear aims, end or sides, it has become – as, for four years, we have more than half expected – a place where bombs go off.

For anyone who has lived in London for more than a few years, the tube map is more than a map on the wall. It burns itself into the brain, like the circuit diagram its design is based on. At news of any disruption, little stretches of it flash red, and almost without thinking, you try to chart a way round the obstruction. For the whole system to be sealed up without warning is to find the ground beneath your feet, paradoxically, to be not so solid as it was.

There was another transport network. Even before Madrid, there was a claustrophobic unease about the Tube, and ever more Londoners were acquiring another mental transport map, the complex map of the city's bus routes. There was a certain pride in knowing how to hop from route to route to get where you wanted without ever going underground. There was a special, slightly chippy pride for us in Hackney, the only inner-London borough without a tube station of its own. And up on the surface, particularly in the light space of the upper deck of a red double-decker bus, looking down on the traffic and bustle in the streets below, you felt safe.

In retrospect, a London bus was an obvious target, a symbol of the city and, coincidentally or otherwise, of 2012 – the Number 30 goes to the heart of London from Hackney Wick, part of the future Olympics site. Terrorists have put bombs on buses in Israel and Moscow. Yet deep down, I suppose, I never really believed a bus would be a target either honourable enough or justifiable enough for a terrorist. It is still a poor person's means of transport. Looking at the pictures of that ripped-apart vehicle I know the cold, cheap feel of those nasty orange poles for hanging on to, and the abrasive feel of the fabric of those nasty blue seats, and think of all the faces of tired hard-working people and student tourists and truanting teenagers looking down from the windows into the prosperous world of Bloomsbury, and just hoping to get on with something good.

London buses, particularly the buses between Hackney and the centre, are also filled with immigrants, and it is very possible that if a bomb exploded in any one of them, it would kill and maim at least one person from every continent and of every major faith. On any busy Hackney bus you'll hear a dozen different languages besides English: Albanian, Turkish, Polish, Chinese, Vietnamese, Hebrew, Arabic, Urdu, French or Yoruba.

I liked to think one of the reasons the Olympics was coming to East London was that every member of every national Olympics committee knew someone who lived there. Sitting at a café in Hackney not far from the Number 30 route a few days ago, just back from the religious strictness of Iran, I watched the different religions pass by: a young girl in a school playground version of the hijab – jeans, T-shirt and a black wimple – and a woman in another, a black chador which only showed her eyes; an Orthodox Jew from Stamford Hill, with his long black coat and black broad-brimmed hat and all the secular post-Christians with their bare heads and hipster jeans. It seemed an idyll of live and let live.

On my way from home yesterday morning I popped in to one of the local newsagents to buy batteries. He was talking sadly on the phone about the atrocities and as he served me I remembered going into the same shop, at about the same time, on the morning of 11 September 2001. The newsagent is Asian and I remembered that while I was in there a white woman in her fifties had put her head round the door and said to him: 'Don't worry, we know you didn't want this.'

It was an uneasy, backhanded sort of reassurance. The kind of 'don't worry' that, if I were the newsagent, would make me worried. Now we are all very worried. Worried about our neighbour and worried that our neighbour is worrying about us. Our neighbour at home, our neighbour on the Tube, our neighbour on the top deck of the Number 30. Live and let live may have won us the Olympics, but live and let live may not be enough. Londoners may have to learn to do the thing they hate more than anything else in the world: talking to strangers on the bus.

8 July 2005

CHANGES TO THE PROGRAMME

Ewen MacAskill

The G8 leaders' meeting at Gleneagles, Perthshire, was disrupted yesterday by the attacks in London. Tony Blair left the summit in the morning to return to London, forcing substantial changes to the programme. Although leaders pushed ahead with as much of the programme as possible, the British government was forced to cancel all its bilateral meetings and the summit group photograph was postponed.

'We do not want to give an impression of giving in to terrorism,' said a G8 spokesman. But the attention of politicians, diplomats and officials was focused on events in London.

The leaders gathered on Wednesday night for a banquet hosted by the Queen, but the opening session of the G8 was not until 10 a.m. yesterday. The agenda was to have been dominated by the negotiation of measures to tackle climate change and foreign affairs, mainly the Middle East dispute. News of explosions in London began to circulate at Gleneagles at about 9.30 a.m. Internal television channels covering events at Gleneagles were switched to news channels as diplomats, policemen, catering staff and journalists crowded round to watch for the latest news.

While the leaders of the eight or, in the case of Mr Blair, his substitutes, continued inside the hotel, discussion among the diplomats, journalists and non-governmental bodies – which would have otherwise been focused on the detail of the draft communiqué on climate change and African aid – was almost exclusively about London. A statement on climate change, scheduled for mid-afternoon, was delayed until today. A series of bilateral meetings Mr Blair had planned with other leaders, including Manmohan Singh, India's prime minister, were cancelled. Some diplomats, including the French ambassador, joined many of the 1,500 journalists who headed from Gleneagles to Edinburgh and Glasgow for flights back to London. Several briefings and press conferences that also had been planned by the various leaders were postponed.

Sir Michael Jay, permanent under-secretary at the Foreign Office, the most senior British diplomat, took over from Mr Blair as chair of what would have been one of the most contentious parts of the summit: a round-table meeting at lunchtime to discuss climate change, on which differences remained. Mr Blair's absence may have meant that some of the more contentious issues were left unresolved.

Jack Straw, the foreign secretary, who had not been scheduled to attend the summit, flew to Gleneagles to chair the afternoon session on climate change and foreign affairs. In spite of the agenda, diplomats and non-governmental organisations lost much of their usual enthusiasm for briefing and counter-briefing. Mr Bush held a videoconference with security officials in Washington.

In spite of the disruption, the leaders resolved to try to put on a show of business as usual. Leaders from African countries flew into Prestwick airport in Ayrshire in the morning for an onward journey to Gleneagles, in contrast with the transport chaos in London. They are due to join discussions on Africa today.

Downing Street insisted that, in spite of the obvious impact of Mr Blair's absence, the agenda had continued much as normal and that today's planned programme, the final day of the summit, would be implemented in full.

8 July 2005

GOING TO THE CAUSE

Robin Cook

I have rarely seen the Commons so full and so silent as when it met yesterday to hear of the London bombings. A forum that often is raucous and rowdy was solemn and grave. A chamber that normally is a bear pit of partisan emotions was united in shock and sorrow. Even Ian Paisley made a humane plea to the press not to repeat the offence that occurred in Northern Ireland when journalists demanded comment from relatives before they were informed that their loved ones were dead.

The immediate response to such human tragedy must be empathy with the pain of those injured and the grief of those bereaved. We recoil more deeply from loss of life in such an atrocity because we know the unexpected disappearance of partners, children and parents must be even harder to bear than a natural death. It is sudden, and therefore there is no farewell or preparation for the blow. Across London today there are relatives whose pain may be more acute because they never had the chance to offer or hear last words of affection.

It is arbitrary and therefore an event that changes whole lives, which turn on the accident of momentary decisions. How many people this morning ask themselves how different it might have been if their partner had taken the next bus or caught an earlier tube? But perhaps the loss is hardest to bear because it is so difficult to answer the question why it should have happened. This weekend we will salute the heroism of the generation that defended Britain in the last war. In advance of the commemoration there have been many stories told of the courage of those who risked their lives and sometimes lost their lives to defeat fascism. They provide moving, humbling examples of what the human spirit is capable of, but at least the relatives of the men and women who died then knew what they were fighting for. What purpose is there to yesterday's senseless murders? Who could possibly imagine that they have a cause that might profit from such pointless carnage?

At the time of writing, no group has surfaced even to explain why they launched the assault. Some time over the next few days we may be offered a website entry or a video message attempting to justify the impossible, but there is no language that can supply a rational basis for such arbitrary slaughter. The explanation, when it is offered, is likely to rely not on reason but on the declaration of an obsessive fundamentalist identity that leaves no room for pity for victims who do not share that identity.

Yesterday the prime minister described the bombings as an attack on our values as a society. In the next few days we should remember that among those values are tolerance and mutual respect for those from different cultural and ethnic backgrounds. Only the day before, London was celebrating its coup in winning the Olympic Games, partly through demonstrating to the world the success of our multicultural credentials. Nothing would please better those who planted yesterday's bombs than for the atrocity to breed suspicion and hostility to minorities in our own community. Defeating the terrorists also means defeating their poisonous belief that peoples of different faiths and ethnic origins cannot coexist.

In the absence of anyone else owning up to yesterday's crimes, we will be subjected to a spate of articles analysing the threat of militant Islam. Ironically they will fall in the same week that we recall the tenth anniversary of the massacre at Srebrenica, when the powerful nations of Europe failed to protect 8,000 Muslims from being annihilated in the worst terrorist act in Europe of the past generation.

Osama Bin Laden is no more a true representative of Islam than General Mladic, who commanded the Serbian forces, could be held up as an example of Christianity. After all, it is written in the Koran that we were made into different peoples not that we might despise each other, but that we might understand each other. Bin Laden was, though, a product of a monumental miscalculation by western security agencies. Throughout the 1980s he was armed by the CIA and funded by the

Saudis to wage jihad against the Russian occupation of Afghanistan. Al-Qaeda (literally 'the database') was originally the computer file of the thousands of mujahidin who were recruited and trained with help from the CIA to defeat the Russians. Inexplicably, and with disastrous consequences, it never appears to have occurred to Washington that once Russia was out of the way, Bin Laden's organisation would turn its attention to the West.

The danger now is that the West's current response to the terrorist threat compounds that original error. So long as the struggle against terrorism is conceived as a war that can be won by military means, it is doomed to fail. The more the West emphasises confrontation, the more it silences moderate voices in the Muslim world who want to speak up for cooperation. Success will only come from isolating the terrorists and denying them support, funds and recruits, which means focusing more on our common ground with the Muslim world than on what divides us.

The G8 summit is not the best-designed forum in which to launch such a dialogue with Muslim countries, as none of them is included in the core membership. Nor do any of them make up the outer circle of select emerging economies – such as China, Brazil and India – which are also invited to Gleneagles. We are not going to address the sense of marginalisation among Muslim countries if we do not make more of an effort to be inclusive of them in the architecture of global governance. But the G8 does have the opportunity in its communiqué today to give a forceful response to the latest terrorist attack. That should include a statement of their joint resolve to hunt down those who bear responsibility for yesterday's crimes. But it must seize the opportunity to address the wider issues at the root of terrorism.

In particular, it would be perverse if the focus of the G8 on making poverty history was now obscured by yesterday's bombings. The breeding grounds of terrorism are to be found in the poverty of back-streets, where fundamentalism offers a false, easy sense of pride and identity to young men who feel denied of any hope or any economic opportunity for themselves. A war on world poverty may well do more for the security of the West than a war on terror. And in the privacy of their extensive suites, yesterday's atrocities should prompt heart-searching among some of those present. President Bush is given to justifying the invasion of Iraq on the grounds that by fighting terrorism abroad, it protects the West from having to fight terrorists at home. Whatever else can be said in defence of the war in Iraq today, it cannot be claimed that it has protected us from terrorism on our soil.

DEATH TOLL PASSES 50 – AND A HUNT FOR THE BOMBERS

Duncan Campbell

A massive police hunt began yesterday for what now appears to be a small al-Qaeda cell responsible for four bombs and the taking of more than 50 lives, as the friends and families of those still missing scoured hospitals in the hope of finding their loved ones.

Early speculation that suicide bombers were involved appeared to be receding, with evidence that the tube bombs had been placed on the floor by the door of the carriages. Anti-terrorist sources said that the main anxiety was that the bombers were still at large and could strike again. Beneath London's streets, hundreds of officers and emergency workers continued digging out the remaining bodies from the tube carriages, and searching for clues that could lead to the prosecution of those responsible. Conditions were difficult and dangerous.

Last night, 49 people were confirmed dead with up to 20 more bodies still in the underground train at Russell Square where the blast seriously damaged the tunnel. Sir Ian Blair, the Metropolitan Police commissioner, said rescuers were involved in a 'job of extraordinary horror'. He said the nature of the incident, the worst terrorist attack on mainland Britain, was becoming clearer. Four bombs consisting of high explosives, weighing less than 4.5kg (10lb) each, were probably carried in backpacks and placed on the floor of the three underground carriages and on the seat or floor of the Number 30 bus that was blown apart in Tavistock Square.

'There is nothing to suggest that there was a suicide bomber,' said Sir Ian, 'but nothing can be ruled out.' The bombers, he admitted, could be at large in Britain, already out of the country, or dead. Nothing could have been done to prevent the attack, he said. 'No intelligence service is perfect. This is an imperfect world and it is an imperfect science.'

The leads now being pursued will come from closed-circuit television tapes, cellphone calls made in the area of the bombs, and from what the police hope will be tip-offs from people who have noticed that a lodger is missing or that a lock-up garage is deserted. Attention has focused on the Number 30 bus and the possibility the bomb there was in transit to another tube train and went off prematurely, killing 13 people. No arrests had taken place by last night.

'Our total effort today is focused on identifying the perpetrators and bringing them to justice,' said the home secretary, Charles Clarke. 'That is, of course, the Number One preoccupation that the police and the security services have at this moment.'

London was almost back to normal yesterday. Most of the public transport system was functioning and Sir Ian urged everyone to be behind their desks at the start of next week. 'This is business as usual on Monday,' he said. 'We go on.'

For the families and friends of those now confirmed dead or unaccounted for, this will probably not be the case. In scenes reminiscent of 11 September, friends and families carried photographs of the missing as they went from bombsite to hospital to television studio, or tied the pictures to railings. The images acted as proof of the extraordinary diversity of the city, and the names provided evidence that those affected came from all ethnic and religious groups. One family hired a private detective, others faxed photos to hospitals. More than 104,000 calls have been made to the emergency number.

'These are seven days that no one will ever forget,' said Ken Livingstone, London's mayor, as he and the commissioner sat shoulder to shoulder and delivered an appeal for information. Mr Livingstone – who, like New York's mayor Rudy Giuliani in the wake of 11 September, managed to articulate his city's dismay and resolve – said that there had been no panic. He proclaimed his belief that London, in all its diversity and with a population that speaks more than 300 languages, 'typifies . . . the beauty of the human race'.

The Queen and the Prince of Wales visited the wounded in St Mary's hospital, Paddington. 'It's been one of the things that many of us have dreaded for a long time,' said Prince Charles. 'What I can never get over is the resilience of the British people who have set us all a fantastic example of how to recover.'

Muslim organisations condemned the attacks amid fears of reprisals on mosques by far-right groups. Sir Iqbal Sacranie, the secretary general of the Muslim Council of Britain, said: 'Our faith of Islam calls upon us to be upholders of justice. The day after London was bloodied by terrorists finds us determined to help secure this justice for the innocent victims of yesterday's carnage.'

13 July 2005

THEY WERE BRITISH

Duncan Campbell and Sandra Laville

Four home-grown suicide bombers, three of them from West Yorkshire and none of them known to the police, carried out last Thursday's bomb attacks on London, police believe. The hunt is now on for the person who police suspect may have masterminded the bombings and who may have already left the country.

'Normality now will not be the same as normality was before,' a senior security source said last night, reflecting on what looks certain to have been Britain's first experience of suicide bombers. The discovery of a bomb factory in Leeds indicates to the police that there were plans for future attacks. Four men, between 18 and 30, three of them with West Yorkshire addresses and all of them British, met up at Luton Station before boarding a Thameslink train to King's Cross last Thursday morning. It appears that the four, described by security sources as 'cleanskins' – with no convictions or known terrorist involvement – reached their rendezvous via two or three hired cars, one of which had been located yesterday at Luton Station. Explosives were found in the car, police revealed last night. Police were also examining a second car found at the station. It was taken to a storage facility at Leighton Buzzard. Closed-circuit television film from around 8.20 a.m. that day shows the four young men, all with identical large rucksacks similar to those carried by infantry soldiers on their backs. The four appeared relaxed.

'You would have thought they were going on a hiking holiday,' said the senior security source, who has seen the footage. It is likely to be released today.

Police were alerted to the existence of one of the four when his distressed family in Leeds called the casualty bureau hotline shortly after 10 p.m. on Thursday. Their son had been travelling to London 'with his mates' and had not returned. A family liaison officer was dispatched to be with the family, as was the case for all those believed to have lost relatives in the explosions. In the meantime, police had found personal documents relating to three young men aged 18, 22 and 30, all from West Yorkshire. A driving licence and credit cards belonging to the 22-year-old whose parents were concerned about him were found on the bus that blew up in Tavistock Square. The documents of the 30-year-old, whose body was found at Edgware Road Station, were discovered both at the scene of that explosion and at the Aldgate bomb scene, where another of the four dead suspects' remains were found. Police believe that the fourth person's remains and documents may still be trapped in the rubble below Russell Square and are hoping they may find those today.

On Monday night came the breakthrough police were waiting for – when the CCTV at King's Cross showed the four young men setting off in different directions. Police yesterday raided three houses in the Beeston and Holbeck areas of Leeds and two in nearby Dewsbury just after 6 a.m. in a coordinated operation involving scores of officers from West Yorkshire and the anti-terrorist branch. They later raided another house in the Burley district after evacuating 500 residents from homes nearby and blasting down the door in a controlled explosion. People who were evacuated in the Burley area were given temporary accommodation as police continued to search an address at Alexandra Grove where a suspicious substance had been found, according to officers. In Dewsbury, officers carried out a meticulous search at a modern bungalow in a middle-class area and forensic teams loaded at least one car on to a covered transporter. At Colwyn Road in Beeston, as police searched a house belonging to the Tanweer family, a car hire firm arrived to collect an overdue hire car. Staff were immediately interviewed by police.

Family and friends of two young British-born Muslims – whose homes were among the six raided yesterday – said they had been missing for several days. Hasib Hussain's parents reported him missing on 7 July. His documents were found on the Number 30 bus which exploded at 9.47 a.m. Shehzad Tanweer, 22, of Colwyn Road, has also been missing since last week. His documents, police said, were found in the wreckage of the Aldgate train. While there was satisfaction within the police and intelligence services that they appeared to have identified a bombing team so swiftly, there were also fears on two fronts: that the finding of more explosives in Leeds indicates that this was not a one-off, and that there could be attacks by far-right groups against ethnic minority communities as it became clear that these were not foreign militants entering the country but home-grown bombers.

The assistant commissioner Andy Hayman of the Met's special operations branch and the deputy assistant commissioner Peter Clarke, head of the anti-terrorist branch, announced news of the breakthrough yesterday afternoon. Last night searches were continuing and police were questioning a relative of one of the four men who had been driven to London. Now the search will concentrate on the 'plotters and planners' who would normally brief and equip a team of suicide volunteers. The normal procedure for such operations, if they involved al-Qaeda or one of its related groups, would be for the chief planner to have left the country before the operations took place. There is a possibility that those who planned it are still in Britain. Police are now checking flight records for suspicious passengers.

Mr Clarke said: 'I would like at this stage to thank the public for all the support and assistance they have already provided. It is invaluable.' Mr Hayman described those who had perpetrated the attack as 'extremist criminals' and added: 'It's at times like these that communities bind together . . . No one should smear or stigmatise any community with these acts.'

There are as yet no indications that any of the four left behind any message about their intentions. The police are going through 2,500 tapes and evaluating more than 2,000 calls from the public. They have more than 100 witness statements. They stressed last night that they were at the start rather than at the end of their investigation.

Hope for the future
A young boy cycles past a mural in Belfast (PAUL MCERLANE)

The Ashes come home
A bus carrying the victorious English cricket team enters Trafalgar Square
(TOM JENKINS)

Goodbye Mo
Peter Mandelson and the late Mo Mowlam, photographed in 1999
(KEVIN BOYES/KEVIN BOYES PHOTOGRAPHY)

Katrina strikes
A New Orleans resident walks through floodwaters covered with a fine layer of oil (BILL HABER/AP)

SECOND TIME AROUND

Owen Bowcott, Vikram Dodd and Alex Brown

Sofiane Mohellebi, a 35-year-old from Paris, stood on the pavement at Tottenham Court Road clutching three sandals abandoned in the panic underground. He had been hoping to find the women who lost them.

'People were trying to pull others down [in the carriage] to get out of the way,' he said yesterday as he stood at the police tape line and looked back towards Warren Street tube station. 'There was no way to get out, but everyone was trying to. I just sat and prayed and waited for it to happen. You don't know what it's like until you are inside. I had been sitting down reading a book, but then there was a smell coming from behind me. The smell was coming from another carriage. There was no smoke. It smelt like rubber or wire [burning] then it got worse. Someone pulled the communication cord. We arrived in the station and they asked everyone to evacuate the train. People were panicking. There was screaming and panic but no one appeared to be injured. They said there had been an explosion and we should evacuate because it wasn't safe.'

Mr Mohellebi, a Muslim from Walthamstow, north-east London, said he had held up an abandoned shopping bag at one point but promptly put it down when other passengers yelled at him that it might be a bomb. 'I don't even know where my mobile is. I've lost it. I saw one guy later telling the driver that he saw a man run away.'

Another passenger, Tammie Landau, boarded the Victoria Line northbound just before lunchtime, heading for Euston. At Warren Street Station her short journey across the city degenerated into chaos and panic. 'I was on the train and people came running through the carriage,' she said. 'Everyone was running really quickly. Someone said duck down. They said something went off with a bang but I didn't hear it.' The shock was evident in her face. 'We had to smash through the train to get to the other end. By the time I was out I was quite scared.' Ivan McCracken, a passenger on one train, told Sky News: 'Some were falling, there was mass panic. It was difficult to get the story from any of them, but when I got to ground level there was an Italian young man comforting an Italian girl who told me he had seen what had happened. He said that a man was carrying a rucksack and the rucksack suddenly exploded. It was a minor explosion, but enough to blow open the rucksack. The man then made an exclamation as if something had gone wrong. At that point everyone rushed from the carriage.'

Other passengers witnessed a chase. Hugo Palit told the BBC: 'I was going into the station, and . . . then I heard noises, like shouting and screaming, and suddenly I saw a guy coming out and people chasing him. He came out from the station, he was running and he was a little bit confused, looking right and left. I couldn't really catch him because I was carrying two heavy bags, and then he passed by me. There was another guy who was chasing him. We saw a policeman, so we waved, like, he was going that way. I don't know if they did catch him or not.'

Many of those who attended a memorial service for victims of the attacks on 7 July at the British Medical Association's headquarters nearby emerged into the chaos generated by yesterday's attacks. One man, 100 metres from the Warren Street tube, said he had smelt smoke in the air shortly afterwards. Max Giacomelli, 21, who works at the University College Hospital, went by the tube station shortly after the alerts. 'I saw a girl coming out,' he said. 'She was shocked. She said she'd seen smoke. She said there was a smell of burning rubber. She saw fire and ran. A man said there was panic: people stepping over each other to escape. I saw a man carrying a shirt and shoes and books that were left behind.'

Jimmy Connor, 32, another passenger, left his bag on the train at Warren Street tube as passengers struggled to leave the carriage. 'People were leaving their belongings. Everyone was just waiting for the bomb to go off. People were trying to make their way to the front of the train.' Mr Connor, from Sheffield, said they had been able to smell burning, like wiring or a fuse box on fire. 'I thought I was going to die, everyone else thought the same,' he added.

Out on the streets of the West End, police began moving crowds further and further back along Tottenham Court Road, setting up wider and wider exclusion zones behind chequered tape. Office workers were evacuated.

'I was on my way back to work,' said David Wilmslow, who was locked out of his recruitment consultancy two blocks from Warren Street. 'Everything was shut down. My keys, wallet, everything is back in there.' In Warren Street, the road that runs beside the station, bomb disposal experts dressed in black overalls and protective masks could be seen preparing to walk down into the Tube. Officers checked basements and cars for suspect devices. Firefighters set up decontamination showers on the street in case there was evidence of chemical, biological or nuclear contamination. These were later removed.

Roger Holloway, 49, the planning manager for a construction company working on the new University College hospital – which treated injured from the 7 July bombs – said: 'I don't know whether I'll be able to get back to my office today. I doubt it, after this. I just hope it's not as serious as last time. The whole thing makes you cautious as you move around.'

In one street three officers detained a 29-year-old Moroccan cleaner, Ahmed Laarbi, from Stamford Hill, who supposedly matched the description of a man outlined in an internal police memo. He was eventually released. He was wearing a blue shirt with an Italian crest – similar to that described in the police memo. 'I am not a terrorist. I am a simple citizen. I'm a Muslim, but I don't like terrorists,' he said. 'Why am I the only citizen questioned? Because I'm black, I'm Muslim.'

A tube passenger, Julie Dube, said yesterday's explosions had hit home harder than the bombings a fortnight ago, despite the low casualty list. 'I'm sad to say that [London] doesn't feel like the safest of places,' Ms Dube said. 'But at the same time, that's not the message I want to send terrorists. It's a strange way to feel.'

22 July 2005

THE BAG EXPLODED

Audrey Gillan

The emergency cord was pulled, and as the tube train drew into Oval Station a man dashed out of the doors and ran. Passengers in the smoke-filled carriage began to give chase, but the man outran them and escaped through the station entrance. Witnesses described how a flower seller outside Oval Station had tried to catch him but failed.

Paul Martin, 32, said: 'People started running out of the station. I saw a guy being chased. It was completely crazy. People were trying to drop him, to rugby tackle him. There was a general mêlée.'

Hugues Caillat, from France, had been buying a ticket in the station concourse when the man ran out. He said: 'Suddenly, I saw a guy coming from the stairs. He was running and at the same time people were running after him. I wanted to catch him but I was carrying heavy bags. The guy said something like "What's wrong with these people?" He was a skinny Asian guy, with a little beard. He was about 19. The guy who sells the flowers was running after him as well. By chance the police were passing by. Both of us waved at them and shouted he's gone that way. Obviously something was wrong, otherwise what's the point of running?'

A witness in the carriage next to the one which contained the bag told Sky News: 'All of a sudden there was a popping, it sounded like champagne popping. I didn't think anything of it at the time but then I heard a lot of shouting from the next-door carriage. People started saying, "Smoke! Smoke!" One of the train guys came through and said "Get off the train, we're evacuating, everyone out!" As we were walking past the carriage we could see the bag sitting on the chair. It was a big black rucksack, like the backpack-type ones that you get. When they got upstairs, people were really distressed. One lady was crying.'

Ingrid Guyon, from France, was also in the next carriage. When it was evacuated she spoke to a woman who had been standing next to the man on the train when his bag exploded and smoke began to fill the carriage. The woman said the man had a backpack. Ms Guyon said: 'The bag exploded. We were evacuated in Oval. We were asked not to panic and just to leave. The guy ran away, people were trying to run after him. There was a terrible smell and a lot of people were shocked. They came running through into our carriage. I nearly fainted because of the smell. I was so scared. It was a terrible smell and there was lots of smoke. It was more like a smoke bomb.'

After emptying the station, police in protective suits entered to check for any traces of chemicals. Sniffer dogs were brought to the scene. A half-mile cordon was set up around the station and surrounding streets, and residents were told to stay in their homes and close their windows. A woman passenger told BBC News: 'It was extremely worrying. No one knew what it was. There was a policeman on his way to work and he took charge. He got us all off. Then the police and the ambulances arrived.'

Last night, police were still interviewing 20 witnesses to the Oval incident.

UNDER ATTACK

Leading article

The shadow of the terrorist bomber fell across a sunlit London for the second time in as many weeks yesterday. This time the city was braced for it, after warnings from ministers, police and security chiefs that such a thing was likely. Rationally, most people understand that civilised life in this country faces a heartless and implacable foe who is prepared to strike as often and as cruelly as possible. Even so, the audacious rapidity with which this latest assault followed the first was shocking and nerve-jangling.

Yesterday's attacks carried several eerie echoes of the 7 July bombings. There were again four attempted explosions – three on tube trains and one on a bus. All the attempts also took place almost simultaneously. (Witnesses reported two explosions and there could have been a third.) Spookily, just like two weeks ago, the bus attack happened on the upper deck. Eyewitnesses said the perpetrators were carrying rucksacks. And the pattern of the attacks was similar too: targets in the north, south, east and west of central London: Warren Street, Oval, Shepherd's Bush tube stations, along with a bus in Shoreditch. Mercifully, as on 7 July, no use was made of chemical or biological elements either.

Thankfully, there were positive differences with two weeks ago too. The explosions had none of the power of those on 7 July. Only one person was hurt, compared with 56 fatalities and 700 injured. The attacks took place at lunchtime, when far fewer people are travelling, not in the morning rush hour when both tube trains and buses are at their most crowded. None of the perpetrators was a suicide bomber – not a successful one at any rate – and some were seen running from the scene. Early evidence suggests that only detonators exploded, not bombs. As a result, both the bombs and the bombers remain extant, a source of vital evidence and potential interrogation (and trial) respectively.

Just as two weeks ago, there are a host of unanswered questions. Were there any links between yesterday's team and the four suicide bombers of two weeks ago? Were they a quite separate team perpetrating a copycat attack, perhaps mimicking what happened on 7 July by deliberately using less explosive power with the purpose of generating chaos and fear? Sir Ian Blair, the Metropolitan commissioner, said last night that he believed the intention was to kill. Yet some explosives experts yesterday suggested the chance of four bombs all becoming accidentally disconnected from their detonators was inconceivable. Was there an al-Qaeda link? Sir Ian said it was too early to answer. There were still doubts on the precise state of the four suspect bombs. The commissioner would not say either whether one of them was a nail bomb.

One other positive difference from two weeks ago is that the police will have better forensic evidence which they can use. Some of the rucksacks were not destroyed and can therefore be traced. So can the unexploded elements found within them. There is likely to be useful DNA that can be picked up. As one former government intelligence officer noted: 'It looks as though the terrorists have put their heads above the parapets – and that plays into Scotland Yard's hands.' Better still, some of the perpetrators were tackled by passengers – acts of bravery that echo 9/11 – and CCTV may once again play a key role in identifying the suspects.

Once again the emergency services responded with admirable speed. The police rightly reminded people who want to blame the Muslim community that the perpetrators were criminals, not a community. But perhaps the best news yesterday was the speed and determination with which London began to get back to normal business, denying the terrorists one of their most fundamental goals: another paralysing disruption of the city.

23 July 2005

FACES OF THE SUSPECTS – AND A MAN SHOT DEAD

Ian Cobain, Rosie Cowan and Richard Norton-Taylor

Police released pictures of four would-be bombers yesterday as the race to capture the gang reached a fevered pitch. The hunt for the men and the larger terror investigation were described by the head of Scotland Yard as 'the greatest operational challenge' that his force had faced in its history. Senior counter-terrorism officials stressed the need to track down the gang as quickly as possible. One said: 'There are a huge number of leads. Events are moving very fast.'

The urgency of the operation – and the determination of police to prevent any further suicide attacks – were demonstrated dramatically at an underground station in Stockwell, South London, yesterday, when a man was chased by officers and shot around five times in the head at point-blank range as he lay on the floor of a train. He was not one of the men who attempted to detonate four bombs around London on Thursday, but came under suspicion after emerging from a property of 'major interest' under surveillance. Police said he ran into the station when challenged and was shot after dashing on to a tube train. Scotland Yard would not say whether he had explosives or weapons with him. The initial suspicion is that he did not.

Within hours, armed police surrounded three properties: first in west Kilburn, to the west, then in Stockwell and Brixton to the south. Each was searched, first by bomb disposal robots and then by explosive experts and forensic officers. No explosives were found, but one man was arrested in Stockwell on suspicion of terrorist offences after another armed raid. No shots were fired. Later, a second man was taken away for questioning. Another address was understood to be under surveillance. In Birmingham, Snow Hill Station was sealed off for two hours while police examined two suitcases. A man was arrested but released without charge.

The pictures of the four suspects, taken by closed-circuit television cameras, show that one bomber, a burly man in gloves and a white cap, had no intention of dying. He left his device on a bus in Shoreditch, East London, and alighted shortly before it exploded. Witnesses have described how the other three were with their devices when the detonators went off, causing small blasts, but failing to explode the bombs. One man was pictured running through Oval underground station in South London shortly afterwards, wearing a distinctive dark top with the words New York across the front. Other CCTV images aboard a train show how a puff of smoke blew from this man's rucksack after he put his hand in his pocket. As some passengers fled in terror, one traveller could be seen attempting to tackle him. Other pictures show the two men who tried, and failed, to kill themselves and other passengers at Shepherd's Bush, West London, and Warren Street, north of the city centre. None of the men is known to the police.

Early examination of the four devices show that they are similar to the bombs used by the four suicide attackers from Leeds and Huddersfield who murdered 52 people in almost identical attacks on 7 July. The possibility that Thursday's attacks were mounted by 'copycat' bombers has not been ruled out, however. Sir Ian Blair, commissioner of the Metropolitan Police, said that officers hunting the gang 'are facing previously unknown threats and great danger'. He appealed for calm around the capital, and said: 'We need the understanding of all communities and the cooperation of all communities.'

Last night in a speech in Atlanta which drew a standing ovation, George Bush said: 'The people of Great Britain must understand how strongly America stands with them during these trying times. I'm confident, like our country, the citizens of that country will not be intimidated by thugs and assassins.'

At Stockwell, bewildered eyewitnesses spilled out of the station and told how they saw the moment, shortly after 10 a.m., when the suspect was repeatedly shot. All described him as wearing a bulky winter coat, despite the warm weather; at least one said he thought he spotted a belt with wires running from it. After leaping the ticket barriers, racing down an escalator and dashing on to a train, he appears to have either fallen or been bundled to the ground by pursuing police, one of whom leaned over and shot him several times in the head.

Anthony Larkin was on the train: 'I saw these police officers shouting "Get down! Get down!" and I saw this guy who appeared to have a bomb belt and wires coming out. People were panicking and I heard two shots being fired.' Mark Whitby, 47, sitting a few yards from the shooting, said: 'I saw an Asian guy. He ran on to the train. He was pursued by three plainclothes officers. As he got on to the train I looked at his face, he looked absolutely petrified. He half tripped and was half pushed to the floor, and the policeman nearest to me had a black automatic pistol in his left hand. He held it down to the guy and unloaded five shots into him. He [the suspect] had quite a sort of thickish coat – it was a coat you would wear in winter, like a padded jacket. I was totally distraught. It was no less than five yards away from where I was sitting.'

At one point, the train's driver was chased by police and had a gun pointed at his head, after he leapt from his cab and ran down a tunnel on hearing the commotion.

The shot suspect was pronounced dead at the scene. The killing has been referred to the Independent Police Complaints Commission for investigation. It said: 'The IPCC will ensure that nothing is done to hinder the urgent police priority of tracking down and bringing to justice those responsible for the recent London bombings and their vital work to prevent further outrages.' Guidance by the Association of Chief Police Officers, which was revised five months ago, states: 'A police officer should not decide to open fire unless that officer is satisfied that nothing short of opening fire could protect the officer or another person from imminent danger to life or serious injury.' The officer, from Scotland Yard's SO19 firearms unit, is thought to have shot the suspect in the head several times to make sure he could not activate any bomb, and also because a shot in his torso might detonate any device.

The Muslim Council of Britain was concerned about a possible shoot-to-kill policy. A spokesman said: 'There may well be reasons why the police felt it necessary to unload five shots into the man and shoot him dead, but they need to make those reasons clear.'

Yesterday a group called the Abu Hafs al Masri Brigade claimed responsibility on a website for this week's attempted attacks. The same group claimed responsibility for the 7 July attacks, but its statement's authenticity could not be verified. Meanwhile, more eyewitnesses told how they saw the terrorists escape after minor blasts blew holes in their rucksacks. At Shepherd's Bush, the bomber appeared to be lying on his back on top of his rucksack, his arms spread out and his eyes closed. 'There was a puff of smoke coming from the bag,' said Abisha Moyo, 28, from Zimbabwe. 'As some people began screaming and others pulled at the emergency cable, the bomber stood up, jumped from the train on to the track, and walked away.'

A man aged 29 arrested in raids in Leeds on 12 July after the 7 July bombings and taken to London for questioning was released yesterday.

THE NIGHTMARE IS REAL

Mark Lawson

At the time Adam Curtis's compelling but tendentious documentary series *The Power of Nightmares* was screened on BBC2 last year, there was some muttering from politicians and commentators about how BBC pledges of political balance could be squared with a series arguing that Tony Blair and George W. Bush had exaggerated the threat of terrorism for electoral gain. The corporation's response was that another series would soon argue the opposite case. Now it has. Peter Taylor's *The New Al-Qaeda*, starting tonight on BBC2, was clearly commissioned as a squabbling journalistic sibling to Curtis's polemical documentaries.

And Taylor – who has spent 30 years making films about first Irish and then Middle Eastern terrorism – was the right guy to reply. The final part of *The Power of Nightmares* sampled soundbites from his previous series on Islamicist terrorism – including a senior British police officer saying that an attack on Britain was a matter of 'when not if' – as an example of scaremongering. In a quiet, coded BBC-colleague sort of way, Curtis was dissing Taylor's work. *The New Al-Qaeda*, in an equally cryptographical way, gives it back to him.

Even so, while *The New Al-Qaeda* was being made, Taylor was only in a position to say that he thought *The Power of Nightmares* was exaggerating the degree of exaggeration. But the London attacks of 7 and 21 July have given the counterblast additional power. The reporter had recorded his final commentary on the evening of 6 July, but has now added a speech to the opening episode in which he rebukes 'those' (code for Curtis) who suggested that the terrorist threat was 'a nightmare dreamed up by politicians'. Yet, beneath this BBC film-maker equivalent of what counter-terrorism experts call 'chatter', the two series are closer than they initially feel. While Curtis's films would have been difficult to screen in New York, Madrid or Bali without arousing outrage, he was not arguing that there is no terrorist threat but that Bush and Blair had encouraged the illusion of a vast, tentacular global al-Qaeda operation, run by Osama Bin Laden from his cave.

Taylor's new series comes to broadly the same conclusion about the nature of the terrorist operation but attributes the lack of an octopus structure not to the fact that leaders have been misleading but to the success of the military action in Afghanistan in fragmenting al-Qaeda's planning and command. What he presents in the opening episode is a much looser system, like some psychopathic version of retail franchising, in which local groups (possibly, for example, in Leeds) adopt the values and techniques of the 9/11 mastermind but never receive coded instructions from a hole in the ground on the Pakistan border. In fact, the twist in the terrorism business that Taylor's first programme chillingly illustrates is that the instruction and arming of Islamicist extremists occurs not through scrambled e-mail messages but in full view on the worldwide web. In a sequence startling even in the work of a reporter who interviewed many Irish terrorists in series including *Provos and Loyalists*, Taylor talks to a London webmaster whose site openly shows footage of beheadings of hostages and the killing by suicide bombers of British soldiers in Iraq. One of many bleak details in the series is the fact that one truck-bombing seems to have been filmed from three different angles for maximum effect: suggesting that some of the al-Qaeda teams in Iraq include a film crew in their planning, with the Internet release of the murders a calculated stage of the outrage.

Journalists in Taylor's line of business are sometimes accused of following too easily the line of the security services (*The Power of Nightmares* seemed to be suggesting this), but his first film includes an interview which MI5 would surely prefer not to appear: the story of a young British man who claims to have been targeted to infiltrate a terrorist cell here. Another surprise is an encounter with an American woman who, apparently operating alone, went online to trap potential American terrorists. And the third programme concentrates on Pakistan: including a very revealing conversation with President

Musharraf about what a difficult political position he would be in if he happened hypothetically to know where Bin Laden is.

The fear of all film-makers is being overtaken by events. But it's a measure of Taylor's achievement that a series on which he has been working for more than a year still stands so powerfully, with minor adjustments, after events which totally rewrote the story of terrorism in Britain.

FAREWELL TO TED

Michael White

It almost rained on Salisbury Cathedral during Sir Edward Heath's funeral yesterday. Somehow that seemed appropriate: the famous spire, solitary and magnificent, beneath a glowering, grey sky. Very Ted. At least 1,500 of his friends and admirers, from all strands of his long life, had turned up to say goodbye. So had some of his enemies, just to make sure it was true.

In the gothic splendour of what had virtually become his own parish church they heard familiar Anglican funeral rites blended with Vaughan Williams and Elgar – a nod in the direction of Sir Edward's musically channelled English romanticism. There was Bach, John Donne (twice) and the mariners' hymn 'Eternal Father' – plus an elegant but slightly perplexing sermon from the Bishop of Salisbury, the Rt Rev David Stancliffe, who invoked Elgar (again) and the sixth-century monk St Benedict, music and politics, sailing, and jolly lunches at Arundells, Heath's handsome home 200 yards away across Salisbury Close. The aim of it all was to capture, and honour, this complex but kindly curmudgeon; a man whose public career crashed when he lost the premiership 31 years ago and the Party leadership a year later, but who willed himself to keep going until his death at 89 on 17 July.

'A notable public life, lived with an integrity of purpose and an unswerving resolve,' was how the bishop put it as he praised the former premier, whose 'vitality of character' would be remembered. But he also acknowledged, as few friends could fail to, that Ted (as the bishop called him) was shy and 'immensely hospitable, but not given to chitchat'. It was a decent Great and Good turnout for a summer holiday occasion. 'You must be going to the funeral,' said the man in the ticket office at Waterloo. And clearly a lot of survivors of the chitchat-free years were heading west.

Since he had insisted on a funeral open to the public, a lot of Salisbury folk queued to be there too. Up to 500 listened outside. Sir Ted was well known in a lot of local pubs, the man from the *Salisbury Journal* confirmed. Michael Howard and Charles Kennedy were among the mourners, though Tony Blair (who saw them both before lunch) was otherwise engaged. The prime minister has a baleful record of non-attendance on such occasions, further evidence of his tin ear for history and institutions. It is his loss, not ours. Jack Straw was reported present, but it was left to Geoff Hoon (not quite the right note) to head the public mourners as they followed the coffin, draped in lilies on the Union flag, out through the great west door. Sir Edward's war medals and the Garter preceded him on black cushions. Next came a frail Lady Thatcher and Mr Howard, Sir Edward's first and fifth successors as Tory leader, followed by the Majors and a clutch of friendlier figures from the Heath-to-Major era: Lords Carrington, Hurd, Howe and Baker. Plus a respectable smattering of Tory MPs, past and present, including Salisbury's Robert Key (who found him Arundells) and Derek Conway, the Eurosceptic who succeeded Sir Ted in Old Bexley and Sidcup.

The Euro-headbangers at the *Daily Telegraph* had thought to mark the occasion by printing minutes of an Anglo-French summit in 1971 at which Sir Edward, as prime minister, promised to abandon the US and take sterling into a single currency if Paris would say *Oui*. The minutes were obtained under freedom of information legislation by – who else? – the Thatcher Foundation. Talk about kicking the coffin!

But this was not a score-settling memorial service, though the Anglo-Catholic Dr Stancliffe must have edged Lady T's blood pressure up a notch by presenting St Benedict's monastic rules as a kind of early EU constitution, and the saint's pan-European vision as the one to which Sir Edward aspired. 'Ted built bridges between countries and nations, between artists and ordinary people, between east and west, between young and old. No one can doubt his lifelong commitment to Europe, nor for that matter to the unity of the world. In this he exerted his fullest force,' explained the bishop, who also risked comparing Sir Edward's skills as musician, sailor and as politician. 'However well the individual voices of your orchestra or choir play, if they don't play in time, there can be no harmony,' Dr Stancliffe ventured. At another point in his sermon he declared: 'No sailor worth his salt thinks that you can just set a course, lash the tiller, and go below.'

Yet that is the charge critics level at him, still shaking with ancient rage. Had the bishop's affection for Sir Edward (who was at Oxford with his parents) not been so evident, it might have sounded malicious about a man whose sense of harmony also produced the three-day week. Yet one thing was indisputable. For a solitary man in so many ways, Ted Heath put down real roots in Salisbury in the last 20 years of his life. And Salisbury, his housekeepers and security men, pub regulars and market traders, shrewdly took him as they found him, chitchat or no. When Lord (Robert) Armstrong, a Heath protégé who became cabinet secretary, read the 'Let Us Now Praise Famous Men' from Ecclesiastes, he mentioned those who 'have no memorial'. Britain in Europe, for better and worse, is Heath's.

26 July 2005

FEAR IN THE CITY

Tim Dowling

I can pretty well pinpoint the moment when my own spirit of defiance started to fade. It was on Saturday morning. I was with the dog in the park opposite our house, chatting to a woman with a boxer while watching two uniformed policemen comb the undergrowth. It's not unusual to see police in Little Wormwood Scrubs – the place has of late become something of a centre of excellence for delinquents. It is unusual, however, to be ordered to leave the area by a plainclothes officer citing the presence of a suspicious device. It is strange to watch the whole park being festooned in police tape, to see cops with machine-guns and earpieces standing on the corner. A huge security cordon was thrown up, with our house inside it.

At this point I was still feeling rather reassured by what I assumed was a ridiculous, if understandable, overreaction on the part of the police. People set fire to stolen scooters in our park, but they do not plant bombs there. We stood out on the front step in order to see what was happening, only to be told by a policeman that we must remain indoors. He was clearly looking for a phrase to describe the seriousness of the situation without telling us any more than he needed to. The words he chose were: 'It's got nails in.' That was when my defiance evaporated.

The spirit of the Blitz was invoked shortly after the bombings of Thursday 7 July, and it seemed to resonate immediately. Those directly affected by the attacks – the injured, the emergency services, the families of those killed or hurt – did indeed behave with courageous stoicism, and Londoners took a little reflected pride in their dignity. Mayor Ken Livingstone, a divisive figure at the best of times, made an emotional statement which perfectly captured the mood of the capital, even though he was in Singapore. 'Londoners will not be divided by the cowardly attack,' he said, his voice angry and raw. 'They will stand together in solidarity . . . and that is why I'm proud to be the mayor of that city.'

The next day people made their way to work, an act that was to become imbued with meaning. In different circumstances a business-as-usual approach to such a tragedy might have seemed callous, but those deeply affected by the bombings and those who were merely inconvenienced (I count myself firmly among the latter: I was in Paris) were united behind the idea that getting on with life sent the terrorists the right message. The buses filled up again. On Monday, Livingstone took the tube to work as normal, elevating the grim grind of the daily commute into a provocative political statement.

At the same time, the hastily set-up website www.werenotafraid.com became a clearinghouse for various expressions of defiance, an almost direct response to the terrorists' online claim of responsibility, which asserted that 'Britain is now burning with fear.' Some of the postings on werenotafraid.com were moving, some were mawkish, a few strayed into reckless bravado, but the overall tone was one of simple solidarity, amplified by the huge number of respondents. And in London things certainly seemed to be getting back to normal. Tourist numbers began to recover. Some 20,000 people turned up to the National Gallery's Stubbs exhibition last Wednesday. Despite stern warnings from the security services about the possibility of more attacks, it seemed like it would be a good long while before terrorists dared to test our vigilance again.

The second attack changed all that. While the display of defiance probably peaked at the impromptu street party in Shepherd's Bush Green, which was brought to a halt after a bomb failed to go off on a nearby tube train, in retrospect this seemed like a slightly giddy reaction to what turned out to be an extremely close call. The half-certainties we had let ourselves adopt were shattered. We had hoped that Britain contained a fairly limited supply of home-grown suicide bombers; it was even possible that the first four had been tricked into sacrificing their lives. We can discount that idea now.

Since Thursday, carrying on as normal has become rather more difficult. No one was injured in the attacks, but I know people in

Shepherd's Bush who weren't allowed to go home for two days. In Kilburn, in Tulse Hill and Stockwell – parts of London previously enveloped in the safety of shaggy anonymity – residents found the anti-terrorist operation had arrived on their doorsteps. If most of us have thus far escaped tragedy, few Londoners remain untouched by fear. On Friday the police shot an innocent Brazilian man in Stockwell Station, and the potential for disaster expanded. It's not enough to spot terrorists on the Tube, you must take active steps to avoid looking like one. Watching events unfold on television (interspersed with long, defiant stretches of cricket) I had the sense of things getting unpleasantly close to home, and that was before someone left a nail bomb in the park where my children play. I know this hardly compares to the Blitz, in which 43,000 Londoners perished, but I still find the idea of exhibiting pluck in the circumstances oddly draining. I feel lucky, but I don't feel plucky.

When Inter Milan tried to cancel its UK tour last week, Livingstone's outraged response rang curiously hollow. 'The terrorists, I am sure, will be celebrating their decision,' he said. 'We cannot allow the terrorists to change the way we live or they will be very close to their aim.' Who in London hasn't changed the way they live, or had it changed for them? I don't know about you, but yesterday I had to go through a police checkpoint to buy milk. People have stopped taking rucksacks out with them. They've stopped riding on the top deck of the bus. When it was first reported that bicycle sales had doubled in the capital, the statistic was interpreted as a plucky response to a badly damaged transport network – people were getting to and from work any way they could – but it may well turn out that a certain percentage of commuters have forsaken the Tube permanently.

On Sunday morning we were woken by the muffled crump of a controlled explosion. Although the bomb has been taken away, as I write this the police are still here and the park is still closed. I don't know whether I want them to stay or not. For the moment I live in unprecedented safety – a veritable gated community – but I must admit I'm now afraid: afraid that another attack is imminent, afraid of the idea of 3,000 armed police on the streets, afraid that London will never quite be the same again, afraid that my children will find out how afraid I am (don't worry, they'll never read this far). Carrying on as normal seems less politically freighted than it did two weeks ago, not least because it's no longer really possible, but you can't say that the terrorists have won just because the cops won't let the postman deliver my Amazon order.

26 July 2005

HUNTERS THEY ARE NOT

Canon Paul Oestreicher

Language betrays us. When the *Sun* talks of hunting terrorists, no surprise. But when that has become the language of BBC reporting and even of the *Guardian*, it is time to stop and think. Language not only reflects a mood but creates it. To speak of hunting human beings, even the most despised, is to embrace the violence we rightly denounce. For our police to be both effective and humane is a daunting task. Hunters they are not.

Canon Paul Oestreicher,
University of Sussex

DEATH OF AN INNOCENT MAN

Mark Honigsbaum

Jean Charles de Menezes, the Brazilian shot dead in the head, was not wearing a heavy jacket that might have concealed a bomb, and did not jump the ticket barrier when challenged by armed plainclothes police, his cousin said yesterday. Speaking at a press conference after a meeting with the Metropolitan police, Vivien Figueiredo, 22, said that the first reports of how her 27-year-old cousin had come to be killed in mistake for a suicide bomber on Friday at Stockwell tube station were wrong. 'He used a Travelcard,' she said. 'He had no bulky jacket, he was wearing a jeans jacket. But even if he was wearing a bulky jacket that wouldn't be an excuse to kill him.' Flanked by the de Menezes family's solicitor, Gareth Peirce, and by Bianca Jagger, the anti-Iraq war campaigner, she condemned the shoot-to-kill policy which had led to her cousin's death and vowed that what she called the 'crime' would not go unpunished. 'My cousin was an honest and hard-working person,' said Ms Figueiredo, who shared a flat with him in Tulse Hill, South London. 'Although we are living in circumstances similar to a war, we should not be exterminating people unjustly.'

Another cousin, Patricia da Silva Armani, 21, said de Menezes was in Britain legally to work and study, giving him no reason to fear the police. 'An innocent man has been killed as though he was a terrorist,' she said. 'An incredibly grave error was committed by the British police.'

Mr de Menezes was shot seven times in the head and once in the shoulder at 10 a.m. last Friday after being followed from Tulse Hill. Scotland Yard initially claimed he wore a bulky jacket and jumped the barrier when police identified themselves and ordered him to stop. The same day the Met commissioner, Sir Ian Blair, said the shooting was 'directly linked' to the unprecedented anti-terror operation on

London's streets. The following day Sir Ian apologised when detectives established that the Brazilian electrician, on his way to a job in northwest London, was not connected to attempts to blow up three underground trains and a bus in the capital. The Independent Police Complaints Commission has begun an inquiry which is expected to take several months. Yesterday it emerged that one armed officer involved has been given leave and two have been moved to non-firearm duties. Ms Figueiredo condemned Sir Ian's decision to authorise the leave, saying she wanted to see the man who shot her cousin, and he should be in jail.

The body of Mr de Menezes is being flown to Brazil tonight for a funeral tomorrow. Simultaneously, a memorial service will be held at Westminster Cathedral, with TV coverage beamed live to Brazil. Ms Peirce condemned Sir Ian's statements on the case, saying there had been a 'regrettable rush to judgement'. She was astonished that the phrase 'shoot to kill' was being used as if it was a legitimate legal term; the family would demand 'transparency' both as to the facts of what had happened and on the policy. She added that the family were ready to cooperate with the complaints body, and she saw no reason for delay: 'They know what their questions are and we see no reasons why they should not be answered.'

A NIGHTMARE ENDS,
ANOTHER NIGHTMARE BEGINS

Jonathan Freedland

One war begins and another comes to an end. That's how it seemed yesterday, as the anti-terrorist branch scoured the streets of Britain looking for the new enemy – just as the old one finally stood down. It was as if one flag was lowered while another was raised. TV news channels alternated between pictures of the current battle – police cordons in Birmingham, CCTV images from London buses – and archive footage of the old: the blood-spattered cenotaph at Enniskillen, the bandstand at Regent's Park, the detonated carcass of Docklands. Britons, Londoners especially, have spent the last three weeks learning to face a new threat. Yesterday they were told their old nightmares could finally be put to rest.

The IRA had last planted a bomb in 1996. And yet it still sounded remarkable to hear the words that came yesterday. They were delivered not in the usual form of a statement from the pseudonymous P. O'Neill, but in a DVD of the former IRA prisoner Seana Walsh reading out a written message – a gesture which seemed by itself to signal a new Provo glasnost. 'The leadership of Oglaigh na hEireann has formally ordered an end to the armed campaign,' he said, words that would once have been unimaginable.

Only two decades ago, this same organisation tried to blow up Margaret Thatcher and her cabinet. They bombed shopping centres and barracks in Britain and killed soldiers every other day in Belfast. Now they promise to be nothing more than an old boys' club for former volunteers. As of 4 p.m. yesterday, promised republican Danny Morrison, the IRA will be about as threatening as the British Legion.

The statement triggered the usual superlative derby, as politicians competed to find words large enough for the occasion. 'A step of unparalleled magnitude,' said Tony Blair. 'Momentous, historic and unprecedented,' said Ireland's Bertie Ahern. 'A defining point,' said Gerry Adams. All of those men were bound to use their most high-blown rhetoric. This project has, after all, consumed their energies for years. For Mr Blair, Northern Irish peace remains perhaps his best hope for an enduring political legacy, with the Good Friday agreement one of the outstanding achievements of his premiership. While the current war on terror brings only anxiety, the one just ending brings a chance for statesmanlike triumph. Amid bombs and rumours of bombs in the London of 2005, what a relief for the PM to declare: 'Today may be the day that peace replaced war, that politics replaced terror, on the island of Ireland.' Not that Mr Blair got carried away. He acknowledged that after so many 'false dawns and dashed hopes', people would be sceptical.

Indeed, a consensus from Downing Street to the White House was that, while the IRA statement was welcome, it will be republican actions rather than words that will matter. In disarmament talks with the Soviet Union, Ronald Reagan's maxim used to be 'Trust, but verify' – and that was the rule of the road yesterday. The message was put most forcefully by unionists. Ian Paisley wanted 'months and years' to monitor the IRA's 'behaviour and activity'. Not for him a rapid thaw for self-rule, which has remained in the deep freeze since October 2002 – but wait and see. Unionists spotted holes in the IRA statement wherever they looked. The promise to end criminality – pertinent after last year's £26 million robbery of the Northern Bank and the pub killing of Robert McCartney – was not explicit enough for their taste. 'Volunteers must not engage in any other activities whatsoever,' the IRA had said, prompting Mr Adams to ask, 'What part of "any other activities whatsoever" do [the Unionists] not understand?'

That oldest and stalest of chestnuts, decommissioning, remains a problem too. 'All IRA units have been ordered to dump arms,' said the statement, pointedly echoing the language when the order was last given in 1962. The dumping will be watched by international monitors, alongside one Protestant and one Catholic clergyman. That does not satisfy Mr Paisley, who repeated his call for photographic proof – a demand that scuppered progress last December. Republican sources promise a 'great acceleration' in disarmament, hinting at large moves in the next week or two. Their hope is that such rapid progress will put pressure on Mr Paisley to return to power-sharing sooner than he would like.

Unionists had hoped yesterday's statement might herald an end to the republican boycott of the Northern Irish police. They were perhaps unaware that, in the last 16 weeks of internal republican debate triggered by Mr Adams's April challenge to the IRA, policing emerged as the most charged issue. Few Provos objected to ending the 'armed struggle' – the hardest hardliners left after the 1994 ceasefire – but they did balk at the notion of backing the police. To that end, Mr Adams is likely to host a convention of republicans on the question next year. Apparently he plans no dramatic shift, but will take instead a series of 'baby-steps', tiptoeing towards an eventual accommodation with the police.

What led to yesterday's move? One factor was a change in republican strategy towards unilateralism. Just as Ariel Sharon has seized the initiative with his one-sided Israeli pullout from Gaza, so Mr Adams realised the power of taking decisive action on one's own terms. In the words of one senior strategist: 'We act best when we act alone.' Ending the armed campaign was not a response to a demand from either Mr Blair, Mr Ahern or Mr Paisley – one that would be contingent on a reaction from the other side. For that makes you a hostage to your enemy. 'This is a republican initiative,' said Mr Adams. 'It's not part of any little deal.'

Unionists will have their objections, that's only natural. But those watching from afar can only feel a twinge of envy at this news. For what wouldn't we all give for a statement like that from the new enemy, promising no more bombs, no more bloodshed and an end to tears?

A SIEGE IN WEST LONDON

Vikram Dodd, Sophie Kirkham, Matthew Taylor, Duncan Campbell, Tim Dowling and Richard Norton-Taylor

It was 9.30 a.m. when the first stages of a dramatic day in the hunt for the would-be suicide bombers started to unfold, as armed police, both plainclothes and uniformed, headed for West London. Their information was that at least two would-be suicide bomb suspects were holed up in two separate addresses and they wanted to bring both of them in alive.

In Tavistock Crescent, near Westbourne Park underground station in West London, neighbours described hearing what sounded like gunshots at around 11 a.m. Charlotte Brown, 16, a student, was at home alone when she heard five or six loud bangs and saw armed police targeting a flat directly below her. Her mother, Mary, a medical secretary, said a second-floor flat in the block had also been broken into by police.

Charlotte said a family with two young children, thought to be from Somalia, had lived in the basement flat for about a year. 'They seem perfectly normal, very nice neighbours in fact.' As police moved in, she said, 'There were about five or six really loud bangs that sounded like gunshots. I was quite scared, so I didn't look out of the window. Over the next hour I heard shouting from the garden where there were police. They were saying something about containers. Then it went really quiet, and I looked out of the window and there were armed police with gasmasks and submachine-guns . . . Then the police knocked on my door and told me I had to leave as quickly as possible, so I just locked up and left.'

By noon, the police had the man they were looking for, a suspect who they believe was linked to an unexploded bomb abandoned and found by a member of the public in Little Wormwood Scrubs last Saturday.

Further west, on the Peabody Estate in north Kensington, sandwiched between the Rootes and the Sutton estates and close to the recreation ground where the unexploded bomb was found, a siege was under way. Armed police, their weapons drawn, sought to persuade the man they were calling Muhammad to come out from a flat.

Zehra Burhan had noticed more police around than usual in the middle of the morning. Rapidly, armed officers in body armour flooded the area around Dalgarno Gardens. Around midday a thundering explosion was heard; some residents thought it was a bomb and that London was again under attack. Ms Burhan said: 'When the explosion went off I heard them say, "Come out, this is the police!"' The assault team began to attack a flat on the fourth flour of block K of the estate, which residents say was occupied by several Somali men.

Lisa O'Brien, who lives opposite, said: 'The explosion shook my flat. Later I heard what sounded like three shots. I was in shock and panicking.' Over nearly three hours confused residents sat in fear as they heard bangs and explosions and feared the worst. 'It's manic, it's crazy, it's like a film,' Ms O'Brien said. 'My daughter, who is 21, said, "Mummy, am I going to die?"'

Josephine Knight, 55, who also lives opposite, said she had seen a man dressed like a bus driver appear to lead officers to the flat, before he was taken away with his hands bound by white plastic ties. Ms Knight said the first loud explosion was the doors being blown off the flat by officers using a low explosive charge. The block had recently been fitted with heavy security doors. On the block's balconies armed officers, some with balaclavas, began to swarm around. Ms Knight said soon after the explosion a man in his forties had come out with his hands up and was led away. Police then warned those remaining inside they would fire CS gas into the flat. When no one emerged, they did. Police sealed off the estate, trapping some children inside the flats. Some residents said they had run for cover, with police training guns on them.

Paul Carroll, 35, was trapped inside his flat just 20 metres away. 'Armed police just blew the door down,' he said. 'They put black masking tape on the door, then they blew it off. Later they fired teargas into the flat. Twenty of them rushed in taking aim at the flat.' Giles and

Mira Craig said they had heard what sounded like three gunshots and then four or five more a few minutes later. Witnesses said they had heard police shouting at those inside to keep talking to them and shouting at Muhammad, urging him to come out. One man said: 'Police were saying "Come over Muhammad", "Muhammad, come out with your hands up." The man replied, "If I do you'll shoot me."' One witness said an officer had replied: 'That was a mistake.' And Muhammad answered: 'You're going to shoot me.'

Towards the end of this exchange a witness said an officer had told Muhammad, who was situated at the back of the flat: 'Strip yourself, nothing is going to happen.' By now police assault teams were also on top of the flat, and officers in biochemical suits were present in case the worst was to be found. Another witness said an officer had told Muhammad to come out in his underwear with his hands up, with the suspect replying: 'I am scared, how do I know you won't shoot me?'

Around 1.30 p.m., four further bangs were heard as police blew off other sets of doors and prepared to end the siege by force. Around 2.30 p.m., witnesses say the final occupants of the flat emerged bare-chested. Officers told them to take off their trouser bottoms, to check for concealed weapons or explosives, and the men obeyed. They then walked along the balcony to police, put on white paper suits and were led away. Ms Knight said: 'They looked like regular Muslim guys.'

At 3.05 p.m. a police van sped through the protective cordons, with a man in the back seat, his face covered by a fluorescent yellow jacket. Ms Knight said by 4 p.m. officers had entered the flat 'gingerly, as if there might be people in there'. The operation had been successfully concluded and police had arrested two suspects, Muktar Said-Ibrahim, the suspected bus bomber, and a man named by police sources as Ramsi Muhammad, the suspected Oval bomber.

A small number of soldiers from the SAS had been present to offer 'technical assistance' to the police – an apparent reference to stun grenades. They were from an SAS squadron based at Hereford, specially trained in counter-terrorist operations. The squadron is ready for deployment at three hours' notice anywhere in the country if the police or MI5 suspect that armed terrorists are in a building, and is understood to have moved to a secret location in London immediately after the escape of the 21 July would-be suicide bombers.

The first arrest was made in Birmingham on Wednesday, by police using a Taser stun gun. Yasin Hassan Omar, 24, who is suspected of having carried the Warren Street bomb, is being held at Paddington Green police station in West London. On the other side of the city yesterday, it was a busy Friday lunchtime at Liverpool Street Station when plainclothes armed police swooped on two women wearing Muslim dress, described by a witness as 'one of African and one of Asian origin', one of whom was apparently standing in a queue at the ticket machine. Travellers gazed on in amazement as the women were made to lie face down and put their hands behind their backs. They were handcuffed and taken for questioning. One of the women had a rucksack with her, according to one witness, and the other a small box.

Both the mainline and underground stations were closed and travellers were evacuated, many people having to abandon their journeys as items were checked. No explosives were found and the stations were reopened. Arthur Yeroshin, who works as a shoe cleaner on the station platform, said: 'There was panic, the girls ran away and the police pushed them to the floor. They kept them there for five or six minutes and then took them away with their bags.' Jaleel Sarwar, 21, who works in Tie Rack just metres from where the arrests were made, said: 'There was a lot of shouting and a lot of noise, then the police were on top of the women to stop them getting away. They were both very little and did not seem to struggle.'

At about 4.15 p.m. yesterday, two hours after the arrests, Liverpool Street tube station was closed and armed officers entered the underground in what police described as a 'firearms incident'. Less than ten minutes later, the armed unit returned to the concourse and the tube station was reopened, just as news came of a further arrest in Rome of Hussein Osman, the man wanted in connection with the bomb attempt at Shepherd's Bush. Seven hours after one of the biggest and most important operations launched by Scotland Yard was set in motion, all five suspects in the 21 July attempted bomb attack on the capital were in custody.

BLACK DAY FOR
THE BLUE PENCIL

Blake Morrison

Has editing had its day? A Dutch publisher recently described to me how a British author had sent her the first draft of his new book. Though a great admirer of his work, she felt that this time he hadn't done justice to his material. So they sat down together and mapped out a different perspective and storyline and he went away and rewrote the book. It's not often you hear publishers speak of being so frankly interventionist – and I wondered if that was why the author had sent his book to a Dutch editor, because this kind of intense collaborative process between author and editor no longer exists in Britain. A novelist friend, hearing the story, said: 'When I hand in a book, I've usually been working on it for several years, so I like to think there'll be little left to do to it. But if I did need editing, I'm not sure, these days, I could get it.'

A graduate student of mine at Goldsmiths College expressed similar nostalgia in an e-mail. 'I have a notion of editors in days of yore,' he wrote, 'being straight-backed and terrifying, all integrity and no bullshit, responding to a vocational calling and above all driven by a love of the word, brave enough not only to champion the best but also to tell their authors whatever might be needed to improve the work. And that now such personalities are as distant a myth in publishing as yer Shanklys and yer Cloughs are to football, that sharp-dressed corporate beasts run the show, reluctant to make decisions of their own, and ill-equipped to challenge those who rule a star-led system, so that everyone from J. K. Rowling to David Eggers suffers from the lack of scissors that might have been to their benefit.'

Just after getting that e-mail, I read about a literary conference at which both writers and agents were complaining that, because of the pressures they're under, modern-day editors simply don't have the time to edit. A news item about an initiative by Macmillan to encourage first novelists left a similar impression – the authors will receive royalties but no advances; however, if their books needed significant editing, they will have to pay for the services of a freelance editor, since no one can do it in-house.

If editing is in decline, that's bad for literature. History suggests that while some authors work alone, more or less unaided, the majority benefit from editors – and that a few are utterly dependent on them. Take Thomas Wolfe, not the white-suited New Journalist and author of *Bonfire of the Vanities*, but the other Tom Wolfe, his outsize predecessor, a man of 6ft 6in, who used to stand up while he was writing, using the top of a fridge as his desk. Clearly standing didn't inhibit Wolfe's productivity. The typescript of his first novel, as submitted to Scribner in New York, was more than 300,000 words – what a contemporary publisher would call 'fuck-off long'. But a young editor at Scribner, Maxwell Perkins, agreed to publish it, if Wolfe agreed to cut 90,000 words, and between them they did the job.

Soon Wolfe was working on a second novel. By early 1933 it was four times as long as the uncut version of the first – and growing at a rate of 50,000 words a month. 'I think I'll have to take the book away from him,' Perkins told colleagues, and invited Wolfe to gather all he'd written and bring it into the office, since he was sure the skeleton was already there. Some skeleton. There were jokes about the typescript being delivered by truck. The bundle stood two feet high – more than 3,000 pages, unnumbered – and this was only the first part of the novel. They began working together, two hours a day, six days a week – then nights, from 8.30 onwards; then Sunday nights as well. It was like painting the Forth Bridge. Wolfe would be asked for a short linking paragraph – and return a few days later with 10,000 words. In the end, while Wolfe was out of town for a few days, Perkins had the typescript set – all 450,000 words. It was published as *Of Time and the River*, and though another of Perkins's authors, Hemingway, said it was 'something over 60 per cent shit', it became a bestseller. Wolfe later wrote an account of its composition, 'the ten thousand fittings, changings, triumphs and surrenders that went into the making of a book'.

There was a sad end to the Wolfe story. First rumours circulated about all the help he'd received, then a damaging piece appeared in the *Saturday Review* alleging that any organisational skills and critical intelligence in his work were down to Perkins. Wolfe grew resentful and paranoid, and in a letter accused Perkins of wanting to destroy him (the letter, characteristically, ran to 28 pages). 'Restrain my adjectives, by all means,' he wrote, 'moderate . . . my incondite exuberance, but don't derail the train, don't take the Pacific Limited and switch it down the siding towards Hogwart Junction'. Shortly afterwards Wolfe ditched Perkins and went round telling people: 'I'm going to show them I can write my books without Max.' It didn't happen. There wasn't the time for it to happen. Wolfe died of TB and pneumonia, at 37.

Wolfe's dependency on Perkins was extreme. It's not so life-and-death with most of us. But all writers need editors. A truism. All writers need editors. So why isn't the matter more discussed? There are several reasons, I think. The editorial tradition, first of all, is for self-effacement. As human beings, editors may be far from self-effacing, but as workers their contribution goes largely unacknowledged – a nod in the preface or a thank you from the author at the launch party and that's it. They're the ghosts in the machine, the secret sharers, the anonymous power behind the throne.

And when they do come out from the shadows to write their own memoirs, they tend to be bland and uninformative. This isn't true of Diana Athill's *Stet* or Jennie Erdal's *Ghosting*, both excellent and at times very funny books about working with authors. But Tom Maschler's recent autobiography is more typical in its unrevealingness. Maschler is an outstanding publisher, whose list at Cape includes Gabriel Garcia Marquez, Salman Rushdie, John Fowles, Kurt Vonnegut, Philip Roth – but none of the many anecdotes he recounts about drinks, lunches, dinners, parties and prize ceremonies sheds light on the process of editing. 'I have often been asked to define what makes one decide on a particular book,' he writes in the closing pages. Ah-ha, we think, here it comes. 'The choice is so personal, so subjective . . . To publish well the publisher must be passionate about the book for its own sake . . . and for me to care I must admire it for its quality.' Well, thanks, Tom, that's really cleared things up.

Writers have done little to clarify the role of editors, either. Where the experience of being edited goes well, they're grateful, but the more publicised cases are when the experience is bad. Henry James called editing 'the butcher's trade'. Byron associated it with emasculation and, he said, would 'have no gelding'. D. H. Lawrence compared it to trying 'to clip my own nose into shape with scissors'. And John Updike says: 'It's a little like going to . . . the barber,' adding, 'I have never liked haircuts.' Or listen to the condescension of Nabokov: 'By editor I suppose you mean proof-reader.' There are, of course, many different kinds of editor – from fact-checkers and OKers (as they're known at the *New Yorker*), to line-editors and copy editors, to editors who grasp the big picture but skip the detail. But in popular mythology they're lumped together as bullyboys, bouncers or, to quote Nabokov again, 'pompous avuncular brutes'. Those who can, write; those who can't, edit – that seems to be the line. I prefer T. S. Eliot. Asked if editors were no more than failed writers, he replied: 'Perhaps – but so are most writers.'

Behind hostile images of the editor lies the pressure of Romantic ideology, according to which the writer is seen as a solitary creative genius or *Übermensch* – and the editor as a meddling middlebrow. 'Invisible behind his arras,' one Victorian critic wrote, 'the author's unsuspected enemy works to the sure discomfiture of all original ability – this fool in the dark who knows not what he mars.' What the editor is accused of marring isn't just originality but that other cherished notion of Romantic ideology, 'the spontaneous overflow of powerful feelings'. By this measure, any sort of interference with a text is a violation. Even authors are castigated for tidying up their younger selves, as Wordsworth did with the 1850 *Prelude* and Auden did by revising or disowning poems he had written in the 1930s. But the real enemies are held to be a writer's friends, family and publishers, whose suggestions can only dilute or contaminate the pure spring of inspiration. The accusation that Ted Hughes was 'suppressing' Sylvia

Plath when he rearranged the original edition of *Ariel* and left out certain passages from her letters and journals was connected to a suspicion that he had driven her to suicide – silencing her twice over. Something similar has been alleged against Percy Bysshe Shelley, for the changes he made to his wife Mary's novel *Frankenstein*, changes which one commentator has described as 'a kind of rape', a 'collaboration forced by a more dominant writer on a less powerful and perhaps unwilling "partner"'. In fact, Mary seems to have been a fully consenting adult, who approached editing as she did parenting – 'the good parent, like the good author, neither abandons its offspring nor seeks wholly to control or shape them' – but the accusation that she was violated remains.

Perhaps I've been unusually lucky, but in my experience, editors, far from coercing and squashing writers, do exactly the opposite, elucidating them and drawing them out, or, when they're exhausted and on the point of giving up (like marathon runners hitting the wall), coaxing them to go the extra mile. And yet this myth of the destructive editor – the dolt with the blue pencil – is pervasive, not least in academe. Perhaps the antipathy stems from the perceived difference between the publisher and the scholar: for whereas a scholarly editor, appearing late in the day and with the wisdom of hindsight, seeks to restore a classic, the publisher's editor is the idiot who ruined it in the first place.

A good illustration of this antipathy is the Cambridge edition of D. H. Lawrence. 'Here at last is *Sons and Lovers* in full: uncut and uncensored,' the editors of the 1992 Cambridge edition crow triumphantly. Their introduction goes on to allege that in being reduced by 10 per cent, the text was 'mangled'; that the editor Edward Garnett's censorship was 'coy and intrusive'; that Lawrence 'reacted to Garnett's decision to cut the novel with 'sadness and grief', but was powerless to resist', and that when Garnett told him further cuts were to be made, Lawrence 'exploded' with rage.

Read Lawrence's letters and you get a rather different impression. 'All right,' he tells Garnett, 'take out what you think necessary,' and gives him licence to do as he sees fit: 'I don't mind what you squash out . . .

I feel always so deep in your debt.' Lawrence was short of money, it's true, and had his mind on other things, having recently eloped with Frieda. Even so, when he writes that 'the thought of you pedgilling away at the novel frets me' (pedgilling, a nice coinage, a cross between pencilling and abridging), the fret isn't what Garnett will do to the text, it's that the task is an unfair imposition: 'Why can't I do those things?' And when Lawrence is finally sent proofs, he's not unhappy. 'You did the pruning jolly well,' he tells Garnett, and dedicates the book to him: 'I wish I weren't so profuse – or prolix, or whatever it is.'

It's true that, just as some writers write too much, some editors edit too much. As the *New Yorker* writer Renata Adler acerbically puts it, there are those who 'cannot leave a text intact, eating through it leaf and branch, like tent caterpillars, leaving everywhere their mark'. When he edited the magazine *Granta*, Bill Buford was sometimes accused of being overbearingly interventionist – in his spare time he hung out with football hooligans, and it was said he brought the same thuggishness to editing, though personally I never found him brutal in the least. At the other extreme are the quiet, nurturing sorts, the editors who ease you through so gently that when they do tamper with the text you barely notice and can kid yourself they did no work at all. Frank O'Connor compared his editor William Maxwell to 'a good teacher who does not say "Imitate me" but "This is what I think you are trying to say".'

When people speak of writer's block, they think of the writer stalled over a blank page or of throwing scrunched-up bits of paper – false starts – into a wastebin. But there's another kind of block, which is structural, when you've written tens of thousands of words, but can't figure out which are superfluous and what goes where. Something's wrong, but you don't know what it is, and that can make you pretty desperate, so that if some new acquaintance rashly expresses an interest in what you've written, as happens to the Californian wine buff and would-be published author Miles in Alexander Payne's recent film *Sideways*, you foist your typescript on them, which in Miles's case means retrieving from the back seat of his car not one whacking heap of pages but two, and even though you know this will (a) place the recipient in an awkward situation, (b) sprain his or her back, and/or (c) ruin a beautiful friendship, still, you do it anyway, because you're desperate. And that's why editors matter, not as butchers and barbers, but because what's wrong with a book can be something the author has repressed all knowledge of, something glaringly obvious which, the moment an editor or other reader identifies it, you think yes, of course, Eureka, and then you go back and fix it. Editing might be a bloody trade. But knives aren't the exclusive property of butchers. Surgeons use them too.

Three major works of early-twentieth-century literature – *Sons and Lovers*, *The Waste Land* and *The Great Gatsby* – were transformed by the interventions of others. The uncut version of *Sons and Lovers* is the one in general use now, so we can see exactly what Garnett took out. Mostly, he pared back passages about Paul Morel's brother, William, at the risk of betraying the title of the novel, which declares this to be a book about 'sons', plural, but mostly with a gain in focus and narrative pace. The censorship, too, is largely innocuous. 'She had the most beautiful hips he had ever imagined,' Lawrence writes, when Paul sees Miriam naked for the first time. Garnett changed 'hips' to 'body', which seems to me an improvement, 'hips' being an odd thing for Paul to focus on and, I suspect, a euphemism, and at any rate not a major breakthrough in sexual candour. The one serious misjudgement Garnett made concerns the scene where Paul and Clara go back to her mother's house, after a night in town at the opera. Paul is invited to stay over and use Clara's bed while she sleeps with her mother. He hopes to have sex with Clara, nonetheless, and it's only when her mother refuses to leave them alone together that he reluctantly makes his way upstairs to Clara's bedroom and undresses. Garnett cut the following: 'Then he realised that there was a pair of [Clara's] stockings on a chair. He got up stealthily, and put them on himself. Then he sat still, and knew he would have to have her. After that he sat erect on the bed . . .'

A braver editor might have allowed Lawrence both his double entendre – 'erect' – and the authentic resoluteness of a man on heat ('he would have to have her'). But the real censorship concerns those stockings. Too kinky, Garnett must have reasoned. The sensible Clara might have thought the same, had she known what Paul was getting up to in her bedroom, and not responded to him as warmly as she does when he creeps back downstairs and finds her naked in front of the fire. (Garnett trimmed a paragraph from this scene too, including a reference to Paul holding a large breast in each hand, 'like big fruits in their cups'.) Still, for us it's an insight into Paul – a clue to his feminine side, perhaps, or closet transvestism or masturbatory male heterosexuality or, on a deeper level, his need to know what it feels like to be Clara. The modern reader wants the stockings and will wonder why Garnett didn't dispense with the Mills & Boon stuff instead ('She gave herself. He held her fast. It was a moment intense almost to agony'). But this is now, and that was then, and by making *Sons and Lovers* a novel which, unlike *The Rainbow*, escaped moral denunciation and legal writs, Garnett did Lawrence a service – as also did Frieda, Jessie Chambers and Louie Burrows, all of whom read the book in draft and made suggestions.

Thanks to the discovery of the original typescript of *The Waste Land* in the New York Public Library in 1968, Ezra Pound's part in the poem's composition is well-known. Most of his comments are plain and workmanlike – a fellow maker offering sound advice. 'Verse not interesting enough,' he scrawls in the margin; 'Too easy', 'Inversions not warranted', 'rhyme drags it out to diffuseness'. He's particularly severe whenever the poem teeters into Prufrockian tentativeness – 'make up yr mind', 'Perhaps be damned' and 'dam per'apsez', he complains. Other cuts are motivated by ear, not logic – Eliot at this point was using quatrains, and Pound chastised him for such old-style regularity. But taste comes into it, too, as when Eliot describes the young man as carbuncular, leaving the typist he has just seduced, 'delay[ing] only to urinate and spit': 'probably over the mark', Pound says, and takes it out, as he also does a chilly, misogynistic account of a woman having a bath. It's good, practical stuff. But not infallible. And Eliot was far from slavish in following Pound's advice. If he had listened to Pound, we would not have the lines about the young man being someone 'on whom assurance sits / as a silk hat on a Bradford millionaire'. Nor would we have those tense snatches of conversation from a couple in bed in Part 2 of the poem: 'My nerves are bad tonight. Yes, bad. Stay with me. / Speak to me.' Pound objected that this was mere 'photography', but Eliot stuck to his guns, preferring to rely on the opinion of his wife Vivienne, who thought the passage 'wonderful'.

Pound wasn't a Redeemer, any more than Garnett was a Mangler. Both had good advice to offer but the integrity of the work – someone else's work – remains. Maxwell Perkins's editing of *The Great Gatsby* is exemplary in this way, too. He had edited Fizgerald's previous two novels, but Fitzgerald wanted this one to be a more 'consciously artistic achievement', and Perkins helped in numerous ways. For instance: (1) The title. Fitzgerald's running title was *Among the Ash-Heaps and Millionaires*. His second choice was *Trimalchio in West Egg*. Perkins didn't like either. Nor plain *Trimalchio*. Nor plain *Gatsby*. A month before publication day, Fitzgerald cabled in a panic from Italy to suggest *Gold-Hatted Gatsby*. Perkins held firm. *The Great Gatsby* was best. (2) Ideas: At an early stage, to spur Fitzgerald along, Perkins showed him a possible dust jacket for the book: two gigantic eyes, brooding over New York. The jacket inspired Fitzgerald to develop a key image and motif in the novel: the billboard of optician Dr T. J. Eckleburg. (3) Length: One week before he thought he'd finish, Fitzgerald estimated *Gatsby* at 50,000 words, more a novella than a novel. Perkins encouraged him to fill the story out, and Fitzgerald spliced in about 20 passages, adding up to 10,000 words. I've never heard anyone complain the book is too long. (4) Character: Perkins thought Gatsby himself too vague: 'The reader's eyes can never quite focus on him, his outlines are dim . . . Couldn't you add one or two characteristics, like the use of that phrase "old sport"?' He also thought readers would want to know how Gatsby got his wealth. Fitzgerald agreed: 'I myself didn't know what Gatsby looked like or was engaged in . . . I'm going to tell more.' And he did.

Fitzgerald had written three drafts of *Gatsby* before Perkins intervened, but then, he said, 'sat down and wrote something I was proud of'. Perhaps there's no better example of the proper balance between author and editor. One little mystery concerns the last page – the blue lawn, the green light at the end of Daisy's dock, and 'the orgastic future that year by year recedes before us'. 'Orgastic' isn't quite a neologism but it's extremely rare, whereas 'orgasmic' and 'orgiastic' are common enough. Was it a typo? Neither Perkins nor Fitzgerald was good at spelling: after *This Side of Paradise* was published, spotting the typos – there were more than 100 – became a parlour game in New York book circles (without his secretary, who saved him time and again, Perkins might have become infamous as The Editor Who Couldn't Spell). But 'orgastic' does work. Perhaps it was conscious artistry.

The years 1912 to 1925 seem to have been the golden age of editing. Most of the publishers I've talked to, both young and old, say it's impossible to do such editing today. However diligent you are, the sheer speed at which books have to be pushed through prevents it. These days you have to be an all-rounder, involved with promotion, publicity and sales – all of which are crucial but mean that when a writer is trapped in a wrong book you don't have the time to sit down together and find a way out. One editor spoke of a colleague who had managed to do brilliant work purely because, having small children, she was allowed to do most of her work at home; were she in the office all day, having to attend meetings and fend off phone-calls, she'd never manage it.

Meanwhile, most people say the real editing of books is now done by agents, since agents offer authors stability, whereas publishers' editors are nomadic, moving from house to house. Does it matter? Books still come out, and if writers these days moan about being edited too little, where once they moaned about being edited too much, well, writers will always moan. By common consent, two of the outstanding debut novels of recent years, Zadie Smith's *White Teeth* and Monica Ali's *Brick Lane*, were insufficiently edited – but that hasn't stopped them achieving commercial and critical success. And who wants to see the return of what Lawrence called the 'censor-moron', cutting whatever he deems improper for us to read?

But think for a moment of another kind of culture, where nothing is edited. A culture where we're all so logorrhoeaic we haven't time for each other's words or books or blogs, where everything goes into the ether – and there's no sign that anyone reads it all. A culture that doesn't care about editing is a culture that doesn't care about writing. And that has to be bad. It seems no coincidence to me that there should have been a massive growth in creative writing programmes in Britain in recent years. That the reason so many aspirant writers are signing up for MAs and PhDs is to get the kind of editorial help they no longer hope to get from publishing houses. If Perkins were alive today, would he be editing texts for Scribner? Or teaching fiction to creative writing students at Columbia University?

'But can you really teach creative writing?' people ask. I like to think so – that certain skills can be passed on. But maybe it's the wrong question. Better to ask: 'Can you teach would-be writers to edit?' Yes, absolutely, yes. Walk in on a creative writing class and you'll hear the kind of babble you might have heard from Garnett with Lawrence, or Pound with Eliot, or Perkins with Fitzgerald: why not think of losing that, or moving that there? Give the reader more signposts. Stop bombarding us with so many characters. Don't parade your research, integrate it. Show, don't tell. Get in and out of the scene more quickly. Is that simile really working? And so on.

Perkins warned editors against delusions of grandeur. 'Don't ever get to feeling important about yourself . . . an editor can get only as much out of an author as the author has in him.' He's right. When a book appears, the author must take the credit. But if editing disappears, as it seems to be doing, there'll be no books worth taking the credit for.

FAMINE IN NIGER

Jeevan Vasagar

She has pipe-stem limbs and displays every rib on her narrow chest, but two-year-old Hasana is not sick enough to be treated in a hospital. Under a white plastic tent, an aid agency doctor has a few minutes to make decisions about the lives of scores of babies. Outside his tent, a sea of desperate mothers queue in the boiling sun, hoping for food for their children.

While aid is beginning to arrive in Niger, the numbers of children needing treatment is still rising. In the last week of July, more than 1,600 children were admitted to treatment programmes run by the medical charity Médecins Sans Frontières in two of the worst affected regions. The seeds of the crisis were sown when locusts and drought destroyed crops and pasture land for cattle in parts of Niger. But it was economics, not the hand of nature, which led to the crisis spiralling out of control. The price of the staple food, millet, has soared, because traders have been exporting grain from unaffected parts of Niger to wealthier West African countries such as Nigeria. While markets here in Yama are filled with produce, the poorest starve because they cannot afford the prices.

'I collect firewood to sell, so I can buy food at the market,' said Mallia, sitting outside the aid agency tent with Hasana, her daughter. 'But I have to carry five loads of wood to the market to make enough [money] for a cup of millet.'

As the crisis grew, the government of Niger at first refused to distribute free food, fearing that it would disrupt the market. But that policy has now been reversed and the first general distribution of free food will begin today.

Hasana is clearly in a desperate state. Lying amid the folds of her mother's yellow-green robes, she weighs 3.5kg. A child of her age should normally weigh 5.1kg. Her twin sister, Huseina, died at the end of last month. Her mother has walked for a day to seek help, and her flip-flops are caked with dirt. But the doctor decides that Hasana is not sick enough to be hospitalised. The infant is given a taste of a nutritional supplement, a sweet-tasting paste that resembles peanut butter. The medical staff note that she is eating well, a sign that she may be able to recover by herself. Child and mother are sent home with several sachets of the supplement, as well as powdered milk and oil.

Johanne Sekkenes, head of the mission in Niger for MSF-France, said: 'I would say that 60 per cent of [the] children will never be admitted into the feeding centre. They are still severely malnourished. They will still die if we don't take care of them. But they are, if I may say so, well enough to stay at home and come once a week [to the mobile clinic], because the mothers are the best caretakers.'

In the nearby town of Tahoua, baby Moussa is one of those deemed sick enough to be brought into an intensive care unit. Lying on a narrow bed, milk has to be fed to him through a tube in his nose. The slender, naked boy with a slightly puffed belly cannot swallow anything because of a fungal infection in his mouth. Moussa's skin is dotted with sores from another infection. Ganda Amadou, a Nigerian doctor at the intensive care unit, said: 'Malnutrition is followed by low immunity. The child is not eating, and if he wasn't here he would die – because how can his mother feed him?'

In Yama, a village of elaborately sculpted mud houses, hundreds of mothers have brought their children to seek help as two aid agencies, MSF and Concern, work side by side. While the medical charity deals with the severely malnourished children, women with children who are slightly less desperate are given food aid by the other charity.

In the sweltering afternoon heat, tensions begin to build. The mothers at the front of the queue to receive food are those whose babies have been identified as malnourished by teams who went out the week before. Each of these babies wears a bracelet to mark them out. Behind them is a press of equally desperate women whose children have not been marked for priority treatment. As all the 'braceleted' babies receive food and pass through, anxiety builds among the mothers at the rear of the queue that they will receive nothing. There is a surge, and the ropes around Concern's tent are knocked down. Swiftly, local elders help to restore order and urge the women back, but the aid workers fear a stampede if they begin the distribution again. Instead, the food is packed away, and driven to local warehouses in a fleet of four-wheel-drive vehicles. It is an illustration of the challenges faced by the charities delivering aid here.

Maureen Crill, a nurse working for Concern, said: 'There were over 1,000 people, and if they started pushing in, we would be asking for people to be crushed, especially babies. I know how horrible it looks. It was a tough decision to make.'

8 August 2005

A CLOSE-RUN THING

Richard Williams

All over England children will be dreaming of biffing a cricket ball delivered by an Australian hand into the top tier of the pavilion, just like Freddie Flintoff does. A narrow victory in yesterday's second Test put England on equal terms with Australia, and may have relaunched a game that not long ago seemed in danger of expiring from underachievement.

Two runs was the difference, after almost three-and-a-half days in which the advantage swung from one to the other and back again. It was the narrowest margin since the Ashes were first contested in 1882, and a wonderful exposition of cricket's capacity for self-renewal. Those twenty-first-century children awakening to the virtues of this arcane and archaic game also have a new, utterly contemporary larger-than-life hero. Flintoff, with his shaved head and his diamond stud, did not deliver the *coup de grâce* yesterday, but he did produce a ball that induced Shane Warne to stumble into his stumps after Australia had scored less than half of the 107 they required to win when the fourth day's play began. That left Brett Lee and Michael Kasprowicz, Australia's last batsmen, needing to make 62 to achieve victory.

It was a distant target, but as Australia summoned reserves of resilience against England's fired-up bowlers it began to seem disconcertingly achievable. A packed Edgbaston, brimming with excitement and confidence at the start of play, fell into a fearful silence broken only by the chanting of the Barmy Army. After an hour in which the tension rose with every ball, Australia's last pair were two runs away from a tie and three from an astonishing win when Kasprowicz fended away a rising ball from Steve Harmison, England's fastest bowler, with his glove and saw the wicket-keeper, Geraint Jones – raised in Queensland by Welsh parents – take the catch.

Claims that cricket's balance of power is shifting back to the game's birthplace had better wait until the outcome of the five-match series is known.★ But after their humiliation at Lord's a fortnight ago, England responded at Edgbaston by attacking from the start. 'We couldn't afford to go two down,' the captain, Michael Vaughan, observed after yesterday's win. A score of more than 400 runs on the first day showed his players adopting the aggressive approach with which Australia dominated world cricket for a decade. The series resumes at Old Trafford on Thursday, with not a ticket left unsold.

★ We won! And what a marathon it was. See page 273.

HYPHENATION

Joseph Harker

So how would you, the reader, feel about being ethnically rebranded? No, please don't look over at that black person in the corner! I mean you, the white one! (Or, should I say, the hyphenated-British one?) That is, after all, what our Home Office minister has just suggested. While her boss, Charles Clarke, has been away on holiday, Hazel Blears has decided that giving us all double-barrelled identities would be a great idea, and would help to make everyone seem valued and included in our modern society. She's apparently been inspired by the US, where descriptions such as Irish-American, Italian-American and African-American have done so much to bring communities together in a big group-hug of brotherly love. Forget marginalisation and discrimination; forget alienation, and how it has helped turn some towards terrorism. All we need now is a neat little addition to our nationality and all our troubles will go far away. It's such a classic spin trick that New Labour's ideologues must have been delighted – although No 10 later backtracked and said the idea was not a proposal.

Ms Blears heads a new government commission on how best to integrate minorities. It is, at least, an improvement on the traditional methods suggested for most non-white newcomers to this country: 'Oi – if you don't integrate we're gonna smash a brick through your window and stick dog shit through your letterbox!' Actually, I did tell a little white lie earlier: according to *The Times*, which broke the story, 'it is unclear whether Irish, Scottish or Welsh people would be part of the exercise.' In fact, it's unclear whether English people would too – but I guess they forgot to ask that question.

The problem is, the minute you start tugging on this idea, the whole thing starts to unravel. Britain is not America. Across the Atlantic, the double identities of the various minorities are a measure of their exclusion from society, not of their integration into it. If, during the US's mass-migration era, the Irish, Italians and Poles had been welcomed into the country and been able to gain a fair foothold, would they have established such tight-knit communities where identity became so strongly bonded over the generations? The hyphenation has merely provided a way for minorities to coexist in their separate ghettoes. Did the British, the Dutch, the Germans and the French who preceded them set such store by their national origins? No, they didn't have hyphens, they had ownership – they were Americans, the country was theirs, and all the immigrants who followed had to accept it. In fact, such was their arrogance that they bestowed a hyphenation on the original inhabitants whose land they'd stolen, now patronisingly labelled 'Native-American'.

Despite being an island, Britain is also a nation of migrants and their descendants. Eight out of ten of us have roots elsewhere. The only thing that marks some people out, rather than others, is skin colour. Five years ago, a Channel 4 documentary, *Untold*, interviewed a number of white Britons who were totally unaware that they had Asian or black family roots. They were people who'd never had to question their identity or nationality; the kind of people who'd have talked about 'immigrants' coming into 'their' country. The kind of people who'd today think of themselves as full-blooded Brits. So what would Blears call them? In her thinking, hyphenation is only for racial minorities – for 'British-Asians' or 'Indian-British'. She didn't talk about 'French-British' or 'British-Australian', for example. No, according to her, they must be full-bloods; nor did she suggest, say, calling the leader of the opposition 'Jewish-British' or 'Romanian-British'. In this act of omission she serves only to reinforce the underlying contradictions that govern so much of Britain's thinking about race. Whites will not have their beliefs challenged – they can consider themselves 'British', with no hyphens. In any case, most would reject out of hand any attempt to put a caveat on their own nationhood. For the rest – you can have a second-tier nationality, which accentuates that you're not like us.

It is this double-standard that causes so much resentment among racial minorities – especially at a time when anyone who looks like a

Muslim is being treated as the enemy within. Why are you questioning us? they ask. Will we always be outsiders? In turn, this forces minorities to examine their own sense of nationhood. When the *Guardian* surveyed Britain's racial minorities just before the general election, fewer than half considered themselves to be fully British. Interestingly, for all the current scare stories, the least-British group were not Asians, but Chinese. And age-wise, despite the fact that the younger generations are far more likely to have been born here, the least 'British' were 25- to 34-year-olds; only among the over-55s did a majority feel British. This is worrying, because it shows that, despite the integration and mixing of races which has taken place over the years, we are somehow heading in the wrong direction. Our ideal should surely be an inclusive nationality that values the different perspectives that other cultures can bring, and doesn't force people to fit into strict Anglo-Saxon norms in order to be accepted.

Ultimately, if we take the Blears route, nearly all of us should be hyphenated, but most of us can get away with pretending otherwise. For those who want to join in, but are unsure of their origins, maybe Ms Blears should come up with some new categories: man-British, woman-British, Arsenal-British, Chelsea-British, Yorkshire-British, Cornish-British or, to tie in with the *Sun*'s current campaign, what about Lawless-British? But if you don't want anything to do with this, and you're quite sure these lands have been yours since your forefathers' time and you don't need to justify your right to a full stake in this society, then that's OK too. From now on, you're going to be Native-British.

THE UNBEARABLE LIGHTNESS OF FLYING

Alok Jha

At 25,000ft the pilot cuts power to the engines. For the briefest of moments there is silence. Then, the world inside the plane becomes a phantasmagoria: people gasp and scream as they are lifted, limbs moving chaotically. Bottles filled with coins rise into the air and the contents begin a serene dance, as if held by an unknown force. Finally, 20 seconds after the Airbus A300 begins plummeting towards the Mediterranean, the engines roar back to life. The people inside, some of whom are pinned to the roof of the cabin, slam back against the floor. The quiet that follows is broken by a sharp hiss. A voice on the intercom crackles 'Next parabola, one minute.'

Feeling weightless is not something you do every day. As such, it is difficult to describe in everyday terms. It is nothing like floating in water. Nor is it like the butterflies in your stomach hurtling down a rollercoaster. It is the single strangest feeling I have ever had – a combination of shock, fear and immense euphoria.

My story began two days earlier at a military research base next to Bordeaux Merignac airport. Though it is part of a sprawling industrial park, the small, single-storey Novespace office sits alone next to the tarmac leading to the airport's runway. When I get there, I find groups of people huddled around bits of foam, metal and plastic. The floor is littered with paper, electrical tape, wires, nuts, bolts, spanners and screwdrivers. Conversations hum in at least half a dozen different languages – these scientists have come from all over Europe to fly their experiments in zero gravity. At one side of the building is a locked metal gate, beyond which rises the unassuming white shape of an Airbus. It wouldn't look out of place at any airport but for the lack of windows and the words 'Zero G' daubed in blue multi-storey letters on its fuselage.

'It's an incredible facility to have,' says William Carey, of the European Space Agency's human spaceflight and microgravity exploration division. 'A lot of scientists who will fly experiments on the space station will test equipment and procedures on a parabolic flight.' Thanks to these flights, scientists can, for 20 seconds at a time, test satellite components or predict problems with experiments destined for the International Space Station before they are sent into orbit. Falling out of the sky in an airplane is the only practical way to experience microgravity without leaving Earth.

At a safety briefing on the morning of my arrival, the pilot explains how the flight will proceed, followed by a doctor who tells us how to survive the experience. Airplanes fly by forcing air over their wings in such a way that there is an excess of the upwards force, lift. While in the air, the plane stays up thanks to lift and moves forward because of the forward thrust provided by the engines. The aircraft battles against two forces trying to slow it down and pull it out of the sky – air friction and gravity. On a normal flight, the amount of thrust will be greater than the friction and the lift will equal the weight so that the plane stays up. On a parabolic flight, thrust is set to equal air friction, while lift is simultaneously removed. This leaves weight as the only force acting on the plane and, like any unpowered object fired into the air, it will move in a parabolic curve as it freefalls. At this point, because everything inside the aircraft begins falling to Earth at exactly the same speed as the plane, the contents act as if they are weightless. That is not to say that the plane and its contents actually are weightless – gravity is still acting on the plane and everything in it.

The effect on a passenger is a wonderful reminder of our animal past. The human brain gets so confused with the shifting sensations that it does what confused brains do best – induces vomiting. The flight doctor explains how the sickness is caused by a conflict between information coming from the inner ear (responsible for balance) and from the eyes. The inner ear can't tell which way gravity is pointing during freefall, whereas the eyes see very little real difference. Cue the sickness.

The experience isn't cheap. Each campaign (usually three 31-parabola flights) costs half a million euros and ESA runs about four a year. As time is precious, most campaigns are limited to ESA-funded researchers. But for the last eight years ESA has run a campaign to give first-timers a feel for space research. The student parabolic flight campaign runs every summer and attracts applications from more than 100 teams of budding space researchers. One of the successful British teams this year was backed by the highly regarded space research centre at Leicester University. Daniel Brandt, Jim Aldcroft, Keith Sprake and Richard Branch – fresh from sitting their Physics finals – joined 28 other teams.

Their journey to Bordeaux had started almost a year before, when Aldcroft and Brandt came up with an idea to test how mixtures of particles of different sizes might settle in zero gravity conditions. 'We're trying to observe segregation of granular matter in reduced gravity conditions,' says Branch. In the presence of gravity, this separation phenomenon is more commonly known as the 'Brazil nut effect', where the biggest nuts in a box of breakfast cereal, for example, rise to the top as the mixture settles. This implies that the sizes of the particles in a mixture determine their final arrangement, but no one has studied the role of gravity in the phenomenon. Out in space, how would a box of cereal settle? The idea has applications for planetologists trying to model how the debris resettles on small moons churned up after meteorite impacts. 'According to our theory, size shouldn't make a difference – what should make a difference is the density of the particles,' says Branch. In zero gravity, Aldcroft and Brandt's idea was that particles of different densities would separate into bands along the length of the box. How could the Leicester team test this idea? Mixtures of materials (ball bearings, sand and simulated Mars dust, for example) were packed into clear plastic boxes and vibrated at various frequencies to force them to settle.

As well as the Leicester physicists, two other experiments from the UK made the flights this year. A team from Imperial College London studied the effects of zero gravity on the brain's ability to process spatial awareness and hand-to-eye coordination, while a group of students from Kingston University tested the practicality of unfurling kites in space.

The morning before the flight is frantic. The 14 experiments on the plane are checked and rechecked by the teams. Most (me included) have barely slept the night before and are nervously pacing the Novespace offices. The rooms fill with the sound of excited chattering. People trade tips and rumours on how to avoid getting sick. Someone mentions eating oranges before the flight (they taste the same on the way out as on the way in, apparently). Another quietly counts the number of people sick on the flights the day before (four). The doctor warns us once more not to move our heads too much during the phases of near double gravity before and after the weightlessness – a sure recipe for nausea, he says. At 8 a.m., an hour before the plane takes off, the flight doctor opens his suitcase of drugs. He places a tiny white pill in my left hand with the word HOPE inscribed on one side – to help ward off motion sickness. In my right he places a much larger pill of caffeine, in case the first makes me drowsy.

I step on to the plane and make for a window seat at the back while flight safety attendants, dressed in vivid orange flight suits, pass through the cabin, handing out sickbags. An hour and a half later, we are in the air over the Mediterranean, with less than ten minutes to go before the first parabola. Not wanting to be held down in a seat for my first bout of weightlessness, I opt to lie on the floor in the central section of the plane, which has been cleared of seats and where the experiments are in place. Seconds before the plane begins to pull up, a conversation with the flight doctor rings in my ears: some people are sick on the first parabola, he had said. They just can't help it. 'Then they are sick for every single parabola after that, too. The flight is not a good experience for those people.'*

And then the engines get louder and I am pushed into the ground, as if someone is sitting on my chest. I try lifting my arm and it feels as if it is made of solid lead. Breathing becomes difficult and I can feel my spine being gently pushed straight. The pilot calls out the angle of the plane: 10, 20, 30. At 40 degrees, he pauses for a breath before calling out 'injection', the signal that the engine power is to be switched off.

And then the magic happens.

'There was a pause between injection and the actual feeling of weightlessness and then everybody just started screaming,' Branch says later. 'Surprise was the thing I saw on people's faces. Surprise and shock. Other people were just laughing because they couldn't believe what was happening to them.'

I had been concentrating hard in the moments before the zero gravity so that I could remember as much as possible. But immediately after the pilot says 'injection', I involuntarily let out a series of gasps. My body begins tumbling uncontrollably around the strap I am now clutching at with all my strength. My legs are moving themselves up towards the roof. Whenever I try to move in any direction (or even just lie still) my body steadfastly refuses to obey. Bodies are being thrown about all around me. And it stops just as suddenly as it started. I crash to the ground and once again feel heavy as the pilot pulls the plane level. At the end of the parabola, I stand up and beam at the people next to me. One down, 30 to go.

Carey, a veteran of hundreds of parabolas, finds it difficult to describe the feeling of weightlessness. 'You're describing something that isn't there. You're describing a loss of sensation,' says Carey. 'The closest somebody has come is like being on the bow of a ship when you get thrown up into the air and come down again.' Branch finds it easier to describe what the feeling doesn't resemble. 'You imagine it's like floating in water without the water there, but it's not,' he says. 'You're not being buoyed up by anything. You don't have the friction of the water to push off.'

Weightlessness is a tremendous shock to the system. Picking something up or moving in a controlled fashion becomes a task of supreme concentration. But once I get used to it, I begin to understand what makes the feeling unique. It is not so much the physical difference but the mental confusion. Between my eyes showing me that things are (mostly) normal and my sense of balance refusing to work at all, my brain is getting a wealth of conflicting signals. Making a coherent narrative from these disparate and nonsensical signals begins to hurt my head. I stay put for the first few parabolas and then begin trying out a few tricks the more experienced crew members are demonstrating – standing upside down on the ceiling, spinning around, flying from one end of the plane to the other. During the tenth parabola, I try staying completely still, as close to the ground as possible. It's tougher than it sounds because as hard as I push, I can't seem to feel the ground beneath.

Working in these conditions takes some skill, but the students on the plane – all of whom had only moments before properly experienced weightlessness for the first time – begin with gusto. By the third parabola they are all busy with their experiments. Carey says that it is an invaluable experience for students to have the 'opportunity to propose an experiment, to build it, to fly it and then to participate in something like a parabolic flight campaign where they get firsthand experience of what being in a non-gravity environment is like.' Another role of the student flight campaign is to tell others what space research is all about. ESA hopes it will turn the students into advocates for their space research programmes. 'One of the problems in Europe is enthusing students and making them interested in science,' says Carey.

The wow factor is enormous. Branch says that even weeks after the event, the flight is at the top of his team's thoughts. 'The word "injection" – when we hear that, we associate it with a euphoric feeling.'

★ Alok Jha did not vomit, not even once.

WARMING HITS TIPPING POINT

Ian Sample

A vast expanse of western Siberia is undergoing an unprecedented thaw that could dramatically increase the rate of global warming, climate scientists warn today. Researchers who have recently returned from the region found that an area of permafrost spanning a million square kilometres – the size of France and Germany combined – has started to melt for the first time since it formed 11,000 years ago at the end of the last ice age. The area, which covers the entire sub-Arctic region of western Siberia, is the world's largest frozen peat bog and scientists fear that as it thaws it will release billions of tonnes of methane – a greenhouse gas 20 times more potent than carbon dioxide – into the atmosphere.

It is a scenario climate scientists have feared since first identifying 'tipping points' – delicate thresholds where a slight rise in the Earth's temperature can cause a dramatic change in the environment that itself triggers a far greater increase in global temperatures. The discovery was made by Sergei Kirpotin at Tomsk State University in western Siberia and Judith Marquand at Oxford University and is reported in *New Scientist* today. The researchers found that what was until recently a barren expanse of frozen peat is turning into a broken landscape of mud and lakes, some more than a kilometre across. Dr Kirpotin told the magazine the situation was an 'ecological landslide that is probably irreversible and is undoubtedly connected to climatic warming'. He added that the thaw had probably begun in the past three or four years.

Climate scientists yesterday reacted with alarm to the finding and warned that predictions of future global temperatures would have to be revised upwards. 'When you start messing around with these natural systems, you can end up in situations where it's unstoppable. There are no brakes you can apply,' said David Viner, a senior scientist at the

Climatic Research Unit at the University of East Anglia. 'This is a big deal because you can't put the permafrost back once it's gone. The causal effect is human activity and it will ramp up temperatures even more than our emissions are doing.'

In its last major report in 2001, the intergovernmental panel on climate change predicted a rise in global temperatures of 1.4°C–5.8°C between 1990 and 2100, but the estimate only takes account of global warming driven by known greenhouse gas emissions. 'These positive feedbacks with landmasses weren't known about then. They had no idea how much they would add to global warming,' said Dr Viner.

Western Siberia is heating up faster than anywhere else in the world, having experienced a rise of some 3°C in the past 40 years. Scientists are particularly concerned about the permafrost, because as it thaws, it reveals bare ground which warms up more quickly than ice and snow, and so accelerates the rate at which the permafrost thaws. Siberia's peat bogs have been producing methane since they formed at the end of the last ice age, but most of the gas had been trapped in the permafrost. According to Larry Smith, a hydrologist at the University of California, Los Angeles, the west Siberian peat bog could hold some 70 billion tonnes of methane, a quarter of all of the methane stored in the ground around the world.

The permafrost is likely to take many decades at least to thaw, so the methane locked within it will not be released into the atmosphere in one burst, said Stephen Sitch, a climate scientist at the Met Office's Hadley Centre in Exeter. But calculations by Dr Sitch and his colleagues show that even if methane seeped from the permafrost over the next 100 years, it would add around 700 million tonnes of carbon into the atmosphere each year, roughly the same amount that is released annually from the world's wetlands and agriculture. It would effectively double atmospheric levels of the gas, leading to a 10 to 25 per cent increase in global warming, he said.

Tony Juniper, director of Friends of the Earth, said the finding was a stark message to politicians to take concerted action on climate change. 'We knew at some point we'd get these feedbacks happening that exacerbate global warming, but this could lead to a massive injection of greenhouse gases. If we don't take action very soon, we could unleash runaway global warming that will be beyond our control and it will lead to social, economic and environmental devastation worldwide,' he said. 'There's still time to take action, but not much. The assumption has been that we wouldn't see these kinds of changes until the world is a little warmer, but this suggests we're running out of time.'

In May this year another group of researchers reported signs that global warming was damaging the permafrost. Katey Walter of the University of Alaska, Fairbanks, told a meeting of the Arctic Research Consortium of the US that her team had found methane hotspots in eastern Siberia. At the hotspots, methane was bubbling to the surface of the permafrost so quickly that it was preventing the surface from freezing over.

Last month, some of the world's worst air polluters, including the US and Australia, announced a partnership to cut greenhouse gas emissions through the use of new technologies. The deal came after Tony Blair struggled at the G8 summit to get the US president, George Bush, to commit to any concerted action on climate change and has been heavily criticised for setting no targets for reductions in greenhouse gas emissions.

13 August 2005

THE MOTORING SEASON

Charlotte Moore

The price of gold hit an eight-month high yesterday of just under $450 (£248) an ounce as the relentless rise in the price of crude sent some investors looking for a haven – an investment 'hedge' against oil prices inflicting serious damage on the world economy. The cost of bullion reached $449.30 in early European trading before sinking back to a little under $447. Prices have risen sharply in recent weeks, gaining 5 per cent during a month when oil prices have risen 10 per cent. Paul Walker, chief executive of the precious metals consultancy GFMS, said: 'I think the rising oil price has restoked investors' fears about the sustainability of the recovery of the US economy.'

Historically, the price of gold bullion has also had a strong inverse relationship with the American dollar. The US currency has weakened against both the pound and the euro in recent weeks as concerns have re-emerged over the size of the US trade deficit. Oil prices reached more than $66 a barrel for the first time in trading on the New York mercantile exchange over concerns of insufficient capacity to pump and refine enough oil to supply the US and China's seemingly insatiable demand for energy. Oil for delivery in September this year yesterday ran as high as $67, with the Brent contract up $1.08 to $66.46.

The price of oil has been pushed up this week by Iran's stand-off with the West over its nuclear plans, refinery troubles in the US, and a warning that production output from Russia and Norway has been disappointing. There was a new problem yesterday at Premcor's Tennessee refinery, which produces 175,000 barrels a day.

Although the oil price has risen by 52 per cent this year, this has had little significant impact yet on either inflation or economic growth. However, the surge in oil prices over recent weeks has caused some investors to worry that this may change. 'I think anyone who says that oil prices of between $60 and $70 a barrel are not going to have an impact on the US economy is deluded,' said Mr Walker.

Gold prices tend to rally in times of economic uncertainty. During the oil crisis in 1979, which was caused by the Iranian revolution, the price of gold more than doubled over the course of the year. Stripping out the impact of inflation, the price of oil is still below the $80 a barrel high reached in 1979. Experts remain divided about how much further the oil price can go. Paul Ashworth of Capital Economics said: 'As it is demand rather than supply that is driving up the price of oil, it can keep rising until it has an impact on economic growth and therefore lessens demand.' Others think the price could fall when the US motoring season ends next month.

13 August 2005

AN UNTIMELY DEATH

Martin Kettle

Less than an hour before he died in the arms of his wife Gaynor a week ago, Robin Cook sent one of his sons a text message announcing that he was at the top of the Highland peak Ben Stack in cloud. 'Weather foul. Wish you were here,' the message concluded. 'He was on the rooftop of Scotland with the woman he adored,' recalled Bishop Richard Holloway at the start of an affectionate but anguished set of funeral tributes yesterday.

Mr Cook never lacked either for admirers or even for self-regard, but even the former foreign secretary might have been surprised and humbled at the palpable sense of raw personal and public loss that cut through his defiantly secular funeral in the heart of Edinburgh yesterday. Mr Cook's wife led the private mourners at the ceremony at St Giles' Cathedral. But the wound to British – and especially to Scottish – public life caused by Mr Cook's sudden death was just as evident in yesterday's markedly political event. It was passionately articulated by Gordon Brown in his funeral eulogy. 'Let us acknowledge Robin's passing leaves a gap that can never properly be filled,' the chancellor told 500 official mourners and a much larger crowd in the street outside. 'I believe it could be said of all of us that we did not value Robin enough in life.' As if to mark their assent at Mr Brown's powerful tribute, hundreds of onlookers burst into applause as the hearse carrying Mr Cook's coffin left the cathedral to carry him to a private burial ceremony in the Edinburgh area yesterday afternoon. Mr Cook, the Labour MP for Livingston since 1983, died from a heart attack while on Ben Stack with his wife last Saturday afternoon. He was 59.

But if the absence caused by Mr Cook's death was inescapably the dominant theme of the day, the more avoidable absence from the funeral of Tony Blair also forced its way on to the agenda when the racing commentator John McCririck, a close friend of the late Labour minister, accused the prime minister of 'snubbing' his former colleague by preferring 'to continue snorkelling' than to break his summer holiday in the Caribbean to return for the funeral. Many in the cathedral and beyond doubtless agreed that Mr Blair should have returned for yesterday's funeral. But there was private consternation and embarrassment among Mr Cook's family and friends that Mr McCririck, who also praised Margaret Thatcher and denounced the European Union in his address, should have used a televised funeral tribute to accuse Mr Blair of an act of 'petty vindictiveness'.

The prime minister was not the only member of the cabinet who failed to attend yesterday but Mr Cook's funeral nevertheless drew a formidable group of political mourners, headed by the deputy prime minister, John Prescott, and the former Labour leader Lord Kinnock. Other cabinet members in the congregation included David Blunkett, Alistair Darling, Lord Falconer, Peter Hain, Patricia Hewitt, John Reid and Jack Straw. The Scottish political establishment was out in force too, headed by first minister, Jack McConnell, and with the Liberal Democrat leader Charles Kennedy and the Scottish Nationalist leader Alex Salmond heading an appropriately pluralistic political turnout. The former foreign secretary, Sir Malcolm Rifkind, who knew Mr Cook from their days on Edinburgh city council in the 1970s, represented the Conservative Party. Overseas mourners were headed by the German foreign minister Joschka Fischer. The former US secretary of state, Madeleine Albright, had been expected to attend, but was ill and unable to travel.

Mr Cook would have been amused and intrigued by the fact that his funeral was being held not just in church but in the most establishment church in Scotland, observed Church of Scotland Bishop Richard Holloway at the start of the ceremony. The former foreign secretary was, after all, a 'devout atheist' who might fear that the 'icy fingers of resurgent religion' were attempting to grasp him at the last, the bishop said. But Mr Cook, like the late Scottish first minister, Donald Dewar, might reasonably be described as a 'Presbyterian atheist', Bishop Holloway added. He would surely have enjoyed the irony of a church funeral in much the same way that he would have enjoyed singing the Red Flag at a New Labour rally, he said.

Mr Cook's sons Chris and Peter read from the former foreign secretary's memoir, *Point of Departure*, and from Zola's *Germinal* respectively. The Labour MP Mohammad Sarwar paid tribute to Mr Cook's work with British Muslims. There was a poignantly personal reading of a Pablo Neruda sonnet and Mr Cook's coffin was carried out of the cathedral to the sounds of the Internationale and the Scottish socialist song 'Freedom Come All Ye'. But Mr Brown's address was the funeral's public centrepiece. Mr Cook was 'the most accomplished parliamentarian of his generation', the chancellor said. He provided MPs with a '30-year-long master class in effective eloquence'. But Mr Cook did not simply make great speeches. He also advanced 'great causes', Mr Brown stressed. His articles in the *Guardian* 'burned as red as his hair'. Mr Brown acknowledged that the two men had had their differences – 'sometimes exasperatingly so'. He was 'never a yes man and not infrequently quite the opposite'. But the chancellor hinted that – if and when he succeeds to the premiership – Mr Cook might have returned to high office. 'In the words spoken long ago of another great life cut all too short: "He had not yet passed on life's highway the stone that marks the highest point."'

OUT OF GAZA

Chris McGreal

It was to be his last day in Gaza, but Sagi Ifrach planted himself on the roof of the only home he has ever known yesterday morning and declared that it would take the entire Israeli army to move him. His parents and siblings had left two days earlier, resigned to the futility of resisting Ariel Sharon's determination to clear Jewish settlers out of the Gaza Strip in a move heralded as historic in many other places, but viewed as akin to treason in the settlements.

Mr Ifrach, 23, was determined not to go so quietly, as 3,000 troops and police moved on to the streets of the largest Gaza settlement, Neve Dekalim, to clear out the remaining 350 families. 'We won't give up without a struggle. The land of Israel is at stake,' he said. 'Generally we obey the law, but this law is anti-Semitic. I won't be coming down until they drag me off.'

Some of his friends joined him on the roof. Yaron Olami, a member of the council in the Israeli town of Herzelia, and Oren Hazan, the son of an Israeli MP, shouted down ringing declarations of defiance after painting slogans on the walls below: *Sharon is a dictator* and *Soldier, look into your heart*. But after five hours in the sun, a policeman shouted up to Mr Ifrach and asked if he wouldn't mind getting off the roof. The young man wrapped himself in the Israeli flag, began to weep and climbed down into the arms of a waiting soldier. The others followed in time.

It was a piece of theatre re-enacted in differing forms throughout much of Neve Dekalim yesterday as the settlers publicly displayed their grief at leaving their homes, and vented their anger at the prime minister, the army and anyone else they thought to blame. But almost all boarded the waiting buses without resistance and left Gaza for the last time. By nightfall, most families had departed. There was almost no violence except when, for the second time this month, an Israeli took out his anger at 'Jews expelling Jews' by shooting Arabs. Mr Sharon condemned the murder of three Palestinians in the West Bank by a settler yesterday as an act of terror. Two weeks ago, an Israeli soldier shot dead four Arabs on a bus in protest at the Gaza withdrawal.

The killings went largely unnoticed in Neve Dekalim, where many families gathered after sunrise for a last breakfast in their gardens, taking in the warm Mediterranean air. Some were slightly surprised to still be there for a last lunch too, but things moved slowly as hundreds of militant young ultra-nationalists who infiltrated the settlement in recent weeks tried to blockade the streets by burning rubbish bins and threatening sabotage. A resident who gave his name only as Michael appeared blind to the reality unfolding around him as he remonstrated with the young protesters. 'I'm trying to convince the youth not to burn the garbage. I was trying to tell them that we will continue to live here. I believe I will be here in a year and my children will marry in Neve Dekalim. And if I'm going to live here, we need somewhere to put our garbage,' he said. 'It's a very difficult lesson we're going through here, but the people who will come out stronger will be the people of Neve Dekalim. The soldier who carries out this order will come out a crushed man.'

The army and police trained for the pull-out for weeks and the young militants were soon corralled around the settlement's synagogue. Scores of those who ventured away were snatched and forced on to buses back to Israel. The settlers tried a mix of pleading for compassion and insults to try to deter the security forces. A handful of elderly women wearing signs saying DESTRUCTION were arrested after confronting the army, formally known as the Israel Defence Force, and denouncing it as the Israel Deportation Force. A girl in her early teens marched up to a policeman, Aryeh Stanger, and presented him with a teddy bear. 'Take that home and show it to your children and tell them what a crime you're committing,' she said to the policeman's blank stare. Infuriated at his indifference, she started shouting 'Kapo! Kapo!', a reference to Jews forced to serve as orderlies in Nazi camps. Officer Stanger was unfazed. 'They like this Holocaust analogy. I think it's a bit exaggerated,' he said. A woman took on another policeman. 'You are expelling Jews for the sake of Sharon's corruption,' she shouted. 'It's for the sake of democracy,' the policeman replied. 'Even Hitler was elected,' she spat.

Shortly after noon the security forces began moving into houses. The routine was the same in each case. A policeman knocked on the door and asked if the family was ready to leave peacefully. Behind him stood 16 other officers and soldiers to make clear that resistance would not work. Most families decided that they had made their point by defying the Monday deadline to leave, and agreed to board the buses. They did not go quietly: there was much loud public weeping, a part of Jewish religious practice, and berating of the security forces. At a few homes, the police had to kick in the door and push the family out, but there was no serious resistance. Some exercised their frustration by ensuring that their homes would not be turned over to the Palestinians intact. One family took to their house with sledgehammers, smashing out the windows and frames, destroying the doors and breaking walls.

Mr Sharon said yesterday he found the scenes 'heartbreaking' and appealed to them not to blame the security forces: 'Don't make it harder for them, don't harm them. I am responsible. Attack me.' The settlers were happy to, but they were more welcoming of a last visit by Amram Mitzna, the ex-Labour Party leader who campaigned at the last election on a platform of unilateral withdrawal from a small part of Gaza, and lost to Mr Sharon, who said he would not give up one settlement. 'The settlers respect me and there's no aggression against me because they say at least I was standing behind what I said from the beginning. Most people here have in mind they were cheated,' said Mr Mitzna.

The police had been worried about the students at the Yamit Yeshiva, a religious school built in the shape of a Star of David. But those studying there, and scores of older Israelis camped at the site in solidarity, decided to go with dignity. The rabbis led a prayer for the dead to mourn the destruction of Neve Dekalim as the death of a part of Israel. Then they led the way, carrying the Torah scrolls, the menorah and Israeli flags. The soldiers saw them on to the buses, waved goodbye and the Yamit Yeshiva was no more.

18 August 2005

SLIPPERY OF THE YARD?

Rosie Cowan, Vikram Dodd and Richard Norton-Taylor

Britain's top police officer, the Scotland Yard commissioner Sir Ian Blair, attempted to stop an independent external investigation into the shooting of a young Brazilian mistaken for a suicide bomber, it emerged yesterday. Sir Ian wrote to John Gieve, the permanent secretary at the Home Office, on 22 July, the morning Jean Charles de Menezes was shot at short range on the London Tube. The commissioner argued for an internal inquiry into the killing on the grounds that the ongoing anti-terrorist investigation took precedence over any independent look into his death. According to senior police and Whitehall sources, Sir Ian was concerned that an investigation by the Independent Police Complaints Commission could impact on national security and intelligence. He was also understood to be worried that an outside investigation would damage the morale of CO19, the elite firearms section working under enormous pressure. 'We did make an error, the IPCC should have been called in immediately,' the police source said.

Later that same day, after an exchange of opinions between Sir Ian, the Home Office and the IPCC, the commissioner was overruled. A Whitehall insider said: 'We won that battle. There's no ambiguity in the legislation, they had to do it.' But a statement from the Met yesterday showed that despite the agreement to allow in independent investigators, the IPCC was kept away from Stockwell tube in South London, the scene of the shooting, for a further three days. This runs counter to usual practice, where the IPCC would expect to be at the scene within hours.

It was also disclosed last night in documents leaked to ITV News that a soldier played a crucial role in the surveillance operation that led up to the shooting. The soldier was stationed outside a block of flats where police believed two terrorist suspects lived. At a key moment in the operation, the soldier was in the process of relieving himself and thus could not turn on his video camera. 'I could not confirm whether he was or was not either of our subjects,' the soldier later reported, according to the ITV News documents. But he added to others in the surveillance team: 'It would be worth somebody else having a look.' This appeared to set in train a chain of events in which Mr de Menezes was followed on to a bus and to the Stockwell tube station, where another two-man surveillance team identified the Brazilian to a police firearms squad. At the point of the shooting, seven undercover officers were all inside the tube carriage within metres of Mr de Menezes. In a further puzzle, the soldier staking out the block of flats identified Mr de Menezes as he left the building as IC1 – police terminology for ethnic white. Yet the suspected Stockwell bomber had already been captured on CCTV and was known not to be white.

Scotland Yard was making no official comment last night, although senior sources stood by Sir Ian, insisting he had spoken in good faith about the shooting. Harriet Wistrich, lawyer for the de Menezes family, said: 'Sir Ian Blair should resign. The lies that appear to have been put out, like the statement from Sir Ian Blair, for instance, are clearly wrong. And nobody has stepped in to correct the lies. From the beginning, the most senior of police officers and government ministers, including the prime minister, claimed the death of Jean Charles to be an unfortunate accident occurring in the context of an entirely legitimate, justifiable, lawful and necessary policy. In the context of the lies now revealed, that claim has become even less sustainable and even more alarming.'

Speaking from Brazil, Mr de Menezes's cousin, Alex Alves Pereira, said: 'The officers who have done this have to be sent to jail for life because it's murder and the people who gave them the order to shoot must be punished. They should lock them up and throw away the key. They murdered him.' Mr Pereira added that both Sir Ian and Tony Blair shared the officers' culpability. 'They are the really guilty ones,' he said.

Whitehall sources disclosed that members of the army's new Special Reconnaissance Regiment had been involved in the surveillance operation. The precise role of the soldiers is unclear. Whitehall officials said the operation had been 'police-led' and that all the commands had been issued by police officers. In the weeks since the shooting, Sir Ian has vigorously defended both the new shoot-to-kill policy as regards suspected suicide bombers, and the firearms officers involved in Mr de Menezes's death.

'Whatever else they were doing, they clearly thought they were faced with a suicide bomber and they were running towards him,' he told the Metropolitan Police Authority on 28 July. 'That is cold courage of an extraordinary sort.' He insisted there was 'nothing cavalier or capricious' about the operation, stressing that the only way to stop a suicide bomber was to shoot him in the head, rather than risk setting off a device strapped around his body. On the day, Sir Ian, who described the shooting as 'directly linked' to the anti-terrorist operation, said: 'Any death is deeply regrettable but as I understand it, the man was challenged and refused to obey instructions.'

MO MOWLAM

Peter Mandelson

Tributes to politicians, often maligned when in office, invariably become glowing encomia when the moment arrives. In Mo Mowlam's case, deservedly, praise and admiration were given during her life. That should not result in the reverse happening now. She leaves a real legacy and strong memory in Northern Ireland. Most politicians, even those who hold the highest office, do not have such tangible achievements to their names. In this, as in so many ways, Mo was different.

The route she took to this accomplishment was both fortuitous and fraught. My reading of her career is that she had a real knack for using political opportunities to full advantage, even when she did not always realise they were opportunities in the first place.

When first offered her Northern Ireland responsibility, she was very unsure about taking it, either because she felt it was not right for her or because she felt it was below her. It turned out to be the making of her. When, after the signing of the Good Friday agreement in 1998, it would have been right for a fresh face to take forward its implementation, she refused the prime minister's offer to move her on. A year later, with the peace process stagnating and her own high reputation affected by this, she flatly rejected the prime minister's suggestion that she run for mayor of London. She seemed slighted by the offer. Actually – again – it would have been the (re)making of her, just as going to Northern Ireland had been. She was a talented, individualistic politician who defied conventional moulds and, as London's first directly elected mayor, she would have enjoyed ruling in her own domain.

From the moment she entered parliament in 1987 she was destined to stand out from the crowd. Her ebullient, sometimes volatile personality made sure of that. She did not have the easiest of starts in

Redcar, her Teesside constituency across the bay from Hartlepool. She was a last-minute selection from a small shortlist imposed by Labour's national executive. Her local party activists did not embrace this shotgun marriage with enthusiasm, giving her a hard time for many years for her ideological ambivalence (Mo never filled the left-wing caricature in vogue in the late 1980s). By 1989 she was quickly moving to the front of the stage. Neil Kinnock, in a move prompted by Labour's chief press officer, Colin Byrne, and recommended by me, appointed her as Bryan Gould's No 2 in the European election campaign of that year. Her role was not major (it was difficult to shine alongside Bryan, whose election performances were magical), but she did not make mistakes and she firmly established the precedent of leading women fronting party campaigns.

She showed her gratitude to me in an unusual way with the gift of a compact TV and radio set that sat by my bedside throughout my time in Hartlepool. I can think of few other politicians making such a kind gesture. She was subsequently rewarded with promotion as the frontbench spokesman on the City in Gordon Brown's trade and industry team. This was not a match made in heaven, as she described in her memoirs. Gordon was totally dominant, leaving little space for Mo, who, in policy terms, did not make her mark. She, in turn, began to complain of being excluded from the 'man's world' epitomised by the impressive rising performers John Smith, Brown and Tony Blair. Mo saw herself in this league. She resented not being part of the gang.

Her second opportunity to leap forward came when John Smith died and she became co-chair of Tony Blair's leadership campaign (a move from which her already fragile relationship with Gordon never recovered). She was ideally suited for the role, embodying the classless, modern, forward-thinking outlook that became Blair's trademark. She happily left the technical management of the campaign to Blair's personal team while busily creating a non-sectarian, feel-good atmosphere around the candidate from which he benefited considerably.

I do not know for sure, but I suspect Mo was disappointed with the outcome for herself. But in 1997, entering the cabinet as Northern Ireland secretary was a triumph for her, not least after the discovery of the brain tumour that affected her personally in many ways. She became unstoppable. Her brazen, nonconformist style broke down barriers in Northern Ireland. She unashamedly and opportunely courted nationalist and republican opinion so as to bring this side of the deeply divided community in from the political cold. She positioned herself against the much-maligned Royal Ulster Constabulary. She shocked loyalists by the directness of her language and behaviour, winning both admiration and abuse from this hard-bitten (and -biting) fraternity. Among mainstream unionists, however, she largely failed to charm. They saw her as a partisan figure, whereas she saw herself as merely correcting a historic imbalance. She made little or no headway with unionist leaders, with the result that first they, then the republican leadership, decided to focus their attention and negotiating efforts exclusively on No 10 rather than on her as secretary of state.

Mo should have left Northern Ireland the moment the ink was dry on the Good Friday agreement, which, through her personality, she did so much to bring about. Without exception, the province tires of its secretaries of state after a relatively short time. But she dug her heels in, believing that she still had more to do. When, 18 months later, I was appointed to take over, our previously close and often fun friendship could have ended on the spot. Instead she insisted on flying over with me on my first trip from Northolt, having invited my partner and I around to her Islington home the evening before to discuss life in Hillsborough Castle with her and her partner, Jon Norton. On the plane she had a pad of A4 paper on her knees with at least 20 items of priority importance on which she wanted me to follow through. Topping the list were enacting the radical Patten police reforms (which I did) and setting up a number of further judicial inquiries into alleged wrongdoings by the RUC and the British army (which I did not). In my view, the already established Bloody Sunday inquiry was enough and, in any case, it was soon clear to me that to implement the Good Friday agreement, instead of keeping it on a pedestal, we needed to restore unionist goodwill, which by then had seriously eroded.

British politicians react differently to being sent to Northern Ireland. Some find it alienating, unenjoyable and, in personal career terms, a dead end. Others throw themselves into it, become absorbed by the place and are sorry to leave. Mo Mowlam was definitely in the second category, which accounts for her success in the job. Her reluctance to depart, though, was not only because she felt fulfilled by the work. She believed she was owed more for her service – she aspired to be foreign secretary – and that her potential was being underrated. Having made such an impact in Northern Ireland, her political morale (and possibly her health) never fully recovered from leaving the place for the Cabinet Office.

As her successor, she talked to me about this. But her disappointment resulted from a misjudgement of her own interests. Health permitting, she could have capitalised on her well-earned popularity to become a leading and influential member of the cabinet. Instead she let her unhappiness show. This, however, will not be what she is remembered for, and her legacy in Northern Ireland will be a permanent tribute to her.

25 August 2005

SLIPPER OF THE YARD

Duncan Campbell

As an encounter, it was the criminal world's equivalent of Stanley finding Livingstone on the shores of Lake Tanganyika. Yesterday one of the participants – the detective who famously remarked 'Long time, no see, Ronnie,' to the fugitive train robber Ronnie Biggs when he tracked him down to a Rio de Janeiro hotel in 1974 – died at the age of 81.

Four years ago, not long after being diagnosed with cancer, Jack Slipper or Slipper of the Yard as he was always known, remarked: 'I am older than Ronnie and it would give me great satisfaction to outlive him to show that my way of life was the best in the end.' In the end, Biggs, now desperately ill in prison and reportedly struck by MRSA, survived the man with whom he will be forever associated.

As a young detective sergeant Jack Slipper had been a member of the squad that hunted the gang responsible for the 1963 Great Train Robbery. Biggs had been jailed with the rest of them, but had climbed over the wall of Wandsworth Prison and disappeared. When he was finally found in Brazil, it was Chief Superintendent Slipper who was sent out to bring him triumphantly home. But Biggs slipped through a loophole in Brazilian law because his girlfriend, Raimunda, was pregnant. Mr Slipper had to fly home with an empty seat beside him on the plane as a poignant reminder of the one that got away. The episode became the subject of a BBC television film over which Mr Slipper successfully sued, claiming that it unfairly portrayed him as 'the fall guy in an Ealing comedy'.

Yesterday one of the first to offer condolences to Mr Slipper's family was Michael Biggs, the son whose birth saved his father from many years in jail. Only in 2001 did Ronnie Biggs return to Britain and give himself up because of illness. 'Even though my father and Mr Slipper were on different sides of the fence, there was a very high and mutual respect between them,' said the younger Biggs, who has been campaigning for his father to be released to spend his final days with his family. 'A clear sign of that is the fact Mr Slipper visited my father twice in Brazil. Our thoughts are with his family.'

'He was one of the old school,' said one retired bank robber, in recognition of the old-fashioned style of a detective who believed in 'coppering' and golf, and who found today's police service 'too political'.

'He was always affable,' said Bruce Reynolds, who masterminded the Great Train Robbery and who described the 6ft 3in ex-RAF Slipper as a 'gentle giant'.

He was famous for his neatly trimmed moustache and military bearing and, although irritated by all the jokes about the 'slip-up' with Biggs, bore no grudges and was always happy to discuss the case, even admitting to a grudging respect for the man who eluded him for so long.

The Metropolitan Police commissioner, Sir Ian Blair, said he was sorry to hear of Mr Slipper's death. 'I served under Jack Slipper's command as a detective constable while he was detective chief superintendent,' said the commissioner. 'I regarded him as the finest detective of his time and it was his inspiration that led me to work in CID for much of my career.'

Other fellow officers joined in the plaudits for a man who also successfully investigated the fatal shooting of three police officers in Shepherd's Bush in 1966. This led to the jailing of three men, one of whom, Harry Roberts, is still in prison.

'Through the illustrious history of the Flying Squad, Jack Slipper is a name that sits above all others as a tenacious investigator and well-respected head of the Flying Squad,' said Detective Chief Superintendent Barry Phillips of the Flying Squad. 'His detective ability, professionalism, commitment and dedication is something that all detectives should aspire to.' Mike McAdam, a former detective chief inspector on the Flying Squad and close friend of Mr Slipper, said he was 'one of the finest detectives in the last century. New Scotland Yard has a worldwide reputation and the name Jack Slipper, or Slipper of the Yard, is synonymous with the Yard,' he said.

As for the 'Long time, no see, Ronnie' remark, that may become the subject for an academic thesis. In his book, *The Train Robbers*, Piers Paul Read suggests that Mr Slipper really said: 'Nice to see you, Ronnie, it's been a long time.'

Mr Slipper, who went on to a career in construction and as a media commentator on crime after retiring from the Met, leaves a wife of 57 years, Annie, two daughters and five grandchildren. His funeral will be held next week.

31 August 2005

KATRINA STRIKES

Jamie Wilson and Julian Borger

Hundreds of people were feared to have died in Hurricane Katrina as more bodies washed up in US Gulf coast cities yesterday in the aftermath of one of the worst natural disasters America has faced in decades. President George Bush will cut short his holiday and return to Washington today to oversee recovery efforts in a region overwhelmed by floodwaters that have sent tens of thousands fleeing and left millions without power.

In New Orleans, those who survived the initial impact of the hurricane faced new dangers yesterday as its dykes gave way under the pressure of the storm surge. With floodwater reaching the eaves of some three-storey houses, rescue workers in boats and helicopters struggled to reach hundreds of victims trapped on roofs. Others were reported trapped in their attics across a city that is 70 per cent below sea-level. There were no official estimates for casualties, but the authorities were thought to be preparing for the possibility of hundreds of fatalities. New Orleans officials moved the city administration out of town, and prepared to evacuate tens of thousands of people who had taken refuge in a sports stadium and in other shelters.

The hurricane's impact was quickly felt further afield. Oil prices surged to record highs above $70 a barrel as the market quailed at the prospect of supply disruptions in the Mexican Gulf. Insurers were flinching at a clear-up cost estimated at $26 billion, which would make Katrina the most expensive disaster in US history.

'Right now, our priority is on saving lives, and we are still in the midst of search-and-rescue operations,' Mr Bush said. 'We know that many are anxious to return to their homes. It's not possible at this moment.'

Many homes in New Orleans were submerged by the surge of floodwater brought on by the storm. The mayor of New Orleans, Ray

Nagin, said bodies were floating in high waters that covered most of the city. 'The city of New Orleans is in a state of devastation,' he said on local television. 'We probably have 80 per cent of our city under water. With some sections of our city the water is as deep as 20 feet [6 metres]. We still have many of our residents on roofs. Both airports are under water.'

On Canal Street, looters waded through hip-deep water and ripped open the steel gates on the front of clothing and jewellery stores. 'The looting is out of control. The French quarter has been attacked,' said Jackie Clarkson, a New Orleans councillor.

In Biloxi, on the Mississippi Gulf coast, hundreds were feared dead after a 30-foot (9-metre) wave surged through the city. Waterfront casinos were torn open and the beach was littered with steel girders. Dazed residents foraged for food and water and sniffer dogs were brought in to help find the dead. 'It was like our tsunami,' said Vincent Creel, the city spokesman. Asked how many people had died, he said: 'It's going to be in the hundreds.'

A Biloxi man, Harvey Jackson, told a local television station, WKRG-TV, that he feared his wife had been killed when she was ripped from his grasp after their home had been split in half by the storm. 'I held her hand as tight as I could,' he said. 'She told me, "You can't hold me." She told me to take care of the kids and the grandkids . . . we ain't got nowhere to go. I'm lost. That's all I had.' In neighbouring Hancock county, 35 people were missing after an emergency operations centre flooded.

Across the Gulf coast, thousands of national guardsmen, some recently returned from Iraq, were mobilised to help with the search-and-rescue operation and to combat looting. However, Katrina could well become the most expensive storm the US has had to clean up, as it laid waste to much of the recent development along the Gulf coast. The region's oil production accounts for a fifth of the nation's needs. Two offshore oil rigs broke free of their moorings, and one hit a bridge in Mobile, Alabama.

Katrina was downgraded to a tropical storm as it moved north into Tennessee and Kentucky, but it continued to wreak havoc, spawning at least seven tornadoes in its wake and emptying heavy rain into the Mississippi. The flooding river was certain to worsen the problems in the Mississippi Delta and in New Orleans. More than 5 million people were left without electricity in Mississippi, Louisiana and Alabama, and in Florida, where Katrina first struck land last week.

3 September 2005

BUSH FLOUNDERS

Gary Younge

George Bush visited the ravaged Gulf coast yesterday amid mounting criticism of his handling of the crisis and a prediction by one senator that the death toll in Louisiana alone could top 10,000 people.[*] As thousands of people sat on the streets of New Orleans, having spent their fourth day waiting to be rescued, the city fell deeper into chaos, with gangs roaming the city and corpses rotting in the sun. Kathleen Blanco, the Democrat governor of Louisiana, threatened looters with a shoot-to-kill policy by soldiers. 'These troops are battle-tested. They have M16s and are locked and loaded,' she said. 'These troops know how to shoot and kill, and I expect they will.'

Last night, amid cheers and catcalls, a military convoy of aid finally arrived in New Orleans to help in the relief of tens of thousands of desperate survivors. Live broadcasts showed a line of military vehicles loaded with crates churning through floodwaters, protected by troops with rifles.

'Lord, I thank you for getting us out of here,' said Leschia Radford, as the convoy arrived in the city centre. But another survivor, Michael Levy, told the Associated Press news agency: 'They should have been here days ago. I ain't glad to see 'em.' Lieutenant General Russel Honore said the priority was food and water; evacuating survivors could take days.

New Orleans has descended into anarchy since it was devastated by Katrina on Monday. Plumes of thick black smoke rose after an explosion in a chemical storage plant, and an apartment complex in the city centre was also in flames. Stunned residents stumbled around bodies that lay rotting and untouched. Others trudged through flooded and debris-strewn streets towards the Superdome stadium, hoping to be bussed to safety. Calling for the immediate deployment of regular combat troops in New Orleans, David Vitter, a Louisiana Republican senator, said: 'My guess is that it [the death toll] will start at 10,000.'

Even before Mr Bush set off, he had to admit the relief effort had been inadequate: 'The results are not acceptable.' Standing by the Republican governors of Alabama and Mississippi at his first stop in Mobile, Alabama, the president said: 'We have a responsibility to clean up this mess. What is not working right, we're going to make it right.' He went on to Biloxi, Mississippi, where he spoke to victims, before heading to New Orleans. After inspecting the disaster scene from the air and on the ground, Mr Bush said: 'I understand the devastation requires more than one day's attention. It's going to require the attention of this country for a long period of time.' Louisiana's Democratic senator, Mary Landrieu, said: 'The president is starting to grasp the magnitude of the situation.'

Yesterday the US Congress broke away from its holiday to agree a $10.5 billion (£5.6 billion) aid package, while the Pentagon promised 1,400 guardsmen a day to stop looting in New Orleans. But these moves did little to quell the mounting anger of hurricane victims and local officials, particularly in the city. At the increasingly unsanitary convention centre, the crowds swelled to about 25,000 as people sought food, water and attention, while dead bodies lay in wheelchairs or wrapped in sheets. At the city's Charity hospital, bodies stacked up on stairways. The airport was a huge field hospital, with fleets of helicopters ferrying the sick for treatment.

Ray Nagin, the mayor of New Orleans, broke into tears on Thursday in a radio interview, saying that federal officials 'don't have a clue what's going on . . . I keep hearing that this is coming, that is coming,' he said, referring to federal aid. 'And my answer to that today is . . . where is the beef?' After 11 September, he said, the president had been given 'unprecedented powers' to send aid to New York. The same should be applied in this case, too, he said. 'Get off your asses and let's do something.'

At a news conference in Washington yesterday, the Congressional Black Caucus criticised the failure to assist many of the mostly poor and black victims. 'I'm ashamed of America. I'm ashamed of our government,' said a Democrat congresswoman, Carolyn Kilpatrick, from Michigan. The Federal Emergency Management Agency director, Michael Brown, defended his record, but said he understood the irritation. Lieutenant General Steven Blum, chief of the National Guard Bureau, said 2,600 further guardsmen would be deployed by tonight, bringing the total number of troops in New Orleans to 7,000. Asked why unrest continued, he said: 'There are not enough police and soldiers to be everywhere all the time.'

Movement of thousands of refugees from the Superdome to the Houston Astrodome halted late on Thursday, after it was feared the Astrodome was becoming a fire hazard. They are being transported to other shelters in Houston. Musician Fats Domino, 77, thought to have been missing after refusing to evacuate, was 'stressed out' but safe after being picked up by a boat with his wife and at least one of his daughters in New Orleans.

★ At the time of going to press the estimate for the number of lives lost was far lower. The current figure stands at over 1,000.

A NEW BEGINNING

THE SHAPE OF THINGS TO COME

Alan Rusbridger

Welcome to the Berliner Guardian. No, we won't go on calling it that for long, and yes, it's an inelegant name. We tried many alternatives, related either to size or to the European origins of the format. In the end, 'the Berliner' stuck. But in a short time we hope we can revert to being simply the *Guardian*.

Many things about today's paper are different. Starting with the most obvious, the page size is smaller. We believe the format combines the convenience of a tabloid with the sensibility of a broadsheet. Next, most conspicuously, we have changed the paper's titlepiece and headline fonts. Gone is the striking '80s David Hillman design – adapted over the years – which mixed Garamond, Miller and Helvetica fonts. In their place is a new font, Guardian Egyptian, which is, we hope, elegant, intelligent and highly legible.

The next difference you may notice is colour. The paper is printed on state-of-the-art MAN Roland ColorMan presses, which give colour on every page – something that sets us apart from every other national newspaper. The effect will be to give greater emphasis and power to our photography and, we hope, make the whole paper a touch less forbidding than it sometimes may have seemed in the past. G2 has also shrunk: it is now a full colour, stapled news magazine with newspaper deadlines. Sport has expanded into its own section – at least twelve pages every day, again in full colour.

As the week progresses you'll notice further changes. There are one or two new sections. There will be new columnists, both in *G1* and *G2* – most notably the pre-eminent commentator Simon Jenkins, who joins us from *The Times* to write on Wednesdays and Fridays. On Saturday there are further changes, including a redesigned and expanded *Weekend* magazine.

The main change – the format – is in response to unambiguous research which shows that readers increasingly find broadsheet newspapers difficult to handle in many everyday situations, including commuting to work. But our research showed equally clearly that there were many things readers didn't want changed, including our comprehensive commitment to news and the intelligence and seriousness of our coverage and comment. They welcomed a wide variety of views, but they wanted news first.

The *Guardian*'s digital edition is now read by nearly 11 million people a month around the world. No other paper in Britain comes close to the size and diversity of our audience. The challenge in redesigning the paper was to remain true to the journalism while making it more convenient to read and handle.

Our ability to plan this new paper and invest in it has been made possible through our ownership structure. The *Guardian* is owned by the Scott Trust, established in 1932 by the same families which had started the paper in 1821. The trust reinvests income from other business to ensure that the *Guardian* can remain a serious, progressive voice in a world in which news organisations are increasingly in the hands of fewer and fewer multinational companies.

No paper ever stands still. The paper you are reading today will evolve. We would like you to be part of that evolution. Because we don't have a proprietor or shareholders our main relationship is with the readers. It's important to know what you make of the changes and how we could improve still further. We promise to read every single response.

We hope you enjoy this new *Guardian*. To those hundreds of thousands of readers who have stayed with us throughout – thank you for your loyalty. To the few who found the old broadsheet paper forbidding or inconvenient – welcome back. To new readers who may have been intrigued enough by the Berliner to buy it for the first time in a while – or possibly ever – welcome, too. We hope the *Guardian* may surprise you.

END OF AN EPIC

John Lanchester

One of the best, and most distinctive, things about watching Test cricket is the amount of time it allows you to spend not watching it. The active bit of any one ball is pretty short – the run-up, the shot, the action, or lack of it. Averaged out, it lasts for about 10 seconds. With 90 overs being bowled a day, that makes 5,400 seconds of action. That's 90 minutes.

But that 90 minutes of action spreads out over a whole day in a manner matched by no other sport. You can watch or listen to the cricket and do other things, and that in turn allows the game to weave itself through your life over the summer, with patches where you are fully concentrating on the contest paralleled by stretches where you are half-watching it while doing, and thinking about, something else.

Not this Ashes series, though. It's been too intense. It's been tyrannical. Leaving aside little details like winning back the Ashes, this is something cricket fans just aren't used to. We're knackered. Also, we need our lives back.

In that context, I would like to boast that in this summer of heroic feats and personal bests – Harmison and McGrath at Lord's, Lee and Vaughan at Old Trafford, Pietersen yesterday, Flintoff and Warne throughout – I have clocked up one of my own. Without planning to, I find that I have followed this Ashes series in the maximum possible number of different media. I've watched it on terrestrial television, satellite television, digital terrestrial, and timeshifted on a Sky+ box. I've listened to it on digital radio, long-wave radio, medium-wave radio, and on TV via digital terrestrial (that was on Saturday, during one of Channel 4's increasingly annoying horse races). On holiday, I listened to it over the Internet. On the Isle of Wight this weekend I was checking on Australia's first-innings progress via Wap on a mobile phone. That's pretty much a full set, I reckon, unless there's some way of keeping in touch via smoke signals or carrier pigeon.

At this point, it would be standard practice to break down and say that none of this is any substitute for being at the game. But that's not quite true. In terms of atmosphere, there's nothing like being at the ground, obviously. But if you actually want to watch the cricket, you get a better view sitting in front of the TV. I first realised this after the Friday of the 2000 Lords' Test against West Indies, the only time in Test history in which parts of all four innings were played on the same day. It was amazing to be there, and I'll never forget it, not least because it was the start of the revival in English cricket which has reached a culmination in this series. But in terms of seeing the specifics of what happened and how the wickets fell, I had a much clearer sense of it after I'd gone home and watched the highlights on TV. Sad but true. In particular, television makes it much easier to see the detail of the contest between the bowler and batsman at the game, and especially from the side, you get the rough gist, but that's about it.

This phenomenon is acted out at grounds in the strange postmodern way the big-screen replay often gets more of a cheer than the actual event. That's because it's only when the replay comes that the crowd can actually see what the hell happened. As I write, there has just been a classic example of this, with the replay of Warne dropping Pietersen off Lee getting a roar roughly twice as loud as the event itself.

And now it's all over. There will be other series, and other heroic feats, but we'll never again get to see this great old Australian team, just off the summit and on the way down, and this great new England team, just below the summit and on the way up, slugging it out over five matches and 25 days. It's hard to take.

Thank God it's only six days until they release the highlights DVD …